Born in Lhasa

Born in Lhasa

by
Namgyal Lhamo Taklha

Snow Lion Publications
Ithaca, New York

Snow Lion Publications
P O Box 6483
Ithaca, NY 14851
(607)273-8519
www.snowlionpub.com

Printed in Canada on acid-free, recycled paper.

ISBN 1-55939-102-2

Library of Congress Cataloging-in-Publication Data

Taklha, Namgyal Lhamo.
  Born in lhasa / by Namgyal Lhamo Taklha.
     p. cm.
  ISBN 1-55939-102-2
  1. Taklha, Namgyal Lhamo. 2. Tibet (China)--Biography. I Title.
  DS786 .T285 2000
  951'.505'092--dc21   2001002170

Table of Contents

Preface

I was standing behind a rack of clothes and planning a new display in the Tibetan Arts and Crafts shop at 693 Madison Avenue, New York City, when a well-dressed elderly man walked in and asked about the origin of our unusual items. He stood in the center of the room, astounded by the colorful paintings and exotic carpets on the wall, the luminous silk robes on the racks, the fur hats with multicolored silk tassels, and the embroidered boots. He approached me and asked where I came from. When I answered "Tibet," he began an almost endless flow of questions. "Is it true," he wanted to know, "that Tibetans drink cup after cup of butter tea, and that they actually fly during meditation?" I tried to answer all of his questions. Before he left the shop, the gentleman gave me some advice: "Young lady, please write your story for us. Don't forget."

These days, I think of all the young Tibetans who live in exile or who live under the Communist Chinese regime. Those who live in exile experience only a touch of their culture, a rich and fascinating culture that is quickly disappearing. They have never heard the soothing swish of Tibet's willow trees. They have never felt the exhilarating breeze of Lhasa on a sunny day, nor have they bathed in Tibet's sparkling streams that run through fields of mustard and peas. Like my own children who were born in exile, they have never known Tibet, our homeland—they are the children of India, of Switzerland, or the United States.

Those children who live inside Tibet are raised in fear and repression and are taught that the old Tibet, before 1959, was backward, cruel, and corrupt. They live with constant mistrust and fear under a foreign government that seeks to destroy the unique Tibetan culture, language, traditions, and even the indigenous race of Tibet.

I would like to give all of these children a glimpse of their homeland and tell them the story of my struggles to build a new life in exile, while preserving the best of our culture and heritage.

I would like to thank Tseten Samdup, who patiently typed the many pages of this book for me almost ten years ago. I am grateful to my friend Whitney Stewart for her encouragement, to Vickie Lewelling for editing this book, and to Carole Wilson, who put me in touch with Snow Lion Publications.

I dedicate this book to the younger generation of Tibetans.

Namgyal Lhamo Taklha
Dharamsala, India

Introduction

The Tibet I knew no longer exists—a free, self-ruled Tibet, isolated from the rest of the world, where simple, religious people spun their lives around harvests, picnics, festivals, and spiritual pilgrimages. With its elaborate and distinct culture, with internal political intertwinings as matted and tangled as yak hair, Tibet fiercely protected its self-determination, and closed itself off from almost all foreign influence.

I was born in Lhasa in 1942, the child of two ancient Tibetan families—Tsarong and Ragashar—whose offspring have served the Tibetan government for generations. I grew up in the house of the Tsarong family, a family which had also produced generations of doctors of traditional Tibetan medicine. My paternal grandmother, Pema Dolkar Tsarong, married the son of a farmer who, in 1910, saved the life and won the great favor of the Thirteenth Dalai Lama. During the Thirteenth Dalai Lama's flight to India, this young peasant led troops who defeated the pursuing Chinese forces at Chaksam, Tibet, thereby allowing the Tibetan ruler to escape safely into exile in India. As a reward for his bravery, my grandfather was made the commander-in-chief of the Tibetan army. He married into the Tsarong family and took this name. Thereafter, the hero of the Chaksam incident was called Dasang Dadul Tsarong. My siblings and I were raised in this household of almost sixty family members and servants, a protective net organized and ruled by our adored grandfather

Tsarong, whom we called Pola—the spark, the power, and life of
our family.

Pola was a broad-minded, forward-thinking patriot who had
observed Russian military tactics while he served during the
Thirteenth Dalai Lama's exile in Mongolia, and trained in British tactics during the Dalai Lama's exile in Darjeeling, India. Pola
unnerved Tibet's monastic "Old Guards" with his plans to modernize the country. Pola wielded great influence in his position
as commander-in-chief of the Tibetan army and as a minister in
the government. He wanted the country to upgrade its defense,
education, communications, and transportation so that it could
prevent foreign military intervention, maintain its self-rule, and
become an independent member of the world community.

Tibet's monastic leaders and a few of its landed aristocrats
panicked at the thought of being heavily taxed and losing government monies that had been generously earmarked for
ecclesiastical services, funds that would now go to civil and military services. The monasteries had a great fear of the weakening
of Tibetan Buddhism, and a few people accused Pola of oppor-
tunism and disloyalty. Despite the accusations, Pola fought
against Tibet's conservatism, and he persuaded the Thirteenth
Dalai Lama to build up an army, to send promising students for
education abroad, and to consider widespread modernizations.

Tibet's development did not last long. During a short period
of peace, monastic leaders and a few conservative civil servants
declared that Tibet had no need for an army and pressured the
Dalai Lama to order the removal of all trained officers from their
military posts. The Dalai Lama advocated change, but he was
unable to steer his country away from the old system before his
death in 1933. As for my grandfather, he was defeated in his
efforts to modernize Tibet, so he turned to the task of educating
his own family members, breaking open for them the world on
the other side of the Himalayas.

Pola fashioned himself into a successful international entre-
preneur. He traded goods with people east and west of Tibet,
and he invited merchants and diplomats of many nationalities
to visit Tsarong House. Scholars, politicians, military officers,
mountaineers, and Buddhist aspirants—the famous and the

unknown—filled our house with stories and images of a world too far away and strange for my siblings and I to understand. We tasted bubble gum from the United States and gawked at issues of *National Geographic*, but we never imagined one day entering the life we saw in these magazine advertisements.

In 1922, my grand aunt Rinchen Dolma Taring was the first Tibetan woman to leave Tibet for an education in Darjeeling, India, a boarding school run by American Baptists. Years later, my father, Dundul Namgyal Tsarong, joined a Jesuit boys' school, while his siblings followed my aunt to Mount Hermon. In 1951, I went to Mount Hermon School in Darjeeling with my siblings.

At the age of nine, I was a changed girl. I went from being a privileged child protected within the comfort, love, and religious idealism of Tibet's bygone era to a minority student in a modern, sophisticated, and international society. I saw my first car, ate my first hot dog, wore my first knee-length skirt, and attended my first Sunday school class. My own clothes became costume pieces; my language was unspoken. Gradually my small landlocked world of Tibet expanded beyond time and space.

I began to study English, Western literature, world history, geography, biology, mathematics, and the Bible with my American, European, and Asian classmates. Having to learn the values and motivations of people raised not on butter tea and Buddha's compassion, but on roast beef and the parables of Christ, I could no longer retreat into my mental shelter of oblivion. I had to learn to be at ease with social unfamiliarity and to overcome my own insecurities.

This lesson, scary at first, was crucial to the rest of my life. Only a few years later everything I had known and trusted became unfastened: my country was invaded, my family members were separated or lost, and my home was taken away. I became a refugee, homeless, stateless, lost amidst the teeming population of India.

When the Communist Chinese took over Tibet in the 1950s, they tried to uproot every aspect of Tibetan culture and to vilify our sacred teachings. While pretending to be the savior of our populace, they worked at breaking us down physically, mentally, and spiritually. Their methods were cruel and comprehensive.

Crazed with hunger from the famine caused by the Chinese, sorrowful at the loss of Tibetan lives, we became suspicious of our own family members, and desolate from the destruction of our cultural and spiritual norms.

Although not all of its members escaped the Chinese, my family—like so many other Tibetan families—fled into exile in India. There we faced an entirely new set of challenges: how to make a home in exile, how to cope in a foreign environment, how to preserve our language, culture and religion, how to help each other with very little money, and, most importantly, how to get our country back from the Chinese. With hard work, perseverance, deeply rooted fortitude, and assistance from all over the world, Tibetans have become a unique community in exile, one that China cannot afford to ignore.

I was fortunate to have lived in India, to have met people from all over the world, and to have been well-educated. Having the skills to help the Tibetan government-in-exile, I began my services as a translator and interpreter at the Bureau of His Holiness the Dalai Lama in New Delhi. Later, I assisted with the rehabilitation of Tibetans in Europe and in health services for Tibetans in India and Nepal.

I married an elder brother of the Dalai Lama, gave birth to two children, and traveled further and further from my childhood world—from India, to Switzerland, to the United States and back to India—but due to my early exposure to foreign customs and my inner strength coming from a spiritual environment, I never felt lost and never abandoned my sense of being Tibetan.

I am writing this book to document Tibet's unique cultural and religious tradition. When I returned to live in a Tibetan refugee community in India after my modern nomadic life, I realized the value of my roots. Mental peace became far more important to me than material acquisitions. In finding a way to care for my countrymen and women, and in contributing to the cause of regaining our homeland, I found a purpose in my life. Now I live with the hope that China will realize the need to settle the Tibetan issue honorably, honestly, and amicably.

1 Born in Lhasa

I was born into the Tsarong family on the 22nd day of the fifth
month of the Water Horse year in the Tibetan calendar (1942).
My family members told me that it was a joyful and auspicious
day not only because I was the first Tsarong grandchild, but also
because the monthly supply of oil, barley, peas, and wheat had
arrived that day from our family estate in Tsang. I suppose my
birth would have been more welcome if I had been a boy—the
heir of the Tsarong family. I could have followed my ancestors
and taken a prestigious position in the Tibetan government.
Nonetheless, I was lovingly received.

My mother often told me about my birth. She was only six-
teen and had been married just a year. As was the custom in
Tibet, the birth was a family affair; no modern doctors or nurses
attended. Assisted by my two grandmothers and a maid, my
mother suffered through thirty hours of labor. Her only comforts were sweet words from her relatives, strong butter tea, the
smoke of holy, sweet-smelling herbs, and her inner strength. As
the excruciating pain prevented her from lying quietly, she paced
around the room, willing me to arrive. When the moment came,
I slipped into my maternal grandmother's hands.

In contrast to the efficient, sometimes impersonal hospital
births in the West, births in Tibet required special rituals. To keep
evil spirits from carrying away the soul of the mother or of the
child, the mother was made to inhale smoke from a burning

mixture of incense and juniper branches, different herbs, and barley powder. Pieces of hair or cloth from holy lamas were also burnt with this mixture, and the smoke was carried around the room. Butter and barley dough were mixed with water and then shaped into a dice or a fish, which the expectant mother was made to swallow while one of her maternal male relatives was called on to recite a special mantra to facilitate the delivery.

In some homes, peacock feathers and hair from a bear were burnt and the ashes were added to a bowl of water. A male relative of the mother was made to say a special mantra, blow on the water, and then urge the mother to drink it. According to Tibetan beliefs, the child is usually born soon after this ritual. Medicines from herbs, roots, and minerals were also given to the mother to ease her delivery.

Tibetans are very superstitious by nature, and there are many superstitions about births. For example, a birth is auspicious if the child is born in an unbroken amniotic sac. My younger brother, Tseten Gyurmey, was born this way, and he was later recognized as a reincarnated Buddhist teacher, the Drikung Kyapgon Chetsang Rinpoche. He was born on the fourth day of the sixth Tibetan month, a very special day according to Tibetan Buddhism—the day when Buddha taught the Four Noble Truths. When my brother was delivered in the sac, he did not seem to be alive. By chance, the English physician of the British Trade Mission, Dr. Guthrie, had been called to attend the birth. When the family thought that the baby was dead, Dr. Guthrie took over. After hanging my baby brother upside down and whacking him on the bottom, Dr. Guthrie displayed a wailing baby boy. My mother is forever grateful to this physician.

After any delivery, a new baby was bathed or oiled and dressed in a soft loose gown and wrapped in a blanket. A tiny piece of butter was put on the baby's tongue before the child was brought to the mother's breast. To revive the mother, relatives fed her hot soup from bone or lamb meat, and melted butter. Traditional Tibetan doctors say that the mother's wind energies are disturbed by the birth and must be resettled with warm food and rest.

Two days after my birth, my maternal grandmother hosted a special purifying ceremony, or *bahng-sel*, for me. The family priest chanted prayers and carried a branch of kusha grass that was dipped in milk and shaken over my mother and me and then around the room. Bowls of boiled rice with raisins and *droma* (a tiny sweet-potato-like root) and butter tea were served to my parents. As they showed me off to their friends, they received traditional white greeting scarves called *khatas* and gifts of silk clothing for themselves and for me.

Because my parents observed Tibetan customs, I was taken on a special outing the first time I left our house. My mother consulted an almanac to see which day would be most auspicious for this jaunt. She dressed me in my best robes, wrapped me in a silk blanket, and embellished my costume with charm boxes, sea shells, specially blessed strings from holy persons and a silver pendant called a *melong*. I was then protected from evil. A smudge of soot was streaked on the tip of my nose as another form of protection from menacing spirits. My mother dressed in her finest silks and jewels and embarked on a day of visits to various temples and to her family home. These same rituals, I am sure, were repeated by my mother with my younger sister, Norzin, and with my three younger brothers.

I treasure my earliest memories of Tibet—my childhood days seem to have been washed in the gleaming Kyichu River, the "River of Happiness," and left to float in the crisp, pure Lhasa air. My four siblings and I were swaddled in familial love and sweet comforts. An active child, I loved to be outdoors or with the adults in my family. I was not popular with our servants because I kept them running. Sometimes, when they needed a rest from the five of us, they locked us in our rooms. I often outsmarted them by finding a knitting needle or some other sharp object and jimmying the door open. Once, when that trick did not work, I climbed out onto a window ledge and shouted at a passerby to help me down outside.

My sister Norzin, who is a year younger than I am, was much easier to handle. Quiet and patient, she never uttered a harsh word toward anyone. Although she was not a pretty child, she became an elegant and beautiful woman. Tsewang Jigme, who was born a year after Norzin, was also quiet and obedient— dubbed "our golden boy" by all of the servants. Next in line came Tseten Gyurmey, who, as I have said, was recognized as a reincarnated lama. He was far more intelligent than the rest of us. The last in our brood was the naughtiest—Tseten Paljor. Seven years younger than I, Paljor was very cute and forever mischievous. He too gave our maids tremendous trouble.

We five grandchildren did not spend much time with our parents or grandparents, because they were often busy. Our elders did have, nonetheless, a great impact on our upbringing. I always think of my father as a man of few words, very kind, gentle, and polite. He was a gentleman with everyone. Often hidden away in his office or his darkroom, he spent hours taking and developing photographs and making films of Tibet. He also loved to tinker with mechanics; he took apart and rebuilt radios, motorbikes, and even a jeep imported from India.

My mother was more outgoing than my father and spent more time with us—often disciplining us and keeping us on a tight rein. Amala (as Tibetans call their mother) was very pretty with translucent skin, a fair complexion, and a small nose. The bridge of her nose was very flat, and she loved to tell the story of how cats had once danced on it and flattened it. She spent hours looking in a hand-mirror, trying in vain to stretch the skin on the bridge of her nose to make it more prominent. She had a passion for make-up, and outlined her small eyes with eye liner from India. Married at age fifteen, she was not educated abroad as were my father and his sisters, but she loved to listen to Western and Indian music. She liked to feel modern and fashionable, and she went to great lengths to dress up for festivals. Glamorous in her brocade gowns and full set of jewelry, she looked like a glittering, movable statue encrusted with precious stones.

Also in the Tsarong house were my paternal grandmother and grandfather: Mola and Pola Tsarong. The management of the household was in Mola's generous hands. Ever busy, Mola could always be found knitting, praying, writing in her account book, surveying the house, or working in the garden. She always dressed in a simple, black hand-woven wool dress known as a *sherma*, and she was so kind and dignified that everyone adored and respected her.

The Tsarong family could be traced to my maternal grandmother's family, who were descendants of Yuthok Yonten

Gonpo, one of Tibet's renowned physicians. However, my grandfather, Tsarong Pola, was the man most respected and considered the pillar of the family. Dasang Dadul, as he was known, was neither a celebrated physician like some of my forefathers, nor a genuine blue-blooded nobleman. He was a commoner from Penpo, a village in central Tibet. It is believed that he was born to a peasant family; his father died early and his mother remarried an arrow maker. Dasang Dadul was commonly known as the son of an arrow maker. At a young age, Pola, as we called him, was engaged as a retainer in the summer palace of the Thirteenth Dalai Lama. The Thirteenth Dalai Lama was so impressed by Pola's intelligence that he made him one of his personal servants.

In 1904, when the British army besieged Tibet under Colonel Younghusband, the Tibetan government implored the Dalai Lama to leave Tibet for his protection. Pola demonstrated his courage and loyalty as he traveled among the Dalai Lama's small entourage to Mongolia and China. In 1909, Pola became a national hero when Chinese troops came to invade Tibet. This time, the Thirteenth Dalai Lama fled to India to fight for Tibet's independence. At Chaksam Ferry, the Chinese troops were on the heels of the fleeing party when Pola and a small band of Tibetan soldiers fought the Chinese back and kept them from capturing the Dalai Lama. Later, Pola was appointed commander-in-chief of the Tibetan army.

When my grandmother's father, Tsarong Shapey, and her brother were assassinated in political turmoil in 1912, the Tsarong family was without a male heir. A close attendant of His Holiness the Dalai Lama who was a Tsarong family friend appealed to His Holiness that Dasang Dadul marry Tsarong Shapey's widow and become the head of the Tsarong family and estate. The request was granted, and His Holiness even gave Pola a dowry.

Eventually, because Tsarong Shapey's widow was not a direct descendant of the family, the senior family retainers insisted that Pola also marry one of the four daughters of Tsarong Shapey. He married the oldest—my grandmother. Later, Pola also married two of my grandmother's younger sisters, one of whom had become a widow at a very young age.

Pola was a man feared and yet loved by all. He was a forward-thinking man who believed in the importance of a modern education and who, like few Tibetans of the era, sent his children and grandchildren to schools abroad. He always made himself available to relatives and friends seeking his good advice. Like most families in Tibet, my grandfather, as the oldest member of the family, was the head of the household. Instead of my parents making the decisions about the children, it was Pola who had the final word.

Pola, however, was more than the family strong arm. He had a tremendous sense of humor and frivolity. He entertained us all and was able to cheer anyone's spirits. A strong man of average height and weight, he had broad, slightly stooped shoulders. His complexion was tan, and his eyes were delightfully expressive. When he was informally dressed, he wore baggy, Western-style pants and coats and a floppy hat. He was very industrious, always writing letters, greeting business partners, planning the next crop of fruit trees, or pruning tomato plants. Pola woke routinely at 3:00 in the morning, lit a kerosene lamp to do some paper work, then washed up and inspected his estate before dawn. The rest of us did not even wake for another four hours.

Our day began with breakfast in bed at seven o'clock. We ate bowls of roasted barley meal (*tsampa*) or boiled rice, and drank hot butter tea. Sometimes, we filled up on leftover fried meat pastries (*sha-bhalib*) or steamed meat-filled buns (*momos*). After breakfast, we were scrubbed and dressed by our maids before we greeted our grandparents and parents. We would then receive a daily supply of treats from my grandmother, who kept a tiny storeroom of delicacies—Tibetan sweet cheese, dried meat, dried fruits, preserved fruits from China, and candies and biscuits from India. Once in a while we would have candy, chewing gum, and chocolate sent all the way from the United States by my grandfather's pen pals—Mr. and Mrs. William Englesman from St. Louis, Missouri. The boxes took four or five months to travel from St. Louis to Lhasa, and we were always excited to open them. Bubble gum was sent with instructions in English that my father translated for us. I remember our servants cheering when my grandfather, my parents, and all the grandchildren held contests to see who could blow the biggest bubble. To me, America was another planet and bubble gum came from the moon.

We children spent most of our time with our nurses and with the children of our staff in our garden and courtyard. For most of the day, our large garden became a fantasy land. We fashioned rags into dolls, drawing their faces with charcoal. We outlined our houses in the ground and decorated ourselves with hats, headdresses, and necklaces of willow branches and wild irises. We romped carefree for hours in our world of stones, twigs, branches, and dirt.

I cherished afternoon tea times when the entire family gathered with guests in our garden or in our grandparents' quarters and sat down to sweet Indian tea, pancakes, buns, and pastries cooked by the chef, Tsering Wangchuk. The adults recounted tales of personal gossip, of business, and of politics, and I ached to hear stories about unknown, faraway places like India, China, and the United States. I was very curious about the outside world.

In autumn, we watched the kite-flying competitions. Kite-flying was a serious sport in Lhasa. If someone was caught flying a kite out of season, he was fined or forced to build roads or public toilets. During open season, the whole town turned out in celebration. Wandering through the market place, or Barkhor, a few days before the start of kite season, you could see all the new kites laid out in preparation. Made of square bamboo frames and handmade Tibetan paper as delicate as Japanese rice paper, these kites were painted in several different patterns: the "bearded one" had two solid borders painted on each side of the kite; the "screwed-eyed one" had two circles of different hues painted on each side of the kite; and the "tailed one" sported a long paper tail. I remember the menacing fighting kites whose strings were coated in glue and powdered glass. When they were sent aloft, they dove and swirled into a tangle of bamboo, shredded paper, and sharp string—the last kite to stay in the sky earned its owner great applause and wads of gambled money. These kite-flying adventures were never without a few mishaps. During all the cheering and running about, many spectators tumbled off rooftops onto the hard, dusty earth.

For an unfailing source of entertainment, my siblings and I often tried to catch Pola in his storeroom. He would set up shop for us and display semiprecious earrings and rings, old tin boxes that once held fancy British cookies, notebooks from India, pencils, penknives and other wondrous knickknacks. He would not give us his goods for free, so we begged our parents or Mola for money and then learned the art of bargaining. Pola was great fun. Once he told us that he was in a trance, and that an oracle spirit had entered his body. He huffed and puffed and chased us all over the house. I remember the time he caught my brothers Jigme and Rinpoche and swatted them forcefully on the bottom. They escaped in tears and ran for comfort to the rest of the family.

Sometimes, we wrapped ourselves up in Pola's loose cloak, and he would tell us dirty tales of the notorious "Uncle Toenpa" of Tibet. My mother used to be furious on such occasions, but she held her tongue out of respect for the head of the family.

On holidays, we often visited my mother's childhood home. My mother's family was descended from one of the oldest noble families in Tibet. The Ragashar family (also known as Dhokar) could be traced from the Ghazie lineage. According to Tibetan lore, the Tibetan people originate from the union of a monkey, an emanation of the deity of compassion named Avalokiteshvara, and an ogress, an emanation of Arya Tara. They had six sons, and the Ghazie family descends from one of the sons; the family is traced back through the male descendants only.

My grandfather, Ragashar Pola, was serious and taciturn, and his behavior set the tone of the house. Whereas the Tsarong house servants (except for the older ones) kept their hair short and were casual, the male servants of Ragashar house were stiff and formal, keeping their hair in long braids and wearing gold and turquoise earrings. Ragashar Mola came from the Sikkimese royal family. She was a tall, heavy woman—very frank, cheerful, and kind. Always in motion, she marched throughout the house with a heavy ring of keys. When she dressed up for holidays, she was massive in her tall headdress and bulky jewelry of the Tsang region—a monument in Lhasa society.

We loved these visits to Ragashar. Mola fed us our favorite dishes and sent us home with special treats. When we were low on pocket money, Pola would reach his hand under his beautiful brocade seat cover and draw out cash notes to give us.

Ragashar House was in the center of the city, and my grandparents' rooms faced the Jokhang Temple and looked right down to the Barkhor. We would spend hours observing the different kinds of people prostrating or circumambulating the temple. We watched as nomads clad in sheepskin robes carried ancient silver prayer wheels. There were peasants from nearby villages in white woolen robes and crushed felt hats, and women and children in black woolen robes. Many monks and nuns strolled around the temple in a mix of maroon and yellow. The fine ladies of Lhasa were dressed to attract attention.

When I was about eight years old, Norzin and I enrolled in a private school in Lhasa. The government schools in Lhasa were founded exclusively to educate men for jobs as monastery officials, lay officials, or doctors of traditional medicine. Co-educational private schools were run by learned men of different backgrounds. Private schools did not charge any fixed sum for tuition, and they were open to children from all social backgrounds. There was no discrimination against anyone. On the day of admission, if the new student's family could afford it, they gave a cash gift to all the students as well as to the teacher. Bags of barley, tea bricks, and clothing were also presented to the teacher. An auspicious day of entrance was chosen by an astrologer and then in a small ceremony, the new student served tea and rice to each student, and presented a ceremonial white scarf (*khata*) to the teacher.

I was not blessed with great powers of concentration, and I struggled through the tedium and difficulties of school. Accustomed to running all over our garden and courtyard, I always felt confined in a school room. The curriculum was rather monotonous. We were taught reading, writing, grammar, and arithmetic, along with many, many prayers. Much of our early years were spent learning the complicated Tibetan alphabets. Sitting cross-legged and hunched over our work, we were made to draw lines on our chalkboards by pressing chalk-covered strings against the board's surface and then copying letters over and over. As soon as we finished one board full of letters and were corrected by the teacher, we started all over again. Eventually we graduated to writing words and then sentences, and after a year or two, if we proved to have decent handwriting, we were allowed to write on paper.

The school administrator was a man named Phala Chantso Kusho, who was the treasurer of a noble family named Phala. Because Chantso Kusho was busy with his duties at the Phala House, his eldest son looked after the affairs of the school and served as headmaster. This headmaster was in his early twenties and miserably strict and arrogant in his constant show of power. If any student giggled or whispered in class, he forced the guilty party to prostrate for an hour. If he was really angered, he would whip the boys and smack the girls on the palms of their hands.

One of his most bizarre rituals took place at the end of the examination period. Students were lined up according to grades and then hit with a bamboo strip—boys on the cheek, girls on the palm of the hand. The student who received the highest mark was hit by the teacher, the second received a whack from the teacher and the student who came first, and so on down the line. The students with the worst grades would end up crying and bleeding from this torture.

Rivalry was very prevalent among the different schools, and street fights often broke out between the older boys after classes. We all carried knives to sharpen our bamboo pens, and these became the weapons of the school wars. I remember one day when boys from the Ngarongsha school stood waiting in an alley for boys from my school. When they confronted each other, they argued and then began stabbing each other. Our maid arrived in time to see the fight and scurried Norzin and I into the next alley and away from the aggressors.

At this time in our life, we witnessed a very important and memorable event—both a happy and sad occasion. When my second brother, Tseten Gyurmey, was proclaimed to be the reincarnation of the head of the Drikung Kagyu sect of Tibetan Buddhism, he was only three years old. There was great excitement when several important-looking monks called on the family to request that my brother be released to their care and taken to

Drikung. Several visits were made. There was whispering among the maidservants that my mother was reluctant to send our little brother to a monastery to live among strangers. After a few days, we heard that my grandparents, especially my maternal grandfather, had insisted that the child be given to the monastery, as the Regent Thaktra had given the final approval for my brother to be the reincarnation of the late Drikung Chetsang Rinpoche. Moreover, my mother recalled an incident that occurred on a pilgrimage she made to a holy place when she was expecting my brother. She met a holy man who told her that the child she was carrying would have an early death or become a very famous man. Remembering this, she worried that if she did not allow my brother to go to the monastery, something harmful might happen to him.

When the time came for Rinpoche to leave for the monastery, he was dressed in a monk's robe, a gold silk gown, and an intricately decorated flat papier-mâché hat. Not all little lamas were permitted to wear this hat; this was special to the higher ranking lamas. It took a little coaxing to get him to wear the stiff leather and brocade pointed boots.

It was a grand ceremony. My grandmother and mother wore full jewelry over their brocade gowns, the maids wore triangular coral headdresses, traditional for central Tibet, and huge gold and turquoise charm boxes strung on different precious stone chains around their necks. The wives of government officials wore the headdress in pearls with huge coral stones sewn on the triangle base of stuffed red felt. The headgear was kept in place by hooks attached to the specially plaited hair.

The farewell for my brother the Rinpoche had to be started by a formal ceremony in the main chapel with the presentation of scarves by the monastery officials to the family members, and the family treasurer presenting scarves to the officials of Drikung Monastery on behalf of the family. Butter tea and raisin and droma with rice were served; singing and auspicious dances filled the corridors. A group of lay people called *shemas* performed an auspicious song and did a very slow dance to the beat of a large drum. They performed only on special religious occasions. Religious music was played on different-sized horns with disparate tones, and cymbals and drums played by maroon-robed monks set the stage for the ceremony.

Our relatives, friends, family retainers, and tenants were dressed up and waiting for the family to come out into the court-yard, the air thick with incense smoke. Out of this mist rode my brother, my parents, and my brother Jigme. Jigme, who was dressed in a yellow silk gown, embroidered boots, and a lovely brocade hat, got to ride on a magnificent brown horse and ac-company the party to Drikung Monastery, about a day's ride from Lhasa. Norzin and I, dressed in beautiful robes and covered in precious jewelry, shed so many tears that they outnumbered all the little gold flowers that decorated our brocade dresses.

Childhood passed, leaving memories of a loving home amid flowers and birds and kind people. Outer walls protected us from unpleasant experiences. An unknown future lay ahead, one that meant I would leave this beautiful world to travel across mountains and oceans to strange and exciting worlds.

2 The Tsarong Home

Most of the wealthy citizens of Lhasa lived in the city, which was very congested. The streets were narrow and the houses were dark and built tightly side by side. The city always seemed strangely crammed together when there was so much space available on the outskirts. Sanitation was very poor in Lhasa, and the public toilets were always neglected. Tibetans kept very much to tradition, were very superstitious, and disliked change. They lived in the same houses for years and years, generation after generation.

The Tsarong family had lived for many generations in an old home in Lhasa, but later built a wondrous home outside the city on the banks of the Kyichu River. Like other houses in Tibet, our house was constructed of stone and wood beams and capped by a flat roof. Multicolored prayer flags fluttered from long poles that extended from each of the four corners of the roof. A mud dome, shaped like a vase, was built in the center of the front of the roof to hold the incense and juniper leaves that were burnt daily to purify the air and appease the spirits.

My grandfather, Tsarong Pola, designed the house and supervised its construction. His influence was easily visible. While the house respected the traditional Tibetan style, it possessed a slight modern flair, incorporating features Pola had admired in houses seen during his travels. He added more windows and overall space to the design and substituted glass panes for the thin Tibetan paper or cloth that was normally stretched across the window frames of Tibetan houses.

The main house had forty rooms and was divided into two wings by two large halls that ran through the middle of the house, one on top of the other. After climbing a flight of steps, one came to the first hall, which served as the main entry to the house. A second flight of steps led to the second floor, and then to the servants' lounge and the Choegyal Khang, the House of the Religious Kings.

All important family ceremonies took place in the Choegyal Khang. Prominent in the room were three four-foot-tall statues made of gold. The figures were seated side by side on jeweled thrones and placed in glass cases. They were adorned in the finest silks, brocades, and precious jewels. The statues were of Tibet's three most important kings—Songtsen Gampo, Trisong Detsen, and Tri Ralpachen—all of whom were instrumental in introducing and propagating Buddhism in Tibet. They were also known as the Religious Kings or Choegyal Mipon Namsum. In front of these statues were large marble-topped cabinets that held 108 large silver water bowls that were changed daily, a huge gold butter lamp, and a beautiful mandala of beads strung with the designs of the eight auspicious signs. There was a parasol to keep away the heat of desires; a pair of fish, symbolizing happiness and freedom from restraint; a sea shell, symbol of the spoken word of the Dharma; a lotus, symbol of divine origin and of purity; a vase, symbol of the treasury of all goods; a banner of victory, symbol of the attainment of enlightenment; a wheel, symbol of the Dharma teachings; and an endless knot, symbol of the law of interdependency of phenomena. Paintings and other representations of the eight auspicious signs were considered lucky and were found on altars, in wall paintings, and on wooden chests and tables. The mandala on our altar was the personal handiwork of my grandmother. Silk and paper flowers from India and China were abundant in beautiful vases. The scriptures, the teachings of the Lord Buddha, were each wrapped in golden silk, patched with brocade, and placed on the cabinets along the walls. A number of rare and beautiful religious paintings (*thangkas*) hung on the walls. The family silver dishes, jade bowls, French crystal, and English china sets, used for special occasions, were locked up in cabinets in this room.

In the western portion of the house were my grandparents' suites, and in the eastern portion were my parents' quarters; we children had our rooms directly below our parents' quarters. Under my grandparents' rooms were the living quarters of my aunt and uncle. Each of the suites included a sitting room, a bedroom, a prayer room, a larger and smaller storeroom, a washroom, and a servants' lounge.

In the lower rooms, grain, flour, tea, raw wool, oil, sugar and many leather bags filled with supplies were stored. I used to wonder what would happen if a few of these bags remained in the corners unopened and neglected for many years. The rooms were pitch dark and could only be traversed with oil lamps or candles. My grandmother or mother used to go every morning with our steward and his assistant to take out the daily supply of rice, flour, sugar, tea, and other goods for the family and the retainers. Once in a while, we would get the courage to sneak into the roasted pea flour bags and take a mouthful. Pea flour is very, very tasty, and one day, in my haste to eat as much as I could, I greedily crammed more into my mouth than I could possibly chew. My mother found me choking, and only the tea from my aunt's nearby room saved my life.

Another favorite room of mine was the Lhamo Khang. Behind my grandmother's suite, the Lhamo Khang housed our family protective deity—the Goddess Palden Lhamo. Soot from the butter lamps and the incense burners made the room dark and black, and the beautiful religious drawings on the walls were barely visible. Entering the room, your eyes were drawn to the altar where an image of the goddess, partly hidden by her colorful silk scarves, was riding her mule and carrying a skull cup. The image was not very large, but its presence filled the room. Numerous other images occupied the room as well, and I always had the feeling that they were smiling at me.

Offerings of water, butter lamps, a mandala, and flowers were spread out in front of the altar. Religious scriptures were lined up on top of the cabinets on the other walls in the room. On either side of the altar, masks of two ferocious looking females, fully dressed in long, dark brocade robes, hung on pillars. Their loose, uncombed hair fell over their shoulders, and they had large, protruding teeth. As I approached Palden Lhamo to receive my blessing, I closed my eyes when I passed these terrifying images, chills running through my body.

Gombho-la, who lived in this chapel, was the monk in charge of offering prayers to Palden Lhamo and the other deities on behalf of the family. He was a comfort, and we used to stay close by him. This room with its dark atmosphere, thick smell of incense, and the constant drone of drums, was not cheerful, yet when I prostrated and prayed and viewed the flickering butter lamps in front of the images of the deities and Palden Lhamo, I felt warm, secure, and holy. I was allowed to visit this chapel whenever I wanted. During each visit, I received holy water and a piece of dried fruit or cheese from Gombho-la. The older members of the family used the Lhamo chapel only during New Year or for special prayers. It was a stark contrast to the main chapel of the Choegyals, but it had a strange warm feeling of awe and comfort and I preferred to make my prostrations and special prayers there.

The Namdzoekhang, or upper storeroom, offered endless possibilities for exploration. Mola always kept the keys to this room with her, and we grandchildren were always ready to follow her inside. When Mola finally led us through the stored boxes, we tiptoed around the dusty bundles that cluttered the floor. Avoiding the bear and tiger skins with their heads and claws intact, we could sift through gramophones, cameras, colorful rugs, maps, photographs, paintings, rifles, swords, rhino horns, elephant tusks, and ancient clocks. I loved the musical clocks more than anything else. Piles of old *National Geographic* magazines revealed to us the splendor of unknown places.

One day, Norzin and I followed Mola inside and then wandered off together into some deep corner. We never heard Mola go out and lock the door. When we realized we were locked in, we cried and banged on the heavy door. I do not remember how long we shouted, but finally a servant heard us and ran to Mola to let us out.

At the back of my grandparents' bedroom was a storehouse of gifts that my family used whenever we celebrated a wedding, a birth, a coming-of-age ceremony, or whenever we gave the customary gift to someone traveling out of town. Because we had many friends and relatives making long journeys, this storeroom was well stocked. Norzin and I often helped Mola find gifts. We cut out silk pieces for new blouses, brocades for new dresses, or folded khatas. Each gift was later packed in stiff, handmade Tibetan paper that was laid out on a tray. On a lucky occasion, my mother was involved in our gift planning, and Mola offered a silk blouse or dress to Amala, Norzin, and me.

With the absence of a modern drainage system and pipes, bathrooms were nonexistent in Tibetan homes. People with servants had water brought up to their rooms where a jug and a basin were kept. Many people washed near wells, streams, or near the kitchen where water was collected in huge bronze or copper pots. In the city, it was not unusual to see dirty water being thrown out of the window after a morning ablution. In distant villages, many people did not wash for months. Baths were taken only in the summer, in the lakes and rivers. The high altitude and the dry, cold climate of Tibet did not allow germs to breed easily.

Separate washrooms were built in our house and furnished with a jug, basin, tin bath tub, and a disposable wooden toilet seat with a chamber pot in the middle. Two-storied toilets were built a short distance behind the house. The ground floor of these toilets was walled in on three sides with a portion of the back left open for removal of the waste material. The upper floors were partitioned into small rooms with hollow slits in the center. The slits were about one foot by two and were framed by wooden panels, which one straddled like a horse. Ash from the kitchen was regularly thrown over the waste to eliminate the odors. When the ground floor filled up, villagers would come from the outskirts of the city to dig out the waste from the opened wall and use it for their crops and vegetable gardens.

Servants had separate toilets, which were similarly constructed, but they were open, without roofs, and had no wooden seats. We children preferred to use the servant's toilets, because we could sit and stare out at the sky. We had to be careful not to fall through the holes though, as there were three or four slits side by side and the holes were larger.

The kitchen was separate from the main house and had three rooms. The smaller was used only for special parties and for Western cooking. Since most Tibetans are of nomadic stock or semi-nomadic agriculturalists, we ate a lot of meat (yak and sheep mostly), butter, cheese, milk, and milk curd. And of course, tsampa is the Tibetan staple. However, Chinese food was usually prepared for special parties, and on occasion Indian curry or Muslim palao. This kitchen was used only for such occasions. The second room or kitchen was for daily family cooking, and the third was the tea kitchen. The tea kitchen also served as the common kitchen. Under the supervision of Wangchuk—a big, sooty man—tea was prepared for the family, and tea and food were made for our retainers, who numbered around thirty (a small staff compared to other Tibetan homes). There was another large room for storing the firewood, brambles, twigs, and animal dung. It was in the common kitchen that most of the commotion took place, always delightfully full of people, noisy, and bustling with activity. In the center there was a huge earthen stove where water was constantly kept boiling to make butter tea. This room, like all Tibetan kitchens, was dark, sooty, and greasy. It had white chalk drawings of signs for good luck, such as the eight auspicious signs. On the eve of every Losar—the Tibetan New Year— new drawings of the same signs would be painted. We children loved this kitchen because it was so busy. Our cooks and their assistants would always chase us out. They scolded us and told us our seats were in the main house, and that we were not to mix with kitchen people.

Along the kitchen, there were a number of single rooms in a long line. These rooms were for guests from out of town, who usually spent a month or two in Lhasa. Offices for the family secretary and his assistant were also there, as well as rooms for the visiting family carpenters and tailors, and living quarters for the servants. The cow shed, a huge pen for the family sheep, and stables for the horses and mules were nearby.

Everyone spent a great deal of their free time working in our garden. My grandparents and parents took great pride in the garden, personally supervising it and working in it themselves. They watered, planted, and mixed the soil and manure, all to the puzzlement and quiet disapproval of the family retainers. The retainers could not understand why the family members did not stay in the house or just enjoy the garden, leaving the manual work to the servants. The senior servants even believed this manual labor by the family members would bring bad luck to the family; it was all so inauspicious.

Flowers of many varieties were planted in neatly arranged beds. We had sweet peas, hollyhocks, dahlias, roses, and pansies, to name just a few. There were fruits, such as pears, apples, peaches, and even grapes, both the green and the black kinds, in our greenhouse, and gooseberries, too. As for vegetables, we grew radishes, carrots, squash, celery, cabbages, and tomatoes. There was also a very delicious small, spicy radish called *labuk kari*, or "small, white radish," a species I have never come across in any country other than Tibet. I believe the Chinese called this the "aristocratic radish" and did not permit the Tibetans to grow it, so now it is extinct. I heard recently, however, that the Chinese were trying to find its seed!

Vegetables were plentiful, and were planted in square lots. Some vegetables, like the radish family, were planted on raised mounds of soil. We used to help the vegetable gardener, a big, square-built woman with a rectangular face, named Yangkyi. She would make holes on the mound of soil with a pointed wooden stick, and then we would put the seeds in these holes and cover them with dirt. There were ditches between the square plots, flowing with water from the well.

A *shogom* was used to dispense water for irrigating the fields. To use the shogom, two people sat facing each other on either side of the well. They grabbed onto strong cords with both hands and with a forward movement, swung the canvas bag into the well. The force of the air pressure dropped the bag into the water, and the bag filled with water. With a backward movement of the body, the shogom was pulled up and thrown out in a square ditch, and from there the water flowed to the fields.

Once, two of my brothers were using the shogom to draw water from the well when one of them fell in. Fortunately, a maidservant was nearby, gossiping with Yangkyi, and they ran for the gardener, who came to my brother's rescue. After this experience, we were forbidden to go near the wells. Of course, from that day on, we itched to get our hands on the shogom.

The flower garden in front of the house had a water fountain built by the Austrian adventurer Heinrich Harrer, author of *Seven Years in Tibet*. We used to love swimming in this fountain in the summer. Harrer, who lived in our house for some time, helped in the garden, brought new ideas to it, and even grafted the fruit trees. Because there was no equivalent term for "grafting" in the Tibetan language, he used to call it "marrying" the fruit trees. This naturally caused a great deal of amusement.

Our compound and gardens were enclosed by mud walls about six feet high. One could only enter the grounds through a huge gate in the east, which was beautifully carved in solid wood and brightly decorated and framed with smooth clay. On each side of the gate, a stone platform was built for mounting and dismounting a horse. My siblings and I used these platforms as a perch for watching passersby.

Many smaller houses for tenants were built along these outer walls. These people came from all walks of life. We had a junior lay official of the central government living with his family on the left side of the gate, my grandfather's sister on the right side of the gate, a monk official of the government (who used to speed around on a motor bike in his monk's robe, a rare sight indeed), our chief cook and his family, and two Moslem traders, who were distinguishable by their long Tibetan dresses, white skull caps, and flowing beards. There were a couple of families living there who worked for us. These tenants paid their rent by services or a small sum of money.

Chantso, our secretary-cum-treasurer, was one of our servants. He had a long, narrow face with a scraggly beard and a long, thin braid. He was known to all as Kusho Chantso-la, but we used to call him Chantso Billy-Goat. While most large families had several treasurers, we had only one Chantso. Next in rank was Nyerpa-la, or the family steward. Both these men were highly respected and were treated like family. They had their own homes and servants in the city, and they were always present during important family discussions and functions. Their advice was sometimes sought on important family affairs, and their words often carried more weight than suggestions from family members. Nyerpa-la had a very kind face, covered by soft, curly white hair. Ever busy, he could be found cleaning the store rooms or keeping accounts or visiting my grandmother. We children loved to visit his store room, which had an endless stash of candy and fruit. Near a festival or our annual summer party, Nyerpa-la prepared *chang*, the barley beer of Tibet. He would clean, wash, boil, and ferment the barley grains from which the chang is strained. It takes a few days to ferment this drink, which tastes similar to champagne but has a higher alcohol content. Nyerpa-la would offer us the fermented barley before the chang was strained, and we would eat it until we got tipsy. He would then give us a hot cup of butter tea and tell us to go straight to our rooms or get lost in the gardens and not go near the adult members of the family.

Next in rank was our chef, Tsering Wangchuk, a stern-looking man. He was an excellent cook and very efficient. He spoke Hindi quite well, as well as a few words of English. He had been trained in India to cook roasts, and make caramel custards, buns, and pastries. Wangchuk could even make ice cream, but only in winter, as we had no refrigerators.

3 Festivals

In the precious garden of Lhasa
Do not say there is not a gem;
If His Holiness is not a gem,
What can he be?
The sky is like the eight spokes of the Dharma Wheel,
The earth is like the eight-petaled lotus,
Between sky and earth flow the eight auspicious signs;
Oh, what a happy place.

The city of Lhasa lies in a wide, flat valley about 12,000 feet above sea level and is surrounded by the highest mountains in the world. Lhasa means the "Abode of Gods." It most likely got its name in the seventh century A. D. when King Songtsen Gampo's Nepalese bride, Balsa, and his Chinese bride, Gyasa, brought images of Lord Buddha Shakyamuni to Tibet. The King built temples to house these precious images. The famous Jokhang in the center of Lhasa city is one of these temples.

At a later date, Balsa built a palace called the Tritse Marpo for the king, which was the foundation of the now-famous Potala Palace. She also built a palace for herself nearby, on Chakpori Hill, which later became the seat of the famous Tibetan Medical College of Chakpori. These two palaces are built on the twin peaks of a small hill that seems to have grown in the center of a valley out of the flat land. The distance between the two peaks is about a mile, and at the midpoint and the lowest part of the ridge, a huge *chorten* (stupa) stands, flanked by two smaller chortens. A large passage is dug right through the center chorten. When entering Lhasa, the sight is truly breathtaking—the majestic Potala poised beneath the awe-inspiring mountains, and the golden roofs of the Jokhang reflecting sunlight as it radiates from the turquoise heavens.

The population of the city in the late 1950s was around 100,000, but during festival times, thousands more gathered there from nearby monasteries, towns, and villages. Because of Tibet's physical isolation, not just from the outside world, but also between towns and villages within the country, entertainment was generally limited to one's own community. Festivals were a time to make the pilgrimage to the holy city.

Religion was the foundation of Tibetan life, and Tibetan art, history, culture, medicine, education, and entertainment all centered around Buddhism. The government was also largely theocratic, headed by Dalai Lamas since the seventeenth century. Prior to the seventeenth century, religious kings or religious sects of the different Tibetan Buddhist schools ruled the country. It is no surprise, then, that most of the thirty-five major festivals in a year were religious celebrations.

My favorite festival centered around Losar, the Tibetan New Year. On the twenty-ninth day of the last month of the year, two days before the New Year, there is a festival called Guthor. During this festival, monks from Namgyal Monastery, the Dalai Lama's personal monastery, performed religious dances at the Potala, which were attended by His Holiness, members of the government, and the public. These dances were performed to exorcise the evil spirits and the bad luck of the past year and to allow the country and its people to be prosperous, peaceful, lucky, and happy in the coming year.

On this particular night, we dined on *guthuk*, a dumpling soup. Every house would offer this soup of small round flour dumplings boiled in shredded radish and meat stock. Some of the dumplings were bigger than the others, and they were filled with different objects that carried a symbolic meaning. One might find a pea, a bit of charcoal or swatch of wool, a hot pepper, a piece of paper, or a grain of salt enveloped in one's dumpling. Family members would sit around a large table, the children laughing nervously and worrying about what their particular dumpling might reveal. As the dumplings were cautiously opened, the contents were examined in front of all of the family members. If a red hot chili or a peppercorn was discovered in the dumpling, the recipient was revealed as having a sharp tongue. A piece of charcoal meant a black heart, while a piece of paper revealed the recipient as being light of character, easily led by others. A few dumplings were shaped to resemble books of scripture, a sun or a moon, and the recipients of these items were cast as good, kind, and religious.

After dinner, small finger-like pieces of tsampa dough were carried out on a large plate by one of the servants and handed to each member of the family, starting with Pola and ending with the youngest child. Each person rolled the dough over themselves from head to toe, squeezed it in the palm of the hand, spat on it, and tossed it back on the plate. This procedure served to rid us of all the illnesses, bad luck, and obstructions of the past year and to bring in health, happiness, peace, and good luck in the new year. Then, in a moment of delightful chaos, a servant ran around the house with a burning torch in his hand, shouting at the top of his lungs to scare the evil spirits out of the house. Fire crackers were set off, and everyone yelled as loud as they could. The discarded dough pieces, a human effigy, and some of the soup were taken to a point where three paths met and then thrown into the torch flame.

A few days before Losar, the entire house was cleaned, the prayer flags were changed, and the *shambus* (colorful banners that hung from the doors and windows) were replaced. The house danced with energy, and we children were overcome with excitement and got in everyone's way. In the kitchen, hundreds of pastries (*khabsay*) of many different shapes with strange names crackled in the boiling butter. Plenty had to be made, because they were used to decorate the front of all of the altars in each living room and were given to our retainers, presented to all the visitors who wished the family a happy and auspicious new year, and donated to the beggars who went door to door. Nyerpa Wangyal-la was busy brewing chang, which was a very important job. The taste of the chang is said to tell many tales; if it is sweet and potent, it is considered most auspicious, but if it is weak and bitter or sour, it is a disaster.

We could hardly get to sleep the night before Losar, and roamed the house in an electrified trance. The main chapel was a dazzling sight; new silk and brocade banners and wall hangings glittered in the lamplight, new carpets were rolled out, and the altar was polished and decorated with stacks of dishes filled with dried fruits, sweets, and pastries. Oranges had been specially imported from Sikkim. The pastries were piled two feet high—flat long ones sat on the bottom, round flat *booloos* were placed in the middle, and criss-crossed, oblong-shaped ones crowned the top. A beautiful elaborately decorated wooden box held tsampa powder on one side and grains of wheat on the other, piled high like a pyramid. A narrow wooden frame, decorated with colorful butter sculptures, was stuck into the top of the wheat and tsampa pyramid. This mixture, along with a silver bowl full of chang, was to be offered to every person who visited the house during the Losar celebrations. The ritual consisted of taking a couple of wheat grains and a pinch of tsampa and throwing them into the air three times to make an offering to the Three Gems—Buddha, the Dharma, and the Sangha—and then tasting a bit of the tsampa. Each person took the fourth finger of their right hand, dipped it into the bowl of chang, flicked it once in the air to make offerings, and then tasted the chang with the tip of their finger. Once these rituals were performed, we repeated "Tashi Delek," meaning good luck and good health. On the altar lay the head of a sheep, decorated with colored butter.

In the early hours of the new day, we would awaken to the cry of the *delkar*—professional beggars who only visited homes on rare occasions or celebrations. These men would don white masks decorated with tiny sea shells and flowing white beards. They would recite ornate verses about their auspicious masks, the auspicious land they had come from, the auspicious day they had come for, and then they would bid us good luck and good health. The delkar would be well rewarded for their wishes with chang, pastries, gifts of money, and a beautiful white scarf.

We breakfasted on hot chang and tsampa brew, sprinkled with cheese, raisins, and droma, served to us in bed. We rose to dress in our finest clothes and prepared to join the adults in the main chapel for the New Year ceremonies. My grandfather and father wore their official golden brocade gowns with round, fluffy, fur hats. They wore long gold and turquoise earrings on their left ears and turquoise beads on their right ears. My grandmother and mother covered themselves in jewels. On their heads, they wore the traditional Lhasa headdress of seed pearls with corals sewn on a triangular felt base. They carried charm boxes studded with jewels and dangled long necklaces made of precious stones that glittered in the light of the kerosene lamps.

We followed the adults into the Lhamo Khang to prostrate and pray before our family protective deity, the goddess Palden Lhamo, and then into the Choegyal Khang, where we were assigned seats according to our age. Grandfather had the highest throne, followed by my father, my grandmother, mother, and so on until we reached the youngest family members. Each of us was presented with a bowl of hot wheat porridge, the hot chang brew, butter tea, and the ceremonial rice. Finally, the servants would bring the wooden boxes of wheat grain and tsampa, and the bowl of chang. Giggling, we would return Tashi Deleks to the bearers of these good wishes.

Scarves were presented by the household staff to the family, going from the oldest to the youngest members, and, with the final serving of tea, the ceremony would come to an end. Pola and Pala would leave immediately for the Lhasa Central Temple to pray before they went to the Potala Palace to take part in the official government ceremony. Mola and Amala would go back to bed and leave for the temple after sunrise, and we would accompany them.

People flocked to the temples in their finest apparel and best jewelry. Mola and Amala were always in full costume. We elbowed the crowd from room to room, prostrating, offering scarves, and praying. Nyerpa Wangyal-la would lead us on our visit, along with a servant whose job was to carry the khatas Nyerpa-la would present to us before we presented them to the numerous deities in the Central Temple.

During the day, we had special food, but had to remain in our homes. It was inauspicious to go out visiting on the first day of

Losar. Firecrackers kept us occupied, and the chang and tsampa brew kept everyone in a festive mood.

On the second day, we received visitors and visited family. In addition to the regular beggars who visited us on Losar, we had visits from a special band of beggars called the Ragyab-pa. The Ragyab-pa were a special group of professionals who were employed by the government to maintain the embankments of the Kyichu River and to dispose of the human and animal corpses in the city of Lhasa. They lived together in a special area established for them. The older males, heads of the family, even wore a *bogdo*, a round, flat, yellow felt hat to show their official status. Their houses were built from the horns of yaks, cows, sheep, and other cattle that they collected from the dead animals. Their community is hereditary, and the head of the family is selected by the office of the city magistrate. The headman collects the donations and distributes them to all the families; he is in full charge of their community.

When there was a special celebration in any part of the town, the Ragyab fathers would first come to beg in a group. They would sing a song of felicitation and request donations for their good wishes. Younger male members were known as the *pedong-nga*; they would come next after some interval, followed by the womenfolk. They were all known to be insistent beggars, and they would forcefully demand substantial "donations." If the alms were not to their satisfaction, they would refuse to leave the house and screech and yell their songs for more money. Even worse, they would sometimes curse the family. At the end of their songs, they would repeat and yell "Wo-jung," but if they were not pleased they left without a "Wo-jung" (meaning "yes, received!"), which signaled bad luck for the family. It was important to obtain this praise, so everyone was eager to please these beggars.

New Year celebrations on the third day generally included a ceremony similar to the one held on the first day in the main chapel of our home. On this day, the retainers of the house received scarves and cash prizes, which were handed out by my father in his full ceremonial costume. Tibetans all over the country celebrated Losar in a similar ceremony, according to their means.

Monlam Chenmo, the Great Prayer, began a few days after Losar to celebrate the victory of the Lord Buddha over the spirits who tempted him during his meditations. During this time, Lhasa was flooded with thousands of maroon-robed monks who came from the nearby monasteries. For three weeks, the city magistrates gave full power of governing to two chief monks, who were known to be very strict and who loved to show their power.

Besides prayers, offerings, and ceremonies, the learned monks from the three largest monasteries of Lhasa—Sera, Drepung, and Ganden—would hold the examinations for the Doctorate of Divinity, the Geshe degree. The examinations took place through theological debates supervised by the senior learned monks. Candidates would sit and watch as the monks stood in front, clapping and gesticulating to question them. At times, the disputes could get quite fiery. These debates served to sharpen the mind and to encourage the monks to read more scriptures.

There is a story about two old Moslems standing and watching this debate. One of them had never seen Tibetan monks debating, so he asked his friend, "What are these monks fighting about?" His friend replied, "They have still not settled some arguments from Buddha's lifetime!"

During Monlam, donations of money and goods were given to the monks and to beggars of the city by His Holiness, by the government, by individual officials of the government, and by the public. Butter tea was served seven times daily, and thick wheat or barley soup was served twice daily to the congregation. Bowls of apricots and buttered rice, sprinkled with raisin and droma were sometimes served, and the congregation received donations of money. Prayers were viewed as very important, and people from other parts of Tibet would come to Lhasa on this occasion to join in the prayers and to be blessed.

The butter lamp festival took place on the fifteenth day of the first month of the new year (every fifteenth day of a Tibetan month falls on a full moon day). This festival took place in the Barkhor, which swelled with all types of Tibetans. After sunset, we would put on our best clothes and accompany Mola and Amala to Nyerpa Wangyal-la's home, which was in the Barkhor.

Besides the temple, there were several government houses and private homes built inside this path. There were also some shops and smaller temples. People circled along the Barkhor for religious purposes, to go shopping, or to visit friends. Buddhists always made a clockwise turn. The counterclockwise turn is known as the outer circle, and believers of other religions were known as outsiders.

There were other shops, Indian tea houses, chang houses, and private homes outside the Barkhor path. For the materially minded, international goods could be purchased, such as the famous 555 and 999 cigarettes, "Evening in Paris" perfumes brought from India, brocades from Russia, China, India and Japan, and cosmetics from France and the United Kingdom. Domestic items could also be purchased, such as *dri* (female yak) cheese and butter from the Changthang and dried meat from the countryside.

Butter statues were beautifully and elaborately sculpted by monks. Some of these sculptures were as tall as seventy feet high. Commissioned by the various monasteries or homes of government officials, each sculpture was made of colored butter, constructed on a wooden frame, and shaped in the form of a person, a tree, an animal, a flower, or an auspicious sign. Some sculptures had strings attached, and when manipulated from the back could move around like marionettes. This display is meant as an offering to the Triple Gem. At the start, His Holiness the Dalai Lama and his ministers and other high lamas would come in a procession to view this spectacle. When the official processions were over, the public, who would be waiting along the side lines, would rush to make the rounds of the butter sculptures, bursting into song and dance along the way.

On the fifteenth of the fifth Tibetan month, in early summer, the whole country celebrated Zamling Chisang, or the day of universal prayer. This day commemorates the appeasing of the local spirits who were attempting to interfere as Guru Padmasambhava propagated Buddhism in Tibet, and Guru Padmasambhava's power over evil when he came to Tibet from India in the eighth century.

The summer picnics began with the government officiating prayers to the local deities and spirits, and the public visiting the various temples and shrines, burning incense, and putting multicolored prayer flags over high hills and mountain tops. The citizens put up tents in the fields and public parks on the out-skirts of the city and moved into them to enjoy the fresh air and the beginning of summer. People bathed in the Kyichu River, in the canals of crystal sparkling water running alongside meadows of dazzling mustard plants.

Men would play dice, an original Tibetan game with many witty verses, and sometimes naughty verses, sung at each toss of the dice. The dice would be shaken in a wooden cup and thrown with great force on a round leather cushion. People would sit nearby just to listen to the witty verses and cheer for the players. Chang and food were passed around generously.

Another festival, especially associated with women of Tibet, is Pal-lhay Ritoe. On this day, the fierce statue of the goddess Palden Lhamo, which resides in the Jokhang, was carried around the Barkhor and briefly put down, facing Vase Hill, a small vase-shaped hill in the southeast direction of Lhasa. Below this hill is Tsechokling Monastery, where the Lhamo's consort resides. Once a year, the goddess in the Jokhang would meet her consort. This day was special for visiting the Jokhang, or any temple with the image of Palden Lhamo, and it was a day for rejoicing and prayer.

One day before the goddess Palden Lhamo made her appear-ance in public, she was taken out of her dark chapel. Her face was recoated with gold paint, she was dressed in new clothing of silk and brocade, and offerings were made to her by the Lacha, the state treasurer. The goddess spent the night outside the chapel of Shakyamuni, the chief deity in the Central Temple. She was placed just outside the iron grille, facing the Buddha.

Early the next morning, members of the Tibetan cabinet came to offer their prayers and scarves and to be blessed by Palden Lhamo. They would be followed by other government officials, and all day a long line of visitors would crowd to meet their goddess. A long human chain of Tibetans from all walks of life would wait to see the goddess, some of them making a lifetime pilgrimage to the Holy City.

During Palden Lhamo's appearance in the city, there were fire ceremonies in four directions that served to purify the air and to get rid of any obstructions. A strong monk was chosen to adorn Palden Lhamo's mask and frame and to make a circle of the inner Barkhor. This monk had to stay in retreat prior to this duty for purification and to invoke the spirit of the goddess within him. After the ceremonies, the goddess once again returned to her dark and gloomy chapel, not to see the sun or to have a glimpse of her consort under Vase Hill for another year. Her chapel is filled with mice who are known to be her army. When I visited this room, the mice crawling all over the goddess sent chills through my body. I quickly slipped into the next room where the peaceful manifestation of the goddess resided without her army.

On this day, the children were given money from older family members and friends. In fact, it was quite appropriate for the children to ask for the gift, which was called *paley thunchar*. My great uncle, who was an old, very kind monk with a gleaming smile, would visit us on this day to distribute money among us children. We would also receive gifts of money from our grandparents and parents. As our collection accumulated to quite a large sum, Amala would put it in our personal bags—sort of old-fashioned piggy banks—and whenever we needed money, we could take it from this bag, which was safely locked up in my parent's living room.

During the summer, the Lhamo was performed. It is believed that during the fourteenth century, a Bodhisattva called Thangton Gyalpo built the first iron bridge in Tibet. In order to collect funds to build the bridge, plays were staged by his workers. The Goddess Tara was said to have provided the seven links of magical iron chain to build the bridge, and Achi Lhamo was the name given to the actors in her honor. Achi Lhamo means "the lady Goddesses."

At the start of a Lhamo performance, an image of Thangton Gyalpo was always placed in the center of the stage, and only then would the show begin. The *ngonpa* (hunters) would come onto the stage and begin the purification dance. They were followed by two stately looking men wearing long gowns and huge top hats and carrying long staffs. Gliding onto the stage, they looked very dignified. The goddesses appeared onstage with long rainbow-colored scarves draped on their shoulders. *Namthar* (songs) were sung, and after a few dances and saluting the guests with bows, the narrator would recite the prologue of the show.

The first performances, very short parts from different operas, would be staged on the twenty-fifth day of the sixth Tibetan month at Kyitsel Ludhing, which is a short distance from Lhasa. This was the palace of the eighth Dalai Lama, Jamphel Gyatso. From here, the opera group performed at the Potala, at Norbulingka Palace, and at Drepung, where there was another palace. At Drepung, the special guests of the monastery were served a lunch of rice, raisins, droma, and *sho drey* (curd and rice). The festival was also known as Shothoen, or "Appearance of Curd."

For four days during the seventh month, the drama companies performed onstage for the public at the summer palace of the Dalai Lama. There was a raised platform in front of the palace where the performances were held. Small canopies were erected on the sides of the stage where the ministers, members of the Dalai Lama's family, the ambassadors of Britain, India, Nepal, and Bhutan, as well as the Moslem leaders, would sit. The remaining government officials sat in their tents nearby. The only women allowed on the stage were family members of His Holiness. Men acted the female roles. The wives of the ministers, in their gorgeous costumes and full headdresses and jewels, would sit below the stage with the public.

There were about a dozen opera groups, but the most famous were Kyumu-Loong, Chungpa, Nyermo, Shangpa and Gyankara, who performed on the stage of the Norbulingka for His Holiness. Different noble houses and monasteries requested the groups to give private shows, and the public was welcomed to these performances. The actors would be paid in cash or with grain and tea, and at the end of the show, each actor would receive a scarf.

These performances provided some of the few opportunities the public had to glimpse His Holiness the Dalai Lama. Another occasion was when he moved from the winter palace, the Potala, to the summer palace, the Norbulingka, and when he returned to the Potala when summer came to an end. The people of Lhasa would line the route His Holiness traveled, dressed in their finest clothing and elaborately ornamented. With much reverence, anticipation, and love for our leader, we waited for the sound of the *dama,* a large round drum. The melancholy "tang tang tang" of the dama, and the sound of the *suna,* a wind instrument, announced the appearance of His Holiness.

The procession was long. It was led by one of the palace sweepers, a man in a long white woolen robe, maroon boots, and a yellow pancake-like hat. He would ride a white horse and carry a pair of tigerskin bolsters with yak tails at each end. He was known as the doorkeeper, and the bolsters were to hold the door open. Following him were several more men on horseback, dressed in brocade robes and carrying different banners. They were followed by senior members of the Tibetan government and His Holiness' personal attendants. His Holiness was carried in a golden palanquin by attendants in golden silk robes, black leather boots and round, red, fringed hats. In a cloud of incense and herbs, the Dalai Lama's bodyguards marched along to the sounds of the military band playing English tunes such as "Auld Lang Syne" and "It's a Long Way to Tipperary."

On the twenty-fifth of the tenth Tibetan month, Tibetans commemorated the anniversary of the death of the great Gelukpa teacher Je Tsongkapa. On this day, new Tibetan officials were admitted into government services and blessed by the Dalai Lama. In the evening, His Holiness and monks from his personal monastery made offerings in the chapel of the Potala Palace.

Lhasa was ablaze with tiny lamps resting on rooftops and window ledges. Children carried special lamps—balloon lamps, made of dried sheep and yak bladders, inside which were small clay oil lamps or butter lamps. The tops had a large opening where strings were attached to the sides, so that they could be carried. We used the lanterns to help light the lamps on the rooftop while songs and prayers of praise were offered to Je Tsongkhapa. The night air was cold, and bright stars glittered in the clear sky. Hot, thick soups awaited us after all the lamps had been lit.

The end of summer was marked by the return of His Holiness to the Potala Palace. Leaves on the willows turned from green to brown, while those from the poplars started to fall. In the early morning hours, an icy chill filled the air. Delights of summer picnics, baths in the Kyichu River, opera and fairies faded like incense smoke. Winter would reign, long and cold.

4　China and Tibet

By the end of 1949, the Communists, under the leadership of Mao Tse-tung, drove the Nationalists out of power, and the People's Republic of China was duly constituted. As soon as they had consolidated their power, the Communists started talking about liberating Tibet from imperialist forces, even though there was no imperialist control over Tibet. In fact, there were only a few Westerners even living in Tibet at the time.

Before the Chinese invaded, strange, inexplicable events began taking place in Tibet. In 1948, a terrible earthquake caused massive damage, displacing mountains and valleys, causing flooding, and killing many people. During the dry summer months, an unusual dripping of water was noticed from the mouths of the decorative stone lions that guard the Central Temple in Lhasa; this was a very bad omen. The women of Lhasa, customarily clad in beautiful, brightly colored apparel, took to wearing black blouses and robes; this too was very inauspicious. Lhasa was cast in deep suspicion, and many unusual events were rumored.

The Tibetan government was very concerned about the threat from China. Tibet had been completely isolated from the rest of the world and was without a proper army to defend the country. The army was more like a police force than a defense against outside aggression; it served mostly as a national guard watching for unauthorized travelers trying to enter the country. Tibet was totally unprepared for a war.

My grandfather, Dasang Dadul Tsarong, believed in the importance of strengthening the Tibetan army and advocated the urgency of training and recruiting a proper military. As commander-in-chief of the Tibetan army under the Thirteenth Dalai Lama, he had managed to send officers to train under the British in India. He had also recruited more men into the army and trained them under a Japanese officer. However, Tsarong's modern ideas were too advanced for the conservative Tibetans. The cost of developing an army would require increasing the taxes of the monasteries and the nobility and this was most unwelcome. Pola was no doubt a patriotic and powerful figure, but his close contact with the Thirteenth Dalai Lama had caused jealousy among members of the ruling elite. Also, he had been born a peasant, and this inclined some of the nobility to regard him with prejudice. The ill feelings towards my grandfather accelerated to such an extreme that he was finally removed from his army post and from the cabinet, and his life was quite possibly in danger. It was rumored that Tsarong wanted to build up Tibet's army in order to wrest power from the Dalai Lama. In such a conservative and religious country, only a fool would take such an action, and Tsarong would never betray his protector. The Dalai Lama had educated him, given him his post, and blessed him to head the Tsarong family. During this crucial period, he left for a pilgrimage to India and Nepal, and his life was saved from his enemies.

There were a number of progressive government officials like Tsarong, young officials wanting to change the old system, but they had to comply with the elders and the religious establishment. In response to the threat from China, the National Assembly met and decided to appeal to the neighboring countries, as well as to the more powerful nations like Britain and the United States. A delegation was prepared and sent, but they only got as far as India. The universal response by the countries approached was that Tibet must try to settle her own problems with China. It was clear that no one wanted to get involved.

Prayers were said, butter lamps were lit, and high lamas and oracles were consulted, but it was all too late. By early in 1950, the Chinese had crossed the Tibetan borders, and by October they had captured Chamdo. Tibetan resistance, with few men and ancient arms, was futile against such a large army, equipped with modern arms and ammunition. A protest was sent to the United Nations against Chinese aggression, but the reply was disappointing. The question was shelved. I often wondered what the United Nations stood for if they could not check the aggression of one country towards another, especially a powerful country asserting itself on a weaker nation. This great body later passed three resolutions on behalf of the Tibetan case, but they did not bother to do more.

The internal situation was not good in Tibet. Regencies had always been very unstable periods in Tibetan history. All intrigues took place during such periods. The country was weak and in chaos, and the Thaktra Regent's court was unpopular. The official oracle of the government announced that the young Dalai Lama, who was only fifteen years old, should be given power to rule the country. Thus, His Holiness the Fourteenth Dalai Lama began his reign in an extremely troubled climate.

As spiritual and temporal leader, the Dalai Lama was the only individual who could unite the country at such a moment of panic and uncertainty. His Holiness was too precious to be left in Lhasa while the Chinese were advancing on the capital. Late in the year in 1950, the Dalai Lama was urged to leave Lhasa and rule from Dromo, near the Indian border, while a lay and a monk prime minister were to remain in charge of the capital.

While my husband Lobsang Samden was alive, I encouraged him to make some notes about his life, but he was a lazy writer. I asked him about the details of the Chinese takeover, because I had planned to write a book about his life. I managed only to extract a few details, but I think they are very important to share. Below are some of his notes regarding the Chinese takeover.

> It was around 1950, in Lhasa, the capital of Tibet, when I first came to know of the rumors that had been going around for quite some time about the Chinese Liberation Army coming to invade Tibet. I was attending Yarkey, the annual summer picnic held for the monk officials of the Tibetan government at Tsedrun Lingka, a lovely park on the outskirts of Lhasa city. Our Austrian friend, Heinrich Harrer, who was then one of only six Europeans in Tibet,

had come especially to deliver this news to us. He had just heard news of the Chinese army's advancement into Tibetan territory on the BBC. This information left us stunned. Much publicity had been made by the Peking government that the liberation of Tibet was to take place, and rumors of their advance had been around for quite some time, but we never expected it to be possible. We never expected it to be so soon and we were totally unprepared for the invasion. Our country's strength lay in the hands of 8,500 men who were equipped with pre-World War II weapons and who had no training in fighting. There was nothing to do immediately but to continue with our picnic, huddled together into groups discussing the latest news.

In the next couple of weeks, a number of meetings occurred among the members of the Kashag, which normally has four members, one of whom is a monk. The monk was Kalon Rampa, and the lay Kalons were Surkhang, Ragashar, and Lhalu. The Kashag met with the four Trungyi Chenmo, the four monk officials from the Yigtsang, the Council of Monk Officers, and the four Tsipon, lay officers from the Tsikhang, the Treasury office. These men also met with the subcommittee of the National Assembly. The meeting created a great deal of suspense in the mind of the public, and the public became aware of the Chinese threat to our peace-loving country. I was eighteen years old and a monk official of the Tibetan government with no significant position, but because I was the brother of the Dalai Lama, I had the privilege of being informed of the various meetings, although I never was present at them. Being so young, I was only aware of the threat to our religion and of the possibility that our peace would be disturbed and we were to be at war. Much fear overtook me. I knew nothing much about the outside world and wondered what would happen to the Tibetan culture and religion and worried about the suffering we would have to face. The outcome of these meetings was that the Tibetan army was to be expanded, and five thousand men were enlisted in a new regiment. Radio Lhasa broadcasted our right to independence and stressed our wish to negotiate with the Chinese on peaceful terms, but we were also willing to fight if China entered Tibetan territory illegally. This broadcast was meant to be in retaliation to a broadcast Radio Peking had made in the Tibetan language.

As time passed, more serious news came to Lhasa from Lhalu, our governor in eastern Tibet, who was stationed in the town of Chamdo. Mr. Robert Ford, a British national who was then employed by the Tibetan government, kept constant radio communication going between Lhasa and Lhalu. One day, a code was signalled from Chamdo that the Chinese were advancing close to our eastern border. The National Assembly, numbering about four hundred, met to discuss this news and made the decision to send delegations to the United States, Great Britain, India, and Nepal to request help and to make our position known to the outside world, which had very little knowledge about Tibet. The appointment of these delegates was made in consultation with the Regent, Thaktra Rinpoche, and the Kashag, Yigtsang, and the Tsikhang. There is a saying in Tibet that to solve a problem, it is better to get guidance from the Buddha and high lamas than from ordinary human beings and then regret the results. Therefore, oracles were consulted and divinations were performed. As was the custom, one representative was not sufficient. It was the rule that a lay and a monk official were paired, and they worked together on any assignment. Before the delegations had even reached the respective countries, replies had been received from each of the four countries, expressing their deepest sympathy for Tibet, but citing the geographical difficulties of reaching it as hindering their ability to provide assistance. India stressed that Tibet should open negotiations with China for a peaceful settlement. Our representative to India got as far as New Delhi, but the talks with the Indian government did not get very far. Ngapo replaced Lhalu as governor, and on October 19, 1950, Chamdo was captured by the Chinese. Ngapo was held hostage, and Robert Ford was captured and imprisoned.

In Lhasa, the government was filled with anxiety and terribly discouraged by the negative responses from the countries from whom we had sought help. The state oracles were being consulted. During one of the consultations of Nechung by the Regent, the oracle expressed that the Dalai Lama should be given official power to rule Tibet, and that he should be enthroned immediately. To many Tibetans, the holy message from Nechung seemed fitting, because the Lhasa government was in chaos and had been in a terrible state of confusion and mismanagement since the death of the Great Thirteenth. Now with the Chinese threat, it was in a sad state. Finally, the Dalai Lama was enthroned on November 17, 1950, at the age of fifteen.

The first official task performed by the Dalai Lama after his enthronement was to write the Chinese government, requesting that they withdraw their army from Tibetan territory, release the captured people, and settle the matter peacefully. Meanwhile, the Kashag had managed to bring the Tibetan case to the United Nations, but on November 24, 1950, discussions on the "Question of Tibet" in the United Nations General Assembly were postponed. Again, we had been left to take action alone, and no foreign government nor any great power was willing to assist us in our fight against the mighty Communist power of China.

To avoid personal danger to the life of the Dalai Lama, the National Assembly met once more and requested that the Dalai Lama hold government temporarily from Dromo, near the border of India. The Dalai Lama appointed two prime ministers, a lay and a monk official, to reside in Lhasa, and he gave them full authority to make decisions regarding the security of Tibet. In December 1950, the Dalai Lama left for Dromo with his party. In the open negotiations with the Chinese, Ngapo was given full authority, as he had requested this from the Dalai Lama. Two lay officials, Tenzin Thondup Sampo and Khenchung Thupten Lekmuen, were appointed by His Holiness to assist Ngapo.

On May 23, 1951, Sampo, Khenchung Lekmuen, Dzasa Khemey, and Secretary General Thupten Tenthar, who joined the former officials in Peking from Dromo, were under pressure to sign the so-called Seventeen-Point Agreement, which was drafted by the Chinese. This agreement would concede the Chinese a degree of administrative and military authority. The Chinese forged new seals of the names of the delegates and forced the Tibetan delegation to sign and seal the documents. The Dalai Lama did not know about the contents of the agreement, nor were the other government officials aware of the agreement, until Radio Peking relayed it on their broadcast. It was only after the Tibetan delegation's return to Tibet that they knew what had taken place in China. Later this agreement was repudiated by the Tibetan government in 1959, at Lhuntse-dzong, near the Tibetan border with northeast India.

Immediately after the Seventeen-Point Agreement was signed, a Chinese general named Chang Chin Wu arrived in Dromo via India and persuaded His Holiness to return to Lhasa. In July 1951, His Holiness and his party left Dromo for Lhasa, as they saw no other choice for Tibet. Tibet was to see a lot of changes, mostly for the worse. A month after Chang's arrival in Lhasa, two Chinese military units, each with about three thousand officers and men, marched into Lhasa as a show of force.

During the Dalai Lama's stay in Dromo, serious discussion transpired among the government officials. There were two parties among these officials, most senior members of the government. The monk officials requested that the Dalai Lama return to Lhasa to negotiate with the Chinese leaders, while some of the lay officials suggested that the Dalai Lama seek refuge in India and not to return to Lhasa. Heated debate surrounded this decision until the Dalai Lama settled on returning to Lhasa, where he had great hopes that, as human beings, the Chinese would settle the matter peacefully. The Dalai Lama and his party returned to Lhasa, while a few of the Tibetan officials decided to settle in India and not have anything to do with the Chinese. A small portion of the Tibetan public made the decision to move to India.

5 In Transit

With the flight of the Dalai Lama and his entourage to Dromo, my family thought it best to leave for India. In December 1950, we gathered the clothing and supplies we would need for an indeterminate stay away from our home, and embarked on a long trek across the Himalayas.

Although I do not recall this journey particularly well, I do remember that our party consisted mostly of children. There were the five children from my family and two of my aunt Betty Taring's children. At nine years old, I was the oldest. My mother, aunt Betty, and my mother's very good friend Mrs. Pemba from Sikkim led a flock of seven small children over strenuous and hostile terrain. Several servants also accompanied us on the journey. My grandfather, grandmother, and father were not with us, as they had traveled to Dromo with the Dalai Lama's entourage.

Strapped in our saddles, we spent many long and what seemed like tortuous hours winding our way toward our destination. Our only comforts were the candies and dried cheese and fruits we kept tucked in our saddle bags. The adults were tired and concerned with the events in Tibet. We talked little, and I ached to be wherever it was that we were going.

One event I do remember clearly happened some weeks into our journey. We had stopped to lodge for the night in a small village. Exhausted after a slow, draining day on horseback, we children were uncharacteristically eager for bed. All at once,

Amala, who had been feeling unwell, became very dizzy and began to lose consciousness. Not knowing what to do and terrified that Amala might be dying, one of us ran for the servants in the lower rooms. They quickly started working their magic on Amala. I remember someone feeling her cold feet and rubbing them, and someone else blowing incense and tsampa smoke in her bed. A warm buttered tsampa dough was applied to her temples and across her forehead, and holy pills were forced into her mouth. Finally, Amala regained her senses, and the heat began coming back in her legs. To our good fortune, Amala made a full recovery, and after a few days we were able to continue on our journey.

When I think back on this episode, I am sure it was the stress of the precarious events in Tibet and the tiresome journey to India that caused Amala's sudden illness. My mother had left behind my father and many family members, not knowing what would happen in the future. It was perhaps the first major upheaval of her life. Before the recent unsettling events in Tibet, Amala's life had been very predictable; every moment at home was completely organized, and everything ran smoothly and efficiently. There was scarcely ever a reason for anyone to raise their voice.

Eventually, we were liberated by officials from the Sikkimese royal household in a formal welcoming ceremony. Just below the Nathula Pass, at Tsogo, under the clear sky and near a sparkling inland lake, these officials greeted us and escorted us to the royal household, where a sumptuous lunch had been prepared. My maternal grandmother and her youngest brother, George Taring—who was my aunt Betty's husband—were from the Sikkimese royal family. Their father, Raja Taring, was heir to the throne, but he had taken refuge in Tibet after a disagreement with the British over their policy toward Sikkim. In addition, my father's younger half-sister, Aunt Tess, was the wife of the Maharaja of Sikkim.

My siblings and I were quite amused by the small, round brocade hats and silk gowns worn by the Sikkimese officials. We could not keep from giggling as we watched them carry out their duties. The lunch was sumptuous, and we ate our fill and then helped ourselves to the irresistible display of sweets. Thrilled to be freed from our saddles, we relished our freedom after such a long trip.

Sometime later in the day, we rode down from the Nathula Pass toward the town of Gangtok, where we were to lodge in the Dak Bungalow, a guest house that was furnished in Western style. This was a thrilling experience for me. Everything was so modern. The furniture was very unlike anything I had ever seen before, and the bathroom was splendid with its shiny china basins and pitchers. What really excited my siblings and me were the roaring jeeps and trucks that sped along shiny, smooth, black roads, nothing like the dusty roads of Lhasa. When the engines roared, we would drop whatever we were doing just to get a glimpse of these moving boxes. Eventually, we were allowed to ride in a jeep that was left at our disposal by the Sikkimese royal family. I was terrified.

In Tibetan culture, it is customary for Tibetans to call on relatives and friends once they arrive in a new town, and to offer khatas and presents. Needless to say, my mother and aunt spent much of their time after our arrival in Gangtok wrapping presents and visiting and receiving friends and relatives at the house. Everyone seemed relaxed and somehow natural, but the situation in Tibet and the uncertainty of events must have been foremost on their minds.

We left Gangtok for Kalimpong where we planned to stay for a while. Kalimpong was an important center for Tibetan trade with India and Bhutan, and many Tibetans lived there. It was also a popular holiday resort for many foreign business people. The town was home to a number of good private missionary schools, and the shopping was excellent. The local market, which opened only two days out of each week, was absolutely charming. The local villagers, most of whom are of Nepalese origin, would bring their goods to the market to sell, and then they would buy their necessary provisions.

Once we were settled in Kalimpong, we were joined by my grandmother and father. My grandfather remained in Dromo with His Holiness. Whereas my parents had visited India earlier and were familiar with the surroundings and the modern facilities and different customs, it was a completely new way of life for my siblings and me. We visited the Dorji family often. Jigme Dorji's mother, Rani Chuki Dorji, was the sister of the Maharaja of Sikkim and was also related to us on my mother's side of the family. Jigme Dorji was married to Aunt Tess and they had three sons our age. We loved spending time with them. These cousins were very mischievous. Accustomed to more freedom than I could ever dream of, these boys were blessed with infinite energy and adventurous spirits. They introduced us to the game of cowboys and Indians and to comics and football games. We sometimes stayed at their home, and the boys' excessively strict servant, Thangchub, would serve us breakfast, which was accompanied by a spoonful of cod liver oil. There was no way to avoid this unwanted dose of the smelly oil, because we were not allowed to leave the table until it had been cleared and we had been officially dismissed by Thangchub.

Soon, other relatives and friends from Tibet came to visit or to settle in Kalimpong. We began to feel more at home in our new surroundings. In fact, life was somewhat carefree for us children. We were mostly oblivious to the situation in Tibet, even though the adults in the family must have existed in a constant state of worry.

Several of my father's siblings—his sisters Daisy and Nancy and his brother Phuntsok—came home from schools in Darjeeling for their winter holidays. My aunts wore those long, full skirts so fashionable in the early fifties. Aunt Daisy even had her hair permed and wore beautiful round gold earrings. She had lots of exotic trinkets stored in various little boxes in her room. These aunts were so pretty and so different from the teenage girls we knew in Lhasa. Norzin and I used to follow them around, and we longed for the days we could dress like them and wear such beautiful earrings and swirling skirts!

Uncle Phuntsok was only four years older than I, and we all had good fun with him. He served as the ring leader for the younger children, and we were happy to follow him around. One day, to the astonishment of my mother and grandmother, Uncle Phuntsok decided to take the younger brood fishing. We fashioned large safety pins into hooks, and then set off on an expedition to fish for goldfish from our neighbors' water fountain.

Uncle caught one and brought it home, only to learn that gold-fish were not edible and to receive a strong reproach from the adult members of the household. Buddhist law forbids the taking of any kind of life, and we got one lecture after another from the older family members. It was a lesson well learned. No more fishing!

Cinema was also a new luxury for us, and it became a weekly activity. In the center of the town, there was an old, decaying movie hall where Indian and English movies were shown. It had a tin roof, and when there was a heavy rain shower it was impossible to hear the film. It really did not matter, as long as we could see the picture. Tibetans loved cowboy movies. We would sit motionless on the hard wooden benches, cheering for our heroes or howling and sobbing at the sad parts. Almost every Indian movie had a tragic part, and it was most embarrassing for my aunts, who used to chaperone us on these excursions, when we broke into loud wailing. This make-believe world was so real to us, and for the short period that we were locked in this entertainment shack we forgot everything else. During intermission, there was enough time to buy peanuts piled in newspaper cones and delicious, juicy oranges from the young, scruffy-looking boys who rushed into the hall during the break. It was most exciting.

It was during this time that the Dalai Lama resolved to return to Lhasa and work with the Chinese. The Chinese remained in Tibet, and their presence was strongly felt as Chinese representatives continued to arrive in Lhasa in large numbers. They seemed genuinely cordial, courteous, and ready to please the Tibetans. It was the mission of these servants of the People's Republic of China to help Tibetans develop the skills they needed for independence and modernization. When their work was completed, they would leave.

For the People's Liberation Army members, the posting in Tibet was a challenging time. Far from China and unaccustomed to the altitude and brutal climate, these emissaries had no experience with the Tibetan language, and adapting to the nomadic diet of the Tibetans was no simple feat. Many Chinese fell sick in Tibet, and they surely felt that the Tibetans were as foreign to them as we felt they were to us.

As the tension in Tibet eased and our leaders returned, many Tibetans who had planned to settle in India returned to Tibet as well, taking with them all of the belongings they had transported with them from Tibet for their brief exile. My family also returned home to Lhasa to wait for the departure of the Chinese and for a free and modern Tibet.

Arrangements were made for Norzin and me to remain in school in India, as my family felt that a modern education was very important. There were very few Tibetan children in schools in India then, among them seven or eight boys who were the sons of government officials sent by the Tibetan government for schooling in missionary schools in Darjeeling. These children were very soon recalled to Tibet.

My family was not popular in Tibet for sending their younger generation abroad for a Western education. It was believed that Tibetans educated out of Tibet, especially in the mission schools in India, would lose faith in the Buddhist religion. With great courage and foresight, my grandfather and my parents overlooked these sentiments and had all of their children educated in India. At times, the elders in my family were subjected to strong criticism and were even labeled as British spies. I am very grateful for my education, without which life would have been very different and much more difficult.

6 Darjeeling—Dorje Garden

In Tibetan, Darjeeling means "Dorje Garden." The *dorje*, a Tibetan Buddhist ritual instrument, symbolizes power, durability, and compassion. At six thousand feet above sea level, Darjeeling sits on the border of India and Sikkim and stretches toward the Kanchenjunga mountain range. This hill station in West Bengal was established by the British in 1835, and became a meeting point for managers of the outlying tea plantations as well as an escape haven for people from the hot Indian plains and the large cities.

During the late fifties, the town was sophisticated and carefree, full of Bengali tourists, American teachers, aspiring Himalayan climbers, swindlers, politicians, Christian missionaries, ethnologists, Tibetologists, imperialists, tea merchants, Sherpa porters, and hotel keepers. With tea shops, movie theaters, a variety of good restaurants, horseback riding, a skating club, dances, opera, and tour companies, Darjeeling attracted a wealthy clientele. Upper-class Asian, European, and American families sent their children to one of Darjeeling's many private Christian schools run by Protestant missionaries, Jesuit priests, or Loreto nuns.

When Norzin and I enrolled at Mount Hermon School in 1951, it was run by American Baptists who looked after the one hundred or so Asian and Western children. There were children from diplomatic, missionary, or international trade families in every grade. Although my father's sisters, Daisy and Nancy, his brother

Phuntsok, and my Taring family cousins were also students at Mount Hermon, Norzin and I were the only Tibetans in the primary school. We could not speak a word of English, and we ached with loneliness.

At the beginning of our first year, Norzin and I suffered great ridicule. We were both quite chubby. Our full, red faces attracted looks of mockery. We were nicknamed "apple cheeks" and "moon face." Nobody could protect us from this name-calling, and with our linguistic disadvantage, we had no power of defense.

The principal and his wife, Mr. and Mrs. Dewey from the United States, knew how far we were from our home, and they were especially kind to us. Most of the teachers at Mount Hermon also helped to create a great sense of family at school.

Norzin was perhaps even more troubled than I was by our isolation and distance from home. At the most difficult point in our transition, she woke in the middle of the night, dressed herself, and crept out of our dormitory room with the idea that she would go to Darjeeling and then home to Tibet. As she started down the stairs, Norzin collided with Mrs. Dewey, who led her back to the dormitory room where the lights were switched on. I awoke to see my sister crying inconsolably. Instead of offering my sister any comfort, I also dissolved into tears. Mrs. Dewey was left with no choice but to wake one of our aunts from the upper school to come and calm us. Eventually, we settled down and fell into a deep sleep, the kind that often follows a traumatic event. I never knew how Norzin intended to travel the two miles from school into town, or what she would have done on the dark streets of Darjeeling without money and unable to speak Nepali or English. She was a brave eight-year-old!

We felt so different in every way. Our clothes stood out. Norzin and I had never worn anything other than Tibetan *chubas*, which hang to the floor. Under these, we always covered our legs with pajama bottoms. At our new school, we felt so bare and chilly in knee-length skirts. Eventually, we came to relish the ease of twirling and flowing in the loose, pleated or flared fabric. After a few weeks, we were no longer embarrassed by our exposed legs. In a strange twist of circumstance, we found ourselves lucky to have our chubas for special occasions. We became the envy of the girls at every formal evening or costume party, dressed in our elegant silk gowns.

Soon we made a few friends, began liking English porridge, and learned to eat with forks. As we learned English, we felt more at ease, and our classmates dropped our nicknames.

Academics at Mount Hermon most likely resembled the standard of international boarding schools organized under some derivative of the British system. We studied Western literature, world history, geography, science, mathematics, music, and the Bible. Because I was a girl with infinite energy, a tomboy really, I was happiest when classes were over and the extracurricular activities began. I threw myself into intramural volleyball, debating, cooking, Gilbert and Sullivan productions, and fencing and soccer with the boys. I could often be found competing with the boys or thinking up pranks that frequently got me into trouble. To the amusement of my female classmates, I was forever being dragged to our matron for a hairbrush spanking on my bottom. I would always scream, "Give me one more chance!" but I rarely avoided punishment.

One of the worst punishments to be doled out at Mount Hermon was to be denied a Saturday outing into town. Every second Saturday, we were given a permission slip and allowed off campus. Dressed in our navy blue shirts, school blazers, black shoes, and white bobby socks, we spent the day shopping, stuffing ourselves with Foo Ying's Chinese chow mein and Keventer's milkshakes, going horseback riding, seeing a movie, or just wandering up and down Chowrestra, the famous Darjeeling mall. We had to be back at school and checked in by five in the evening. The day went by quickly, but it was one release from the highly restricted world on campus.

Once, because of a zestful prank, I was denied permission to go off-campus, and was thrashed with a belt and made to sit alone in the gloomy telephone room that looked more like an isolation cell. I had been trying to help a classmate, Heather, who was in a desperate state. Whereas I was thirteen and one of the oldest in class three, Heather was younger and sometimes defenseless. One day, she was dying to go to the bathroom before the start of Miss Penn's English class. Miss Penn was a hard-boiled

woman who intimidated most of us. Heather's thick and slug-
gish body prevented her from racing to the bathroom and back
before Miss Penn arrived, so she burst into tears. Some of the
boys suggested that Heather pee in the wastebasket, so we girls
stood between Heather and the class, with our skirts outstretched
for privacy. Despite our efforts, some of Heather's urine trickled
out of the wooden box and trailed all along the floor. What to
do? I came up with the bright idea of spilling the flower vase
from the teacher's desk. That took care of the water part, but
there was still a faint smell of urine that we had to hide. I dashed
up to the first floor dormitory, grabbed some cologne from a
bedside table, and then spilled some on the classroom floor. Of
course, when Miss Penn entered the room, she did not miss the
water on the floor nor the scent. Our deeds were exposed.
Heather got off lightly, but I got walloped.

Despite having heard countless sermons on the fires of hell
awaiting those who do not accept Christ as a personal savior, I
had no intention of converting from Buddhism to Christianity. I
was nonetheless shaped by the ethics and values of our teachers. I dodged the Fishers of Men who were desperate to convert
students like me, but I understood and accepted the value of
having love for all mankind and having patience and perseverance in life. I also believed in the comfort of prayers, even if my
personal prayers were Buddhist instead of Christian, and were
recited on my rosary. A few biblical stories got their hold on me,
and I still love Christ's Sermon on the Mount. Once, in my final
year of school, when I received the award for female student of
the year, I actually chose a Bible from the offered prize books; I
read that Bible from time to time until my father gave it to a
Christian friend.

After several years at Mount Hermon, my aunts, uncles, and
cousins all returned to Lhasa to settle down and start families.
Although these relatives had gone to boarding school late, and
still had not finished by the time they reached their late teens or
early twenties, they believed they had all the modern education
they needed. My female relatives planned on marriage and
motherhood, and my uncle knew he would join the Tibetan
government, so an advanced degree from a Western school was

not necessary for any of them. With the departure of these older family members to Lhasa, my siblings and I were the only Tibetans at Mount Hermon. We still missed our parents and bemoaned the six- to eight-week mail delivery time between Lhasa and Darjeeling, but despite our isolation we eventually fell into a comfortable pattern at school.

When I think of the warmth of friendship, I remember a trip to Sikkim that I took with some classmates during the traditional Puja holiday for Hindus. A group of about twelve girls, three Sherpa porters, and our nurse, Ms. Digby, set out on foot from Darjeeling to Sikkim. I still remember the wooden hut where we spent the first night at Sandakphu. A clear night sky was overhead, and the stars were beautiful. We were at an elevation of almost 12,000 feet, and despite our weary bodies, we cooked a light meal, helped by the porters, and then remained outside in the huge silence. Every morning for ten days, I loaded a small pack on my back, grabbed hold of a sturdy walking stick, and started out with vigor on the dusty mountain trail. I felt so close to home looking out on a slope of grazing yak, or looking up at a craggy, snow-covered pinnacle. We stepped carefully over dry shrubs and through pine and juniper trees and tried to hold onto our nerve when we crossed swinging rope bridges that carried us above thundering rapids.

Two strong Sherpa men and one woman carried our food supplies: tea, powdered milk, sugar, canned sardines, cheese, ham, flour, and rice. Being of Tibetan origin, the Sherpas felt like close friends to Norzin and I; our languages were close enough that we understood each other. The Sherpas helped us build a cooking fire at the end of the day, and then Norzin, Cherry from Sikkim, and I cooked Tibetan rice or flour soups called *thukpas* for the group of German, Thai, Indian, Australian, and British friends.

Namche Bazaar in Sikkim was the largest town we came to after leaving Darjeeling. There we replenished our stock of food, took a day's rest, and visited the small town and a Buddhist temple where an old monk and a child monk greeted us with much curiosity. I guess very few visitors from the outside passed through this part of the world. The Thai girls were also Buddhists, and we went inside the temple together for prayers and blessings. Our Christian and Hindu friends joined us, too, with respect. From the quaint town, we made our return trip to Darjeeling by a shorter route, with warnings from villagers of bears.

Brown and tawny from the hot Himalayan sun, with sore legs and feeling fatigued, we got back to school. We were delighted to find that most of us had lost weight, but poor Gisela and her sister Ingrid from Germany were so sunburnt that Gisela had to stay in the school infirmary for a couple of days with tea packs on her face.

Other memorable events from my Darjeeling days included our stay with a very interesting family in Kalimpong who looked after us when my mother could not join us for the entire three-month winter holiday we had from school or when she arrived late for the holidays. The Macdonald family owned the Himalayan Hotel. David Macdonald, known to all of us as "Daddy," was the son of a Scottish father and a Sikkimese mother. Married to a Nepalese woman, he had three daughters who helped run the hotel. Actually it was Annie, the oldest daughter, who ran the hotel. She was well built, quite tall, rather dark in complexion, looking more Nepalese than Scottish. She was very liberal and free-spirited. Annie had a loud, husky voice and was always dressed in pants. She let it be known that it was she who wore the pants in the family. Daddy Macdonald was rather old and had a hearing problem. Aunt Vicki and Aunt Vera, the two younger daughters, ran a local arts and crafts center, which produced some lovely handwoven crafts—cotton prints and pretty bags and scarves. This center was started by the daughter of a missionary, Dr. Graham, to give jobs to the local people. Dr. Graham also started an excellent mission school for needy children, which later accepted many students from all over India.

Aunt Vera never married. She was fat and cute with a puff of hair, which fit well atop her smiling, chubby face. She always wore too much make-up and had plenty of magazines. We loved her room and her company. We loved to touch the perfumes and nail polishes on her dressing table, try on her colorful crocheted shawls and blankets, and peruse her *Daily Mirrors* and *Women's Own*.

Daddy and Annie and Vicki and Vera were like our second family. They had long been friends of our family, and Daddy had been especially close to my grandfather. Often boring the hotel guests, Daddy could talk incessantly about Tibet and the Tibetans. As a younger man, he had been employed for some years by the British government to work in their trade office in Yatung, and he loved Tibet and its people.

At the hotel, there were always many guests from different walks of life and from all over the world. There was a great room where the guests mingled, played gin rummy, drank tea and rum, or chatted with other guests. Sometimes, Norzin and I sang and showed off the exquisite folk dancing steps we had picked up at school.

The variety of guests at the hotel included local English tea estate managers or international scholars on the Himalayan kingdoms, among others. Tibetologists and retired British nationals who lived in the Darjeeling area would meet at the hotel for a game of cards or a glass of rum or a cup of tea. The Aunties made the place very comfortable, and it had a very personal and homey atmosphere.

Once Kalimpong earned the reputation of being a "nest of spies." There could have been a lot of informers during the early period of China's claim to Tibet. I remember here a very amusing incident. One morning, Norzin and I were reading some of Aunt Vera's magazines on the front lawn while Jigme played in the bushes nearby. A few of the guests were relaxing on lawn chairs and enjoying the luxurious Himalayan sun when Jigme, who was crazy about cowboys, suddenly lassoed me. He had a thick rope around my neck and was pulling me as I began to suffocate. A guest rushed toward me to loosen the cord. He scolded Jigme and asked him why he did such a dangerous thing to his sister. Jigme replied that he was practicing his lasso skills so that he could lasso the Chinese when he returned to Tibet. Alas, Jigme did not realize that he was talking to Mr. Wang, a Chinese banker who worked in Calcutta for the Bank of China. Mr. Wang was a perfect gentleman, a smooth talker, and a very kind and gracious man. He was always neatly dressed and always had chocolates and sweets for us. Mr. Wang became our favorite guest at the hotel. Later we learned that he was an agent of Communist China.

The Macdonalds were Christians, so they always celebrated Christmas and had a lovely Christmas tree with lights and decorations and gifts scattered all around the tree. Each Christmas Eve they held a party. They had a couple of children from their family, children of close friends, and of course, my siblings and me. It was with the Macdonalds that we were first introduced to this birthday party of Christ. The great excitement of seeing Father Christmas and getting presents was like celebrating one's own birthday.

Dressed in fancy party clothes, all the children would collect in the lounge near the tree to sing folk songs and Christmas carols. Norzin and I did our number—a favorite song and dance called "Cindy" and it went something like this: "I wish I had a nickel, I wish I had a dime, I wish I had a pretty little girl to love me all the time!" Cindy was the horse we galloped on, and it was our tradition to do this dance, until we were too old and embarrassed.

We ate sandwiches, cakes, and other pastries, and swilled lemon drinks until we were ushered by Aunt Annie out to the front porch to welcome Father Christmas. The poor, tired old man in the red suit with the long white beard and the sack on his back entered the room ringing a gong. I used to think that he must have come all the way from England to visit the Macdonald family. I was quite frightened of him. Later I figured out that it was one of the Nepalese bearers of the hotel, dressed up for us. With Aunt Annie leading the way, we followed Father Christmas to the lounge where he would give us our presents. We could not sit still until we had opened our parcels—lovely handkerchiefs with our names embroidered on them, small bags and purses and scarves from the arts and crafts center. After all this gift giving, inspecting our bounty, and thanking each other, Father Christmas would leave us and the party would come to an end.

7 Lhasa Under Red Army Boots

In the winter of 1953, Amala made the long trek over the Himalayas to our boarding school as she always did during our winter holiday. This year, however, she had come to take us home for good. Arriving three weeks before our planned departure, Amala busied herself buying provisions and presents to take back to Tibet, organizing the packing, and calling on her relatives and friends. She had had little rest since she arrived and was exhausted even before we started our trip home.

The journey to Lhasa was long, cold, and monotonous. During the month on horseback, we passed many wandering hermits and camped in remote villages. We crossed treacherous passes and rivers, and each evening, after a full day's ride, fell exhausted into our beds. For much of the ride, my siblings and I were preoccupied with thoughts of home and the infamous Chinese Red Army that had moved into Lhasa. We knew that our Lhasa would be different now that the Communist Chinese were entrenched there. I understood almost nothing about the Chinese or what they were doing in Lhasa. I remember asking my mother if they really had red faces, red hair, and red clothes. Amala kept telling us that the Chinese were human just like ourselves, but I did not believe this. Red monsters could not be ordinary people. From the bits of conversation that I had overheard about the "Red Chinese," it appeared that Tibetans did not trust them. It frightened me to imagine standing face to face with these Chinese soldiers and having to shake hands with them, or worse, having to bow to them.

When we arrived at the last village before the city, my father was waiting for us. With my mother's brother, Ragashar Ashang-la, Pala had arranged a welcoming picnic. There was food to cheer and fortify us, and friends and family to greet us with khatas. Such was the Tibetan custom of seeing travelers off or welcoming them home. It was a joyous occasion, but I felt a little unsure of myself. I was self-conscious when people commented on my growth or when I was stumped to find a word in Tibetan. I had forgotten some of my mother tongue during the three years I was away.

After our picnic, we traveled the last bit home—a winding trail around an endless rise of mountains. As we traversed the last switchback, we stood in awe of our holy city. There, before us, was our greatest welcome. I could hear my heart pounding as I lifted my eyes toward the massive Potala Palace, its gleaming golden rooftop piercing the clouds above. Standing across from the palace was the high Chakpori Hill where the medical college was built. Two bulwarks of our city, offering only imaginary protection against our new invaders.

In the first few weeks, everything seemed both foreign and familiar, and I was alternately bewildered and charmed. I had to get used to wearing the uncomfortable Tibetan chubas again, instead of the simple dresses or pants I had worn in India. The weather was different from India; I suppose I had forgotten that Lhasa's daytime heat dissipated with the setting sun, and the nighttime air was icy. It was as if my mind, body, and spirit had to shift again.

At home again, after so much time away, my siblings and I spent hours rediscovering the house and property. We went to the stables and the kitchen and then searched for familiar servants and their children. Chungla, our chef's daughter, had been sent to study in China, but some of the younger children were home. I also saw a few new faces. Metok, the new gardener hired to help dear Yangkyi, was a great comic. She was petite, with a friendly smile that displayed two long, shaky fangs protruding from her gums. On occasion Metok was toothless, and I was told that she had lost her own front teeth, and so she tied two incisors from a dead sheep onto her molars.

We brought roller skates from India, which we tried out in our front hall. Showing off for the servants who had never seen skates before, we danced and twirled for our amazed audience. When we were not playing with the servants and their children, Norzin and I hunted down Aunt Nancy. She had returned from Mount Hermon School a tall, elegant, educated young woman. For hours, we used her make-up, tried on her earrings, and helped her clean her wardrobe that held beautiful clothes. We idolized Aunt Nancy and longed to be her enviable age of twenty. Before leaving Aunt Nancy's room, we always raided her collection of romance novels and read them in secret, far out of my mother's sight.

Walking through the streets of Lhasa was different. I felt lost in all the traffic, the rush of bicycles spinning around, and so many pedestrians, everything making so much noise. My eyes couldn't help fixing themselves on the Chinese soldiers. Outfitted in khaki and green cotton uniforms and fur-trimmed hats or Mao caps, most of the soldiers rode bicycles and kept white gauze over their mouths to keep out the dust. I could identify the officers; their uniforms were better made than those of the ordinary soldiers. Only the officers wore wool in the winter.

Clad in drab blue coats and pants and rubber gym shoes, the Chinese civilian men and women looked nearly identical except for their haircuts. The women went without make-up and wore their hair braided or in a short, blunt cut. Only the children wore bright colors. Chinese babies wore vibrant jackets, and young girls often tied huge, colored bows onto the ends of their braids. Although they appeared dull, the Chinese seemed very friendly. Quite a number of them visited our home and brought candies for the children. My relatives were always gracious to the Chinese who arrived at our house unannounced, but they seemed relieved when these visitors departed. I wondered why all my relatives looked startled and frightened when they talked about these Red Chinese. Why all the hushed conversations?

Amala would not let us stay idle for very long, and she insisted that we continue our studies. Our Chinese visitors persisted in the view that my grandparents should send us to the new Lhasa Primary School, which was run by the Communists. Unlike the Tibetan schools, students were not required to offer gifts and khatas to the teachers. The curriculum, however, was not unfamiliar. Each morning we recited prayers, such as the "Kyabdo" (taking refuge in the Buddha, Dharma, and Sangha) and studied Tibetan grammar. We also had classes in Tibetan, math, science, music, dance, elementary Chinese, and sports. We brought our lunch with us or went home to eat; only the Chinese teachers and a few of the resident Tibetan teachers ate in the school canteen. At the start, we wore our own Tibetan clothes, and then the school provided uniforms. For some reason, students were paid to attend the primary school.

Naive as we were, my siblings and I saw nothing peculiar about the Chinese-run school. To us, school was school, and if it was fun, so much the better. The lack of social segregation and the relaxed curriculum impressed me; I loathed the monotony of the standard Tibetan educational program. I looked forward to basketball games and school dances, and did not mind the requirement of sweeping public streets or school grounds from time to time. Some children from noble families were prohibited by their families from sweeping or carrying brooms; their personal maids accompanied them to school to carry out these tasks. When the school was started, teachers gave no lessons on politics, but we were taught many Chinese propaganda songs that we sang without concern.

After a few months of school, I began to realize that something was wrong. A few times, returning home from school, we were taunted by hidden stone-throwers who shouted "greedy students" and "running dogs of Chinese beggars." An ineffable evil began to haunt our city, our school, and our home.

The Tsarong house gradually became solemn, full of whispers and broken conversations. Our elders kept us children at a distance; they feared and distrusted us, and we did not understand why. The Chinese seemed to be forever in our home at odd hours for tea and small-talk. One day, I found my young aunt crying after having been scolded by my grandfather for encouraging visits by the Chinese.

I did not perceive the ominous tension between the Tibetans and the Chinese. I did sense an overall distrust within our family and between neighbors, but I could not grasp the reason. My parents and grandparents revealed nothing to my siblings and me. At school, we were told that the Chinese had come to liberate Tibetans from "imperialists." The word "liberate" became an essential word for the Chinese. Liberate and modernize Tibet. Tibet was a backward country, claimed the Chinese; it needed a better education system, better roads, and a more modern health-care system. When all these improvements were made under the joint leadership of the Dalai Lama and Chairman Mao, the Chinese would then leave our country. Or so they said, again and again. We students believed the Chinese proclamations; we saw the modernizations under way, so we had little reason to doubt that the Chinese were helping Tibet. We were easily swayed.

Once the Chinese settled in Lhasa, they organized a variety of public associations to aid in Tibet's modernization. Every Lhasa citizen was persuaded or pressured to join an association—the families of Tibet's government officials and business leaders were rigorously coerced to join in order to set an example for the general populace. There was a Tibetan women's association, a youth association, cultural groups, drama groups, and later a Communist Party association. We had friends in these associations, and we were glad to help modernize Tibet.

The younger generation of Tibetans now had a freedom never known before the Chinese arrival. Tibetan parents were, as a rule, strict with their children, and the children were quite obedient. Children had to go to school and study or they had to help their parents in household or business affairs. The elders were especially strict with the girls, who were not permitted to roam around the market or to visit restaurants or tea shops unless they had some errand to perform. An obedient girl who was always at home was an asset for a young man looking for a bride. The Chinese changed this when they arrived.

Against the wishes of my parents, I joined a politically active drama group. I loved being busy and performing with this group—once our school drama corps even performed for His

Holiness the Dalai Lama on the Norbulingka stage—a first for Tibetan women.

I remember an extravagant event when the Tibetan Youth Party hosted a youth conference in Lhasa. Delegations came from all over Korea, China, Sinkiang, Mongolia and from other areas of Tibet. We performed for them and acted as hostesses for the evening dance parties, which the Chinese loved to arrange. At this particular meeting, people were eagerly awaiting the arrival of the guest of honor, the older brother of the Dalai Lama, Lobsang Samden. I too was edgy, and I underestimated the reasons why.

The organizers needed two girls from the drama troupe to sit at the guest of honor's table, and I was chosen as one of the lucky girls. I was very young, maybe the youngest in the group, and self-conscious about eating with the Dalai Lama's brother. At such parties, people drank heavily and made long speeches and each toast or speech was followed by a fresh drink. The Chinese had little trouble imbibing their harsh *mao tai*, and then forcing it on everyone else. Lobsang Samden was a monk at that time, so he stuck to Chinese tea. He left the party promptly after the dinner and the speeches.

Not long after they arrived in Lhasa, the Chinese began meddling in Tibetan governmental affairs, demanding land for their military camps and food for their soldiers and their work animals. This caused supply shortages and price increases on daily household goods, something the Tibetan people had never had to worry about in the past.

This "peaceful liberation" of Tibet by the Chinese began to look like the forced occupation that it was, and Tibetans became openly resentful. The Chinese pressured the Dalai Lama and his cabinet to remove Tibet's two prime ministers, Lukhangwa and Lobsang Tashi, from office because they strongly opposed the way in which the Chinese were handling Tibetan affairs, and because they openly expressed their disapproval of Chinese policy. Lukhangwa was very brave and loyal to Tibet, predicting wisely that the Chinese planned a political takeover after they had established complete physical domination of the Tibetan government and country. He openly demanded the withdrawal of Chinese forces, and the Chinese delegates countered by pressuring the young Dalai Lama, who still believed he could find a peaceful solution to the Chinese demands, to ask the prime ministers to resign. The Dalai Lama regretted doing so, but he saw no other way to maintain peace between Tibetan and Chinese politicians.

In 1955, the Peking government proposed to set up the "Preparatory Committee for the Autonomous Region of Tibet." I was one of fifty to sixty young Tibetans selected to travel as a political representative to nearby Tibetan villages. Because I had only traveled to and from school in India, I jumped at the chance to visit rural parts of Tibet. Divided into groups of ten to fifteen, we traveled in trucks, or on foot when our vehicles broke down, and we took turns talking to villagers. We were meant to inspire the villagers and give them cause to celebrate Chinese aid. Urging people not to fear or obstruct the Red Army, we explained that the Chinese would free villagers from their indentured labor and give them their own land and liberty.

Our journey was vigorous. At times we had to wade through the swift, waist-deep water of the Tsangpo River. Linking ourselves hand in hand, we swayed, balancing backpacks stuffed with food, tea, drums, cymbals, blankets, pots, and pans, over rocks and through the current. Some of us sacrificed dry shoes; our bare feet were too tender for the river rocks.

Early in the trip, I realized that the traveling was not our greatest challenge. The river was nothing compared to the fear and apprehension of the villagers we met. Upon seeing our troupe enter their town, the locals ran indoors and refused to come out until we lured them with our colorful dancing and our vivacious music blasting through loudspeakers. When the villagers finally stepped into a circle around us, a quiet, curious audience, we began our prepared speeches about Chinese reforms and then solicited comments from the villagers. Our enthusiasm was met with silence and wariness. Their eyes held back any commitment of thought. We could do little to gain their trust.

Mistrust increased—mistrust between the youth group and the villagers, between the Chinese and Tibetans, between the Tibetan government and the populace, and between family members. I believed I was part of a group of energetic youths ushering in the modern world and helping Tibet. The elders in my family questioned my loyalties and refrained from openly discussing the Chinese with me in case I reported family conversations to my youth group. They were not unnecessarily cautious; the Chinese did indeed cultivate spies who repeated private conversations and thereby incriminated family, friends, and neighbors.

I was eager to spend time with my peers, eager to envision myself as a national volunteer laboring for Tibet, to plant vegetation in barren parts of Tibet, to dig irrigation ditches, to build up my country with Chinese aid. I saw no further. I did not analyze Chinese motives, nor see their clever policy of using Tibetan youths to establish their occupation of Tibet.

With an absence of public media, and with the powerful reticence of older Tibetans to voice their fears about the Chinese in front of the youths working with the Chinese, we young people did not fully comprehend China's betrayal. We knew nothing of the brutal methods of the Chinese who had already taken over our eastern Kham and Amdo regions, nothing of the murders, rapes, torture, and mass suicides of desperate Tibetans.

By this time, we had moved to the Lhasa Middle School. This was the first Chinese-run middle school in Central Tibet, maybe in the whole of Tibet, so we had students from all over the country. Some came from as far as Kham and Amdo. The school was situated at the back of the Potala and even before it was completed, we had to move in from the primary school. We lived in the school as boarders, and, as there were only a few classrooms built, the girls slept in these bare rooms while the boys slept outside in tents. We were permitted to bring our bedding, a change of clothing, and a dish and a spoon, in addition to our toiletries.

We left home anxious and tearful as my grandmother wished us good-bye. This boarding school was very new to her, and it was difficult for her and her close-knit family to accept this move. My mother cried, and so did our old maidservant. My sister Norzin and I were sad to leave home, yet excited about the adventure ahead of us. Being so young, very curious by nature, and rather popular with my classmates, I was rather looking forward to living at school.

When we arrived, we laid our bedding on straw mattresses, which covered every square foot of the bare floor. The mattresses were the only furnishings in the huge room, which had many glass windows, naked without curtains. Several girls brought camp beds but were quickly ridiculed by the Chinese teachers. The girls were told that they were the spoiled products of capitalist-minded parents. These girls were so tormented by the other students that eventually they got rid of their beds. The room was so crowded that you couldn't move without waking your neighbor at night. In the tents, the boys didn't have the luxury of mattresses, but slept packed together like sardines on plain, wooden planks on stilts.

The excitement quickly wore off, and we were feeling the hardship. However, Norzin and I were determined to bear our plight bravely. We had convinced ourselves that we were doing this for the future of our country and our people. Moreover, we had made this move against our parents' wishes and were not anxious to admit we had made a mistake.

Our bathing facilities consisted of two pots of hot water to be shared among all the boys and girls. There was always a stampede for the warm water, and the girls were generally pushed aside by the boys and subjected to bathing in frozen water. If we wanted to wash our hair or take a bath, we had to go to the canal behind the Potala.

The sanitation of the school was horrific. Due to the lack of hygiene in Tibet and the cold weather, people were careless about their personal habits. The toilets were built about thirty yards from the school buildings, but when winter approached, the girls were too cold and lazy to run to the toilet at night. There were no lights outside, so the grounds just outside the dormitories were used as latrines.

Mealtimes offered no comfort either. Breakfast consisted of a plain watery rice soup and a mug of hot water. Lunch and dinner consisted of plain steamed bread or tsampa, a plate of vegetables to be shared among a group of eight to ten students, and a mug of hot water to wash down the coarse tsampa. The tsampa was mixed with barley husks, sand, and stone. Once, when a servant came to visit us with some bread and cheese from home, he cried when he told my mother about our lunch. He told the family that he had never eaten such tsampa in his life.

There were many children from well-off homes—children of the nobility, government officials, and businessmen. Periodically, the Chinese teachers would come around during meal times and ask us to comment on the food just to annoy us. The general atmosphere among the students was very friendly and coopera- tive. We made friends with everyone, but remarks such as, "Do you feel comfortable eating from the same plate as the street children?" alienated and humiliated us. This, of course, was the intention. Moreover, there had never been any animosity or division among the students, yet these tactics were used as an attempt to divide the Tibetans.

This school was the first of its kind in Central Tibet—an "ex- perimental" boarding school. Most of the teachers were new ar- rivals from China, and they were less personable than the Chinese who had lived in Tibet. They spoke no Tibetan and only a very few of the teachers were Tibetan. The school was not well organized, perhaps even a bit chaotic.

On Saturdays, we had to attend group meetings where we reported on our weekly assignments, such as planting trees, sweeping the school premises, washing the windows and so on. We then had our "criticism campaign," which was an open fo- rum for criticizing fellow students for their perceived misdeeds. Once, I was criticized for being too proud to attend school dances. These meetings generated animosity and promoted personal vindictiveness; I saw no gain to the school or the community in holding such sessions.

Norzin and I always looked forward to Sundays when we could visit our home. One Sunday, we had a terrifying experi- ence. A group of us girls were chattering and walking from the foot of the Potala towards Lhasa, when we had stones thrown at us from behind. Luckily no one was hit. Seconds later we heard shouts and the rattling of chains. When we glanced back, we saw a small group of wild-looking men in chains with bushy, uncombed hair running after us. We realized that we were being chased by prisoners. The day must have coincided with an aus- picious or holy day on the Tibetan calendar. Typically, prisoners with lighter sentences could be let out for the day from the prison in Shoel town. The prisoners were usually tied in pairs with iron handcuffs. Prisoners with heavier charges would have wooden frames around their necks.

Most citizens of Lhasa and Shoel, including our parents, did not like our attending the Chinese schools, but the invading Chinese party was too strong and powerful now to be opposed. My family had no choice but to send us to the Chinese-run school. It had become a nightmare. Students had become restless in the wretched living conditions. Food was still meager; the boys still slept in the tents; the new Chinese teachers were unfriendly and arrogant. Slowly the Chinese altered traditional Tibetan school policies; morning prayer was abandoned. Teachers scheduled more time for Chinese language studies than for Tibetan.

Because most of the students were in their teens or early twenties, they comprised an unruly group. Courageous and contentious Tibetan students acted out anonymously. During one evening screening of a Chinese propaganda film, someone threw a stone at our Chinese teacher's head. With a bleeding wound, the teacher had to be taken to the hospital while the assailant fled from the outdoor theater. Later, another Chinese was stabbed with a knife by an unknown assailant who also got away. Serious trouble had begun.

With these events, my parents became increasingly worried about my sister and me. My grandmother cried every Sunday when we returned to school after spending the day at home. I dreamed of returning to my beloved school in India. Yet, India seemed so far away, beyond mountains and across rivers and plains. The journey seemed too long and arduous.

On one visit to our home, I remember participating in the "Taytha Tsichu" or Monkey Year Tenth Day religious celebrations. On the tenth day of the Monkey Month, which was the seventh Tibetan month during the Monkey Year, all the oracles in and around Lhasa met at different places and entered into trance. Amala took my sister, brother, and me to witness this rare event at Nechung Monastery. A distant relative of my mother was one of the four female oracles who gathered at Nechung Monastery; she was the medium for the Pari spirit. The well-known Terma spirit, a guardian of Tibet, was the only female oracle officially acknowledged by the government of Tibet, and that spirit's medium was very pretty.

In our fine clothes and jewelry, we left very early that morning to visit the home of Pari. We called on the lady of the house and her husband, who was a junior member of the Tibetan government staff. We were served tea and breakfast, and then we proceeded from the Nechung Monastery courtyard to the tent of the Pari oracle, where we waited for the oracles to gather.

Colorful cloth tents with multicolored appliqués of different auspicious signs and symbols were pitched side by side around the courtyard. We struggled through crowds to find the right tent as people in their finest garb congregated in and around the tents.

Twelve to thirteen oracles, all guardian spirits of Tibet, would gather at Nechung on this day and go into trance in their individual tents before they would make a round of the courtyard and the monastery. Amid billowing incense smoke and the sounds of religious music and chants, the oracles were invoked so the spirits of the protectors could enter the mediums. Our gentle and mild hostess, dressed in a special brocade costume, turned into a completely different person in a few minutes. It was astounding. She became strong, bold. Just looking at her power, one felt a bit afraid to go near her. The tent was crowded, and we pushed ourselves further away from the oracles and wished we had not come into the tent in the first place.

Nechung, with his beautiful brocade gown, blazing gold breast shield, and gold headdress topped with fluffy cotton balls, led the other oracles around the courtyard and made a round of the temple. All the oracles wore brocade costumes, gold ornaments, swords and headdresses. It was a dazzling sight. The sound of religious music in full blast, the anxious attendants, and the smoke from herbs and incense made everyone a bit tense and excited. I was glad to have been a part of this ceremony, because no such gatherings of oracles ever took place again.

On this day, all of the oracles in the whole of Tibet were said to have gone into trance. A twelve-year cycle had come, and soon the Monkey Year passed into the Sheep Year. Many changes and upheavals were to be expected in Tibet. Of course, no one took much heed, but before the great Thirteenth Dalai Lama left this world, he predicted the following:

> The present is the time of the Five Kinds of Degeneration in all countries. The manner of working among the red people is the worst. They have seized and taken away all the sacred objects from the monasteries. They have made monks work as soldiers. They have broken religion, so that not even the name of it remains. Have you heard of all these things that have happened at Urga? It may happen that here in the center of Tibet the religion and the secular administration may be attacked both from the outside and from the inside. Unless we can guard our own country, it will now happen that the Dalai and Panchen Lamas, the Father and the Son, the holders of the Faith, the glorious Rebirths, will be broken down and left with only a name. As regards the monasteries and the priesthood, their lands and other properties will be destroyed. The administrative customs of the Three Religious Kings will be weakened. The officers of the State, ecclesiastical and secular, will find their lands seized and their other property confiscated, and they themselves made to serve their enemies, or wander about the country as beggars do. All beings will be sunk in great hardship and in overpowering fear; the days and nights will drag on slowly in suffering.
>
> Do not be traitors to Church and State by working for another country against your own. Tibet is happy, and in comfort now; the matter rests in your own hands. All civil and military matters should be organized with knowledge. Act in harmony with each other; do not pretend that you can do what you cannot. The improvement of the secular administration depends on your ecclesiastical and secular officials. High officials, low officials and peasants must all act in harmony to bring happiness to Tibet; one person alone cannot lift a heavy carpet; several must unite to do so.

The Thirteenth Dalai Lama left us, the Tibetan people and the Tibetan nation, with this prediction that was realized in our time. He had envisioned our plight, but I had no idea at the time of my youth work with the Chinese that I would soon live as a refugee, a survivor, and a fighter for truth, justice, and the right to regain my country from its invaders.

8 Freedom at Last

Smoke from the incense swirled in the cloudless, blue sky, and the sweet smell of burning juniper and fragrant herbs filled the air. All of Lhasa had turned out to bid farewell to His Holiness as he began his long journey to India. The occasion for which the Dalai Lama was traveling to India was the Buddha Jayanti, the 2,500th anniversary of the birth of Lord Buddha, celebrated in 1956. Many people wept as the Dalai Lama and his entourage passed. The Chinese presence in Lhasa had become like a bad, ripe boil on raw skin. Outbursts of temper and small skirmishes between the occupied people and their aggressors were becoming more common. Without the calming presence of His Holiness, it seemed only a matter of time before something bigger and more violent might happen.

Not long after the Dalai Lama left on this journey, our servant Kunga arrived at school with a letter requesting that Norzin and I be allowed a leave of absence for a few months so that we could go on pilgrimage to India, during the holy year. We were instructed to pack up our clothes and bedding, to leave our wash basin and eating utensils at school, and to come home immediately.

Norzin and I were overjoyed. This was the most wonderful news we could have gotten; we would have welcomed any excuse to get ourselves out of such unpleasant living conditions. Never had we gotten ourselves packed and ready with such alacrity. I did not even take the time to bid farewell to all of my friends. Of course, the letter had mentioned that we would be back in school after a month or two, so I expected to see them upon my return.

When we reached home, Amala informed us that we would be leaving for India within two days. It appeared that my parents were worried that a delay of a few days might hinder our journey. Early on the morning of our departure, we visited the Jokhang to pray for a safe journey, and in grand style we left Lhasa, accompanied by a senior Chinese officer, two guards, and two drivers in a large Chinese army truck and small jeep.

At the time, Ragashar Pola was chief of the Tibetan army. The Chinese had given him a title and placed a car and a few body-guards (that we secretly referred to as spies) at his residence. Pola was attending His Holiness in India, so Mola was planning to travel with us as the head of the family. The Chinese attendants were there for her honor. The Chinese wanted us to return to Tibet after the pilgrimage, and this was their way of showing that they could be obliging and helpful. My parents and four of us Tsarong children accompanied my grandmother, my mother's sister, her husband, and my uncle's daughter, Tseten Ragashar. There were also a few servants with us, besides the party of Chinese.

As we prepared for our departure, we said farewell to our Tsarong grandparents, our maids, and our playmates. Drikung Kyabgon Rinpoche, our younger brother, was staying behind with our grandparents. On the morning of our departure, Mola fainted while bidding us good-bye. It was heartbreaking to see her in such a state. We filed by her one by one, touching our foreheads to hers, as is the traditional Tibetan greeting or part-ing gesture between loved ones. As I touched Mola's head to mine, I felt her tears on my cheek. My nose and eyes were run-ning too, and all the water mixed to a salty taste. The separation was very painful. That was the last time I saw her.

Once we reached the border town of Dromo, the vehicles could travel just a few miles up the pass, and from there we had to continue on horseback. Somehow, it was sad to say good-bye to our Chinese officer and the guards. They had been sincerely kind and helpful on the journey. Shao Kwee, the youngest guard, was crying like a baby at bidding us farewell. He had been living at

Ragashar house for a couple of years, and everyone had shown him affection. I guess he accepted the people at Ragashar as his adopted family. Mola told us later that he had quietly approached our Ragashar maid, Dawa, to request Mola to take him with us to India.

We reached the highest point of Nathula Pass, about 14,300 feet above sea level. The crisp, cold air brushed our exposed skin. We placed prayer flags in the ground and added extra stones to the large pile already put there by passing travelers as offerings to the gods. We shouted "Lha Gyalo," or "Victory to the Gods," at the top of our lungs. Because Buddhists believe that certain deities protect high mountain passes, travelers place prayer flags and chant prayers in order to receive the blessings of these deities. For us, this was a ceremonious way of asking for luck for ourselves and for our country. Some members of our party threw tsampa into the air, and then we rode merrily towards Gangtok with sprinkles of powdered tsampa in our caps and on our horses.

We traveled on narrow paths above deep gorges that were thousands of feet below us. The sky was a deep turquoise blue and accented by tiny white clouds. Reaching the Sikkim side of the pass, we glimpsed Tsogo Lake, which was dazzling in the strong sun.

We were met by attendants from the Sikkimese royal family and treated to a lavish lunch at the Palace. Maharaja Tashi Namgyal—who was Ragashar Mola's uncle—his son Thondup, and his beautiful Tibetan wife, Sangdi-la, were our hosts. The Queen Mother lived at another palace; she was separated from the King. We went to visit her as well, because she was Ragashar Pola's sister.

Lunch was served in Western style, and the menu was continental. It was all very formal. The service was elaborate, and we children were quite intimidated by all the silver and china spread before us. The servants were dressed in elegant robes and wore round brocade caps, and they moved softly up and down the room as they carted huge silver dishes. We watched the adults and shyly picked up our knives and forks, which we had not used in the past two years of our stay in Tibet.

The Maharaja was a tiny, delicate man with fragile features. He moved slowly and had a soft voice. Sitting at the head of a large table, dressed in silk and a round brocade hat, he looked like an exotic bird perched on a huge tree. He spoke in almost-whispers, so those of us sitting furthest from him could hardly hear what he said. When we did hear pieces of the conversation, we realized he was referring to the spirits in the palace who visit him. He must have had a fair amount of alcohol during lunch, because when the meal was over and we were going to the living room for tea and coffee, he wove down the narrow corridor as if he were following some imaginary crooked path. Norzin and I were trying our best not to giggle. We liked him.

The Maharaja was an excellent artist who lived in a world of spirits. He lived alone on the top floor at one end of the Palace. We made it a point to visit him one day with our cousins Soden and Chemi Phunkhang, whose mother was the eldest daughter of Tashi Namgyal. He told us that he had a thigh bone and every evening when he blew on it, the spirits came to his call. Strange, but I learned that his wife also saw spirits often, and she always slept with her bedroom lights on.

From Gangtok, we moved to Kalimpong, where we stayed in a rented villa for a few weeks before we began our pilgrimage in the plains of India. Having been forewarned of the fevers afflicting travelers in the plains, we had to endure a number of dreadful injections at the Mission Hospital. In Kalimpong, we were joined by more cousins from Tibet, as well as two interpreters—a Nepalese trader named Sotha-la, and our cousin Kyibuk.

On pilgrimage, our first stop was Bodh Gaya, where Buddha attained enlightenment under the Bodhi Tree. When we arrived by train just outside Bodh Gaya, we were met by throngs of squabbling coolies who fought to carry our luggage. We found a rickshaw to take us to the small town of Bodh Gaya, and upon our arrival in the dusty, dirty village, we were accosted from all directions by hordes of beggars, many blind or maimed. Entering the dimly lit temple near the Bodhi Tree and looking up at the face and statue of the Lord Buddha was like entering a different world. It was so calm and serene—there was certainly a different energy in the room. Next, we visited Sarnath, where

Buddha gave his first sermon. The garden, with its ancient, round stupa, was grand and solid and extraordinarily beautiful. It was in Sarnath that we caught up with the Dalai Lama and his party and attended the public audience. Pilgrims from all parts of the Himalayas had come to receive the blessings of His Holiness. Police and security people were scattered all over. The Panchen Lama was also present. Ragashar Pola was accompanying the Dalai Lama, so we were able to visit with him briefly. We did not know that this would be the last time we would see him. Sometime later, he died on his way to an official visit to Nepal.

We went to Lumbini, where Buddha was born, and to Kushinagar, where he died. In Kushinagar, we visited a Sikh Maharaja who invited us for tea and took us around his sugar factory. The melted canes gave off a very strong, pungent, and unpleasant smell. It seemed that this Maharaja lived alone in his beautiful palace. He had invited His Holiness to visit his palace and the factory, and very proudly he showed us his guest book with His Holiness's signature.

After visiting the Buddhist pilgrimage centers in India, my family wanted to travel to Nepal to pay homage to the Great Baudha Stupa in Kathmandu. We reached Raxaul on the Indo-Nepal border by train and for a short distance rode in a bus that was so rickety I was afraid one of the wheels would fall off. When we got off the bus, we learned that the aircraft to Kathmandu had just crashed a few hours earlier. Discouraged by this news, we decided to return to Kalimpong after a short stay in Calcutta.

Traveling in India was great fun in those days. We booked the whole train compartment and brought our own food. Servants also traveled with us, and the journey was like a picnic on wheels. Every station had peanut and fruit vendors, people selling tea in small red clay cups and shouting, "Chai," along the platforms. We loved the comics and the Indian movie magazine *Filmfare*. The adults gave us their small change to distribute among the many beggars who stretched their emaciated hands through the car windows. When the train moved, we would toss our banana and orange peels out of the windows, targeting the squatting men who perched their bare, brown bottoms along the train tracks to take care of their personal business. We only saw men inclined to such a ritual and wondered if women in India ever defecated. Later, we learned that they wait to do their job at night, or in the fields in case of an emergency.

Before reaching Calcutta, the train halted for a moment on a long bridge, giving us a glimpse of the large city and preparing us for the chaos of one of the busiest stations in the world. Our interpreters got off of the coach to stretch their legs, when suddenly the train lurched forward. Being rather slow-motioned by nature, and not as fast and adept as the local passengers who could climb on the train while it moved, they were left standing on the bridge. So, we reached Howrah station in confusion amidst swarms of people without our interpreters. The crowds and the noise and the chaos were all quite intimidating.

Many Tibetans who had been on pilgrimage in India were ending their journey in Calcutta. As Tibetans had the reputation of tipping well, the coolies fought to carry our bedding and trunks. With some of us children speaking English, and Amala with her smattering of English and Hindi, we managed to find the hotel we had booked in advance without the assistance of our interpreters. Fortunately, Amala had the address with her.

Continental Hotel was in the center of the new part of Calcutta, on the famous Chowringhee Street. The traffic was heavy, and all the famous shops were convenient. We spent hours just looking down from our hotel windows at the speeding cars and the throngs of people. Nighttime was even more beautiful, with the car lights and the neon signs advertising movies, shops, and goods, such as Horlick's beverage to give strength and Colgate toothpaste for beautiful smiles. Some of the light bulbs were burnt out, and the Colgate mouth looked as if it were missing some teeth.

Indian ladies in gorgeous silk saris shimmered side by side with half-naked men, and the fashionable young people in Western clothes paraded about like peacocks in a garden. The Bengali *babus* made us giggle as they lifted the sides of their starched white loin cloths daintily into the air. Such sights we had never seen before. We spent hours just observing and soaking in all the newness. It took a little time to adapt to the noise and the crowds and to digest everything that was happening all at once.

Once we grew familiar with our new surroundings, so different from Lhasa or Darjeeling, we would lose ourselves in the large shopping center called New Market, or stroll along Chowringhee Street window shopping. Never had we seen so many shops filled with so many goods; nor so much pageantry next to the poverty of the general populace. The beggars were haunting with their emaciated bodies covered in rags; tiny babies gazed out with huge, lifeless eyes. There were storytellers on the streets, parrots who picked up cards to make divinations, wise-looking, well-fed men in *lungis* who read your future from the palm of your hand, jugglers and magicians on every street corner, and pickpockets waiting to snatch your wallet or bag. Stray cows and bulls strode calmly along in the middle of traffic, oblivious to the cars. They seemed quite self-assured, as if they were the ones who owned the road. Policemen in immaculate white uniforms directed the traffic with little notice to whether or not the animals obeyed the traffic rules.

We left Calcutta for Kalimpong, where, to our delight and relief, Norzin and I were told that we would be going back to school in Darjeeling. It was decided that Jigme was to join the Jesuit boy's school, St. Joseph's, where my father had once attended school for a few years and where our cousins, the Dorji boys from Bhutan, were now studying. Our youngest brother, Paljor, was to be with us at Mount Hermon. He was about seven, and my parents thought that the older sisters could keep an eye on him.

In March 1957, Mount Hermon School welcomed us with open arms. We were especially appreciative of the comfort, cleanliness, and efficient routine of the school after the lack of organization and hygiene at the Lhasa Middle School. Mount Hermon had changed in the two years we had been away. There were more Indian teachers, and the foreign teachers tended to come from Australia and New Zealand, rather than Britain or the United States. More of the students hailed from Southeast Asia, and there were even a handful of other Tibetan students enrolled. The American informality was missing; all the students wore navy blue uniforms with white shirts and blue and gold striped ties. The rules were more rigid, but we soon adapted to another system of schooling and another way of life.

March 1959 brought sad and shocking news from Tibet. I was in the dressing room after gym class when a friend relayed the news she had read in the daily newspaper, *The Statesman*. The

Chinese army had bombed Lhasa. I was stunned. I raced to the library to read the news for myself. My first thoughts were of my grandfather and other family members. My brother, Drikung Kyabgon, was only ten years old. As the reality started to sink in, the pain felt like a knife in my stomach. I was overwhelmed with grief at the thought that I might never see my country again. The thought of losing my loved ones was devastating. My feelings alternated between anger and hurt that Tibet had been so viciously attacked by the Chinese. I felt betrayed and cheated. The friendly Chinese teachers and visitors to our home used to say that they were in Tibet to help us develop the country. I believed them and even worked with them, and now they were killing the same people they had come to help and destroying our homes and monasteries.

I felt so helpless. Every day Norzin and I rushed to read the papers. We learned that the Dalai Lama had managed to flee Lhasa, but otherwise, the news continued to be gloomy. Thoughts of our homeland were fixed in our minds. It was difficult for us to be so far away; there was really nothing we could do but go on with our daily school routine and pray for our people in Tibet.

From the newspaper, we also learned of the death of Tsarong Pola. The year before, he had been in India and many friends and relatives, even my father, had tried to persuade him to remain there, as the situation in Tibet was getting tense and revolt was imminent. Uprisings and violence, sparked by Tibetan rebels in Eastern and Central Tibet, had already begun. The rebels had attacked the Chinese army and China was growing increasingly more impatient with the situation. Pola was in his seventies, and losing his strength, but he was determined to return to Lhasa to help bring His Holiness the Dalai Lama out to the free world. No one could dissuade Pola from going back to Lhasa. A group of Tibetans in India, including His Holiness's elder brother, Gyalo Thondup, had asked Pola to stay in India to lead them in their fight for Tibet's independence. Gyalo Thondup and some other Tibetans had started a Tibetan freedom movement at Kalimpong and needed Pola's expertise, but Pola was determined to return to Lhasa. He told my sister once that he wanted to go back to Lhasa because if he was to die, he wanted to die in his own country.

Because of the continued violence and an increasing fear that
the Chinese had plans to capture him, the Dalai Lama, members
of his family and his closest associates fled Tibet for India. Tibetans then waged a full-fledged revolt. During the revolt, Tsarong
Pola was elected to serve as one of the Tibetan People's Representatives. Before any negotiations could take place, however,
the Norbulingka was bombed, the Tibetan government was dissolved, and the members of the Tibetan People's Representatives
were arrested and imprisoned by the Chinese. I found out many
years later that Pola was scheduled to go on public trial, but
died in his sleep the night before. The prisoners were watching
a movie. Pola was holding the famous Tibetan heroine Kunsang-
la's small daughter on his lap, when he turned to Sampo Kungoe
Depon, a fellow prisoner, and offered him the few cigarettes he
had left. Sampo Kungoe was curious as to why Pola had given
him the cigarettes; they were the only comfort Pola had in prison.
Kunsang-la, who was Pola's niece, was also imprisoned, but she
was kept in an isolation ward. Kunsang-la was executed for leading the women's movement against the Chinese in March of 1959.

I am thankful that Pola did not undergo the trial. During these
public trials, called *thamzing*, the victim was abused, humiliated,
and beaten. The Chinese would find people who had grievances
against the victims, and these individuals would participate in
the abuse, thereby getting their "revenge." Many people were
willing to torture a victim in order to gain the favor of the Chinese. Pola was a proud and patriotic man, and I am sure he would
not have wanted to die at the hands of his own countrymen,
under the instigation of the enemy. Instead, he died a noble death.

9 Tibetan Refugees

Following the Dalai Lama's escape to India in the spring of 1959, thousands of Tibetans fled to the neighboring countries of India, Nepal, Bhutan, and Burma. China's meddling in Tibetan affairs had reached a dark climax, resulting in a forceful domination of the country, the persecution of thousands of innocent Tibetans, and the destruction of monasteries and sacred places of worship. Ultimately, the Chinese occupation of Tibet threatened to erase the Tibetan way of life.

By the summer of 1959, about eighty thousand Tibetan refugees had escaped from Tibet, taking with them only those belongings they could strap to their backs or carry in their arms. Before they could reach their freedom, the refugees had to make a treacherous, almost impossible journey. Those who managed to leave made the long trek on foot or by pack animal. The overwhelming difficulties of their flight were compounded by an oppressive fear of being captured by the Chinese. Traveling with few supplies and no definite route to follow, those who survived the journey arrived at the border stations mentally and physically devastated. Many were in shock.

Samten Dolma, now a nun in her late seventies, remembers the flight from Kongpo:

> There was hardly any proper path we could follow. We
> had to climb high mountains, sometimes with the help of
> rope ladders made from the vegetation we collected. We

> crossed roaring rivers on thin bamboo bridges, and I
> sometimes wonder how so many of us reached India. I
> remember the escape was full of hardships, but the fear of
> being captured by the Chinese was greater. Many of us
> were so exhausted and miserable that we cried every day.
> The road was so bad, and we had to walk and carry what
> load each could possibly manage to bring along.

Many people died en route from starvation, exposure, and exhaustion. Countless stories are told of the grave hardships suffered by the survivors; stories of people rescuing babies from the arms of dead mothers, others having to shoot injured or dying family members, and still others having to leave family members and small children behind.

Once the refugees had reached their destination and were safe from the Chinese, they had to endure other adversities—adjusting to a different environment and hostile climate, new diseases, and foreign languages and customs. When His Holiness learned of the mass exodus of his countrymen—most of whom were the common people of Tibet and who would be completely devastated without assistance—he appealed to the governments of India, Nepal, and Bhutan for help in resettling these refugees.

Although the government of India now shared a common border with China and was nervous about showing open support for the Tibetan cause, they were extremely generous in their provision of land for refugee settlements. In addition, His Holiness was given housing in a villa belonging to the wealthy Birla family in the hill station of Mussoorie. From this villa, His Holiness focused his energy on sheltering the Tibetan refugees and garnering world support for Tibet's struggle for independence.

Subsequently, two transit camps were opened near the borders in India, one in the plains at Missamari in Assam and another at Buxa in Bengal. Each camp was staffed by an Indian government officer who served as the camp commandant, and by a Tibetan leader.

The first group of refugees arrived at the camp in Missamari during April of 1959. They were sheltered in hastily constructed bamboo huts, each of which housed about fifty to sixty people. Within a few weeks, six thousand people had reached Missamari and another thousand, mostly monks, arrived at the camp in Buxa.

International organizations, different societies, and individuals generously provided aid to the refugees in kind, cash, and care. The attention and help from the outside world fueled a spark of hope in the spirits of the refugees.

In spite of his own weariness and anxiety about the future of Tibet, the Dalai Lama put the plight of the refugees first, and worked hard to bring some measure of comfort and leadership to this tired, displaced, and depressed lot. We are forever grateful to the Dalai Lama for his leadership, his compassion, and his advocacy for the refugees, and to those Tibetans who gave up their own comforts to assist the refugees in their fight for survival.

My cousin, the late Phurphu Samdup, was an officer at one of the camps. He said,

> Life at Missamari was intolerable. The climate was hot and unbearable, the mosquitoes feasted on the little blood we had left, and many people died from malaria and diarrhea. The few interpreters who were helping in the camps could not cope with the diseases, the deaths, and the dire situation; they ran away, leaving me alone for some time. The sight of rice and dal (lentil soup) still nauseates me, because this was all that we ate day after day.

Days led to months and the camps were increasingly overcrowded; many people were dying. His Holiness asked the government of India to move the Tibetan exiles to cooler regions in the mountains. There they could be relieved from the oppressive heat and occupy themselves with work instead of spending anguished days worrying about their families and friends in Tibet. The Indian government granted this request, and soon groups of families were moved to cooler regions in the Himalayas and put to work building roads. Many of the roads high up in the Himalayas were built by these Tibetan refugees. Orphans were collected and sent to a nursery in Dharamsala, India, that the Dalai Lama had founded with his older sister, Tsering Dolma, who looked after the children. Older children were sent to a school started in Mussoorie, run by my great uncle and aunt, Jigme and Rinchen Dolma Taring.

Our people soon had to seek more permanent homes and jobs. Work was irregular, and the workers had to move from place to place, living in shacks or makeshift tents. Many of the workers had small children with them, and life was exceedingly difficult. During the monsoon, when rain fell in torrents in the Himalayas, water gushed into the tents. It trickled down from the openings of the tents, drenching every piece of clothing or bedding. The powdered milk from CARE would mold, and legions of mountain rats as big as kittens would steal the crumbs saved for the children. One mother stated, "I saved some powdered milk for my son, but when it got mildewed, I cried and cried out of anger and frustration."

Most of the refugees were farmers and nomads from Tibet, unskilled in any sort of mechanical work. In addition, there was the language barrier, which made it difficult for these people to find permanent employment. His Holiness did not lose hope, and once again he appealed to the Prime Minister of India, Pandit Nehru. Mr. Nehru wrote to the ministers of the different Indian states, asking if land was available for cultivation by the Tibetan refugees. Mysore State in South India affirmed that three thousand acres of land would be leased to the central government of India, and, subsequently, 666 Tibetans arrived in Bylakuppe on December 16, 1960. Funds for this project were released by the government of India, as well as from various international voluntary organizations. The Swiss were especially helpful in the cultivation of these jungles.

On life in the jungle, my colleague Deki Khedrup states,

> Bylakuppe was a thick jungle when I worked as an interpreter for the camp leaders. Tigers, elephants, wild boars, snakes, and jackals were all over. I was lucky not to meet any wild animals other than a group of wild elephants who were feared by the people. I took care not to go far from the tent I was living in. Most of the refugees were in tents or busy felling the jungle to grow crops and to start a new life all over again.

Settlements spread to northern and central India. Our people, being industrious, optimistic, and eager to settle down in a permanent place with a proper roof over their heads, toiled very hard and became an example to the world of a well-organized refugee community. In fact, many people from around the world came to see how well the Tibetan refugee communities in India and Nepal had succeeded and to learn from our experiences.

In Darjeeling, Mrs. Thondup, the wife of the Dalai Lama's elder brother Gyalo, gathered some of the poorer Tibetans who had arrived there and opened a Tibetan handicraft center. This was the first craft center founded by Tibetans in exile. It is still in existence and now supports a large number of families by exporting Tibetan crafts all over the world. There are now a number of other such centers. The students at Mount Hermon School performed a few plays to raise funds for this self-help center. We also helped the center to sell tickets and programs during a Tibetan opera they put on for the town of Darjeeling. It seemed like we could do very little for our countrymen, but it gave us a sense of satisfaction to make some contribution at such a difficult period in Tibet's history.

At the end of 1961, I completed my senior Cambridge exams. Finally released from school uniforms and examinations, I felt liberated. It was many years before I could bring myself to wear navy blue again. At the same time, I was very sad to leave Mount Hermon, the massive stone building with the grand, ivy-covered entrance where children from many different parts of the world entered a new world with apprehension. It was a world of its own, and so many events in my life took place in its dormitories and classrooms, experiences shared by friends who are now scattered all over the world. A beautiful chapter in my life had come to an end, and I was innocently stepping into adulthood. I started to ask myself what I should do next; should I serve the Tibetan refugees or should I continue my studies?

My parents were living in Calcutta at the time. With the influx of Tibetan refugees into the free world, and most heading to India, my father, as a Tibetan government officer with a knowledge of English, was recruited to work at the Tibetan Bureau in New Delhi. He was to help in resettling the Tibetans, but was transferred to work under the Dalai Lama's older brother, Gyalo Thondup, and a senior monk official. Their task was to sell some Tibetan treasures. My father implored the council of ministers to relieve him of such a heavy responsibility, but there was no way out of this post. He was told that because there were so few Tibetans with any knowledge of the outside world, someone with his experience was needed to work in rebuilding a Tibetan community in exile. My father had no choice but to move to Calcutta.

The proceeds from the sale of these treasures were used to fund the Tibetan government-in-exile in India, to open Tibetan offices in New York and Geneva, and to bring the Tibetan issue to the United Nations. Some funds were invested in projects, such as an iron and steel company in Bihar, where my father worked as manager. A paper factory was started in Bhopal in Madhya Pradesh, and a wood factory was set up in Bangalore. None of these large ventures met with success. Gayday Iron and Steel was started in a partnership with Belgium. Production was initiated, but more funds were required and loans from the Reserve Bank of India were not forthcoming. The government of India was facing a financial burden after a Chinese attack on the northeastern frontier, and the competition with the Birla Iron and Steel Company in the same state of Bihar was not foreseen. My father was a very gentle man without a knowledge of modern management techniques. At the same time, some of his Indian counterparts were shrewd businessmen and not always honest.

To compound Pala's stress, the family resources were running low, as he had four children to educate, and he was sponsoring two orphans at a Tibetan school in Dharamsala. He was not receiving a salary for his services at the company, and the heat of Calcutta was beginning to take a toll on his health. The chairman of the company, Mr. Gyalo Thondup, was by this time spending most of his time with the Tibetan guerrilla movement based in Mustang, Nepal. Kungoe Gadang and Kungoe Mindong Senpo Khenpo, who were involved earlier in the sale of the treasures, had moved to Dharamsala after the project was completed.

Eventually, my mother had a severe nervous breakdown which lasted a few years. Later, the accumulated stress of his responsibilities as well as the failure of the company caused my father's health to give out, and he had no option but to resign from the company. My father suffered a nervous breakdown and was hospitalized in the Christian Medical Hospital at Vellore. My mother was in one bed and my father in another at the same hospital.

After graduation, I was not sure what to do next. I was rather insecure. I was a refugee and had no certain future. Despite my parents' health problems, they were trying to help the many relatives and friends who had arrived from Tibet penniless and weak.

A number of new refugees were also housed with my family. There was really no occasion for us to discuss the future. Moreover, in the Tibetan custom, children were there to be obedient, not to mix with the adults. Like many Tibetan youngsters, I did not have a very intimate relationship with my parents during my early years. At nineteen, I was still considered a child.

I enrolled in a secretarial college and was taking French courses at the Alliance Française in Calcutta when Colonel Ilya Tolstoy, the grandson of Leo Tolstoy and a family friend, visited my parents. He was in India to see the Dalai Lama and was on his way to visit Tibetans in Darjeeling and Sikkim. Ilya had come to India with plans to resettle a large group of Tibetans in Wyoming. He had been a family friend since 1943, when he came to Lhasa as a representative of the United States government and had called on my grandfather with some gifts from President Roosevelt. They had remained friends over the years.

Ilya offered to help get me into Pratt Institute for Design in New York City. I thought design would be useful in preserving and propagating Tibetan handicrafts, and was seriously considering this possibility when some members of His Holiness the Dalai Lama's family approached me with the suggestion that I marry His Holiness's immediate elder brother, Lobsang Samden.

Lobsang was in the United States at that time, having immigrated earlier to join his oldest brother, Thubten Norbu. He had been employed for a short period in the training of Tibetan guerrillas. Having felt that this was not a pragmatic solution to the Tibetan cause, he was studying English at a college in Pennsylvania while working as a waiter to pay his tuition. By now Lobsang had given up his monk's vows. Norbu had recently gotten married, which was very sad as he was a Rinpoche, or reincarnate lama. The family realized that Lobsang would follow in the same footsteps and was worried that he would bring back an American bride. Lobsang's younger sister, Jetsun Pema, was a good friend of mine, and she suggested that I marry Lobsang. At the same time, Lobsang's friends suggested that he marry me. One day his older brother, Gyalo Thondup, called on my parents to ask for my hand in marriage for his brother. I had met Lobsang earlier; but the last meeting was in Calcutta when he was twenty-seven and I was seventeen.

This was a big decision. I was very lucky to have parents who were broad-minded enough to leave the decision to me. I thought that I should meet Lobsang again before considering such an important life commitment. My father warned me that being married to the brother of the Dalai Lama would not be easy. My mother said that she had seen many different events in the marital lives of my father's sisters. She felt that this proposal was best left to my judgment.

Lobsang and I met in Calcutta. He was handsome, very friendly, pleasant, and had a zest for life. He had traveled extensively, had a wonderful sense of humor, and was very open. Almost immediately, his frankness, sincerity, and simplicity won my heart. I was smitten. We met in March and were married by the end of August, 1962.

According to the Tibetan calendar, 1962 was a black year, an inauspicious year when no ceremonies were to take place, and definitely no weddings! Lobsang's mother and older sister wanted him to wait until the next year. The Choegyal of Sikkim and his American fiancee, Hope Cooke, had already postponed their marriage. By this time, His Holiness had moved to Dharamsala, and a Tibetan administration had been set up at that location, so Lobsang was working there in the home department. I later discovered that Lobsang had told his mother that I was pregnant, and that we had to have the wedding soon. It was a clever story that Lobsang had made up, and we had many laughs about it later.

We were married in a simple ceremony at my brother-in-law Gyalo Thondup and his wife Chutan's home in Darjeeling. Being young and just out of school, I was very shy and nervous on my wedding day. I had to meet many friends and acquaintances who came to greet Lobsang and me with scarves, gifts, and good wishes. Before I left my home in Kalimpong with a party sent from Darjeeling to accompany me, we had a simple ceremony at my home with our friends from the Himalayan Hotel, including the kind Aunties who had looked after us when our parents were in Tibet, and Major Cann, our teacher. Major Cann was a Buddhist from Canada who earned his living in Kalimpong as a private tutor. He brought me a beautiful yellow orchid, which he pinned to my green brocade dress. I felt very sad about leaving my home. With tears streaming down my face, I bid farewell to my parents, who were also in tears, especially my dear father.

In Tibet, marriages were usually arranged. Sometimes, families committed their children to each other when the children were very young. The older members of the family or family friends made the decision to find a bride for their sons. Names of young girls, usually from the same family background, would be chosen, making sure that the family was honest and religious. Four or five names were selected by the older members of the family. The son was lucky if he had a say in the selection. These names were then presented to a holy man for selection by divination, and astrological calculations were sometimes done for the final choice. Calculations had to be done so that the groom and the future bride would be compatible. Family members or close friends would be sent to ask for the hand of the selected bride.

We had a very jolly and mischievous grandaunt, a sister of Tsarong Pola, who was sent to marry the chieftain of Poyul, a region near the border with northeast India. The people in this region were known to be fierce, and they lived in the jungles. These tribal people were causing many problems by evading taxes, harassing their neighbors and refusing to talk with the central Tibetan government authorities. In an attempt to elicit some peace and cooperation from these people, my grandfather sent his beautiful sister as a bride to the tribal chieftain. Pola was very powerful, and my poor aunt had no way to get out of this marriage. She often told us her story, "I came as a bride with much apprehension and fear, having learned that these tribes ate people and were truly wild. I had no choice but to come to this land. On the wedding day, I surreptitiously peeked at the chief. What a relief that he was not ugly."

In spite of the marriage, the tension remained, and the tribal people continued to harass their neighbors. Eventually, troops had to be sent from Central Tibet to subdue them. The chief fled over the border into India and Aunt Zheyshi returned to Lhasa. The government gave her a small estate called Zheyshi, and she came to live in one of our outer houses. She was a lot of fun and loved wearing gobs of make-up, although she was not so young.

Everyone enjoyed her company, and she used to leave us in stitches with her wild jokes. In front of my grandparents, she was very meek and quiet. Her new husband was rather strict and possessive. She could never openly talk to another man as her husband was likely to beat her. Whenever he turned his back, she slyly flirted with every young man in sight.

Wedding ceremonies are basically the same all over Tibet, except for slight differences according to local customs and the wealth of the families. After the selection of the bride, and with the consent of the bride's family to the marriage, a date is set for the engagement. On the engagement day, or "Longchang," translated as the "Beer Begging Day," representatives of the groom, usually relatives or close friends, go to beg for the bride and beer. Many gifts are taken, such as khatas or money wrapped in a paper folder and presented to the mother of the bride as repayment for nourishing the girl. This payment is called *nu rin*, or the "breast payment." There is no fixed sum of money, and most marriage contracts are drawn up during this occasion. This contract includes ways to find an amicable settlement should there be a divorce, so that the bride is well taken care of in the future. If there are children, the daughters live with the mother and the sons live with the father in the event of separation. The engagement day is also a day for feasting and drinking.

The wedding takes place on an auspicious day, fixed by an astrologer. The representatives of the groom's family come to the house of the bride with a full set of clothing and jewelry and a *dhata*, an arrow, bound and knotted with scarves of the five colors of the elements—white, yellow, blue, green, and red—ornamented with precious gems and a round piece of metal called a *melong*. The party is welcomed with a ceremony of droma, rice with raisins, and tea. Early the next morning, the bride is dressed in the clothes and jewelry sent from the groom's home, and she is taken to the family chapel to bid farewell to her family protective deity. A ceremony of serving tea, droma, and rice with raisins to all the members in the home and the visitors from the groom's home takes place. Scarves are presented to the family of the bride by the husband's representatives, and the dhata is stuck on the back of the bride's robes. This symbolizes that the girl now belongs to the owner of this arrow, and that she should bring luck to her new home. When the bride leaves her house, the dhata belonging to her family is waved in a clockwise motion behind her so that the bride does not take the family good fortunes to her new home.

There are no dowry systems such as the ones in India, but the bride's family sends clothes, bedding, household utensils, jewelry, and money with the bride. There is also no fixed number of such gifts. A painting of a Wheel of Life is carried with the bride at the head of the wedding procession when she leaves for her new home. Every house has a painting of a Wheel of Life, or *Sipa Khorlo*, which brings luck and obstructs misfortune.

When the bride enters the groom's home, she is met by the mother of the house, who offers her a jug or bowl of milk to welcome her. There is also a box of wheat and tsampa as well as the bowl of chang to wish her well. She is first taken to the family chapel, then to the living room where she joins the groom and his family in the tea and rice ceremony. Following this is the presentation of scarves by family members and friends. The parents do not accompany their daughter to the new family or participate in the ceremony, but join later in the day or days of feasts, songs, and dances.

If the bride was unhappy in her new home or the husband did not treat her well, she could always return to her own home. Of course, relatives and friends would try to counsel the husband and the wife, but divorces took place and there were no stigmas attached to such decisions. The partners remarried or lived alone. If one of the partners died, the other was permitted to remarry and was often encouraged to marry a younger member of the family. Polygamy and polyandry were practiced, and it was rare that there were fights in such arrangements. Usually, two or three brothers would marry one wife, or one man would take two or three sisters as brides. Love marriages and elopements also took place. In the present day, most Tibetans marry for love and seek their own partners in life.

10 New Delhi

Before our marriage, Lobsang worked in the Tibetan rehabilitation office in Dharamsala. Instead of joining him there, I received a letter from the Tibetan cabinet appointing me to work in New Delhi! Here we had been married a mere six weeks, yet Lobsang was to return to Dharamsala, and I was to live in New Delhi. This was unexpected and unthinkable. We were inseparable by then, and I was very unsure of how to manage my own life. I had never lived alone. Lobsang decided to take a long leave and requested a transfer to Delhi. While I went to work, he kept the house and did the cooking. This was long before the women's liberation movement, but I had a husband who was understanding, kind, and practical.

We lived in an apartment in Delhi owned by my brother-in-law and his wife. They lived in Darjeeling and only used this apartment during the winter months. My salary was only 75 rupees per month, and I usually went back to our flat to join my husband for lunch, paying more than my salary for the transportation. A Mongolian lama named Zurki Rinpoche also lived with us in this apartment as the caretaker. Tall and thin, with a gaunt face and a shrill, husky voice, Zurki Rinpoche was funny to look at, a funny man and a wonderful companion. Kind and humble, he had been a high lama in Amdo before leaving Tibet. He loved to joke, and he made delicious Mongolian meat pancakes. On Sundays, we would go shopping for vegetables and then come home and cook exotic dishes, which Lobsang enjoyed very much. Lobsang loved food and was a wonderful cook. It was a learning experience for me. I had never had to cook anything, and my culinary skills consisted of making fried eggs or omelettes. No matter how hard I tried, everything turned out very bland. I was a better dishwasher than cook!

I was assigned to work as Mr. Ngawang Choesang's translator at the Bureau of His Holiness the Dalai Lama in New Delhi. Mr. Ngawang Choesang was a Tibetan monk official in his mid-thirties. His head was shaved, but he did not wear a monk's robe; instead he dressed in trousers and a bush shirt. Having recently come out of Tibet, it is possible that he did not own a monk's robe or have the funds to make one. His huge eyes and broad nose were quite prominent on his tanned, round face, which was always very greasy. He was an eloquent orator with a flair for words. He traveled to the road camps, to the settlements, and to points where new refugees arrived. He made reports that were sent to the home office of the government of India and to voluntary agencies helping the refugees. It was an extremely tedious job for him as well as for me, because I had to translate his reports. Having come to India at a young age, my Tibetan was very poor. I could not read his reports and had to ask him to read them out loud. The writing was in the classical, official language, so different from the spoken language used in everyday life. I had to request that he convey the message to me in more ordinary, colloquial language. He was very kind and patient, and I learned a great deal by working with him. Sometimes I had to type the reports of other officers and take the telephone calls as well.

By then, the seat of the Tibetan government-in-exile was in Dharamsala, and all the various departments had an officer in charge at the Bureau in Delhi. We collected information for the educational, religious, resettlement, health, and other development needs of the Tibetan refugees, and passed the material with project reports to the outside world in order to seek assistance. We also maintained relationships with the diplomatic missions in the capital, trying to gain their assistance in seeking support for our cause. Tsepon Shakabpa, a seasoned diplomat, was in charge of the Bureau, and we had about a dozen staff members working there. My husband was later appointed to assist Mr. Shakabpa. We decided it would be more economical and practical for us to move into the Bureau house.

New Delhi was lovely. In those days, the monstrous, ugly concrete buildings that are so visible now were rare sore spots in the beautiful park-like city. Well-kept houses with miniature gardens were set among lovely old mosques, forts, and lush green parks. Each enclave had a well-organized shopping center that catered to an international clientele. The old city oozed with people and antiquity. Going to Sadar Bazaar was like entering the world of Ali Baba. Ancient houses lined narrow, filthy streets in which cows, dogs, and people competed for foot space. Rickshaws pulled by thin, dark men with wiry legs struggled along at a snail's pace through the congested corridors. Colorful saris dazzled the eye, and the aroma of fried potato pancakes competed with those of the tangy oranges and fragrant mangoes, sending our taste buds into a frenzy. Exotic incense lingered around every shop entrance, and the shouts of hawkers could be deafening if you went too close.

Vegetable sellers roamed the city with their fresh and plentiful goods. Even in the winter, many varieties of vegetables were available. It was a pleasure to catch the "sabjeewallahs" and to choose from the goods on the colorful wheeled carts they pushed through the neighborhoods.

The common people were very friendly and helpful. On the other hand, the well-to-do people and the government officials of Delhi were stiff and formal. The latter were still clinging to British social habits, and they seemed neither at ease with their Indian heritage nor comfortable imitating the British rulers. Our neighborhood vegetable seller, the dry cleaner, and the indispensable electrician as well as the *dobi* (the washerman) were very natural and friendly, especially when we spoke Hindi.

The Dalai Lama's Bureau was a large two-storied rented house with a small garden in the front. The living room in the upper portion of the house was made into the office, where each desk represented a different department. We had two officers to each desk, and needless to say, we were crowded. The rest of the rooms were living quarters for the senior staff members. The down-stairs rooms accommodated our common living-cum-dining room, and the rest of the staff had their living quarters there. We were each provided a bed, a table and a chair, and were happy that each room had built-in cupboards. Some of us were lucky enough to have our own bathrooms, which was a luxury.

There were about a dozen of us, and I was at that time the only female on the staff. We also had a cook and an Indian driver. The gardener and the sweeper were part-time Indian workers from Delhi. We worked together and ate together and were like a large family. The Bureau served as a center for Tibetans going through Delhi, so it was always filled with people. Some mornings, we would wake up and find people sleeping on the flat roof or on the verandas! We ate from a common kitchen where we paid minimum charges, and we would find at least three or four new faces daily.

Lobsang found the food at the common kitchen extremely boring, because we had noodle soup or rice and dal with a veg-etable dish every day at every meal. We bought a small electric stove and did some of our own cooking in the bathroom during the weekends. Squatting on the bathroom floor, being very care-ful to cut the ingredients as far from the toilet bowl as possible, and hunching over a small electric stove in the Delhi heat was one of my most agonizing household chores.

Our pantry was in our bedroom. Lobsang and I bought some cups and saucers, colorful tablecloths, and bed covers. I always found fresh flowers at reduced rates at the end of the day, and our little bedroom-cum-living room was cheerful and clean. I have some very happy memories of that small space. It was also in this room that our daughter Chuki spent her first two years.

My husband had to attend a number of diplomatic cocktail and dinner parties, and I accompanied him on these outings. When I first arrived in Delhi, I loved to dress up and go to these events. It was all very glamorous. However, such occasions gradually became boring and superficial. Everyone seemed to say the same things, and many of these guests drank more alco-hol than they could hold. Underneath their strained, artificial smiles and the polite chitchat, most people looked as if they had only come for the free drinks and food. Of course, it was not all for nothing. I am sure some important deals were made during such parties—development projects were planned, people got to eat, the greedy got to pocket part of the spending marked for the poor. It is said that governments can be built and governments can be toppled during a good party.

Summer was approaching, and I was dreading the dry, dusty heat of Delhi. I felt lethargic and exhausted. I was feeling so tired one day that I decided to visit the Holy Family Hospital. Because I was very shy, and brought up in a sheltered home and a conservative school, I asked for a female physician. To my surprise, I was examined by a Catholic nun, who terrified me when she told me that I was expecting a baby in a couple of months. When my husband heard the news, he began to treat me as if I was a precious object. Immediately, I became very fragile. We went straight to a bookshop after the hospital visit to read up on pregnancy and babies. The shopkeeper gave us Dr. Benjamin Spock's book, which was very useful in preparing me for motherhood. This book helped me in raising my children, and I carried it with me from India to Europe and to the United States. When my daughter became a mother, I recommended that she read Dr. Spock. A friend told her that such books were out of date, but I feel thankful to have had Dr. Spock. If he is alive, I am sure he will be happy to learn that my babies were healthy and happy, both physically and mentally.

People in the East were reluctant to talk about pregnancy and sex, and my knowledge about pregnancy was very vague. We never could have asked our mother about sex and babies. At Mount Hermon, our biology teacher, who was Bengali, was too shy to explain the chapter on reproduction to the class. What luck that we didn't have any questions on the subject on our final examination! I was twenty years old, and my only experience with childbirth was hearing our maid deliver a baby with Amala attending. Amala wanted my sister and me to help her. The mother, who was howling in such pain, got us so scared that we would not even go near the room. We did see the baby after the birth. Little Dolma Kyi was so fat and fair and beautiful. She was a living doll for us.

On May 29, 1963, our daughter Tenzin Chuki was born. I returned to my parents' home in Calcutta so the baby could be delivered there. The night before our daughter's birth, my mother dreamt of my paternal grandmother, to whom I was very close. When my mother went to the New Market to buy flowers to take to me at the hospital, the only kind she could find were lotuses. She thought this to be rather strange, as the florists in the New Market always had many varieties of flowers for sale, but on that morning only lotuses were available. In Tibetan, the word for lotus is *pema*, and Pema was my grandmother's name. My mother believed Chuki to be the reincarnation of my paternal grandmother. It is quite strange, but Chuki is very close to my father.

Chuki was a very beautiful baby, born with a head full of black hair and dimples on her chubby face. She was a favorite in the hospital ward. The day she came home from the hospital, she cried and cried until I was so disturbed that I cried with her. Nothing would stop her from crying until my father dipped his little finger in a jar of honey and let her suck on his finger. That kept her silent for a little while. Even to this day, that was the only time Chuki gave me any reason for worry. My husband and I were really lucky to have the experienced help of my parents. Tenzin Chuki, meaning "Holder of the Faith" and "Happiness," was named by His Holiness the Dalai Lama.

It was in June, just a month before the outburst of the monsoons, that we came to Delhi. Our little room was like a furnace. We put wet sheets over Chuki to keep her cool, but in a few minutes the sheets would be dry. The fan in the room blew more hot air on us and the first few nights in Delhi poor Chuki cried nonstop. Calcutta had also been hot, but at least we had had air conditioning. We welcomed the showers of the monsoon and the loud claps of thunder and the streaks of lightning in the dark, brooding Delhi sky.

Another daughter followed Chuki. I was back in Calcutta, and my husband had gone to the States because his reentry permit was about to expire. The baby came prematurely and I did not inform Lobsang that I was in the hospital. I had a well-known German physician and my parents nearby. I was admitted to the hospital because I was bleeding profusely and was in a great deal of pain. My doctor was busy seeing his patients in the clinic, so I was left unattended for several hours. The nurses were helpless, as they could not even prescribe aspirin without an attending physician. When my doctor arrived, I was rushed to the operating room. As I was entering the room, my husband arrived straight from the airport. When I woke up from the effects of the anesthesia, I asked for my baby. I had tubes attached to different parts of my body and was groggy and in pain. From what seemed like a far away land, I saw my husband near my bed. He was holding my hand, but my thoughts were on the baby. Before I could ask about my baby, I returned to a dark, unknown world. Finally, when I returned to consciousness, I pleaded to see my baby. My husband told me that the baby had been stillborn. By then, the tubes were out of my mouth, and I could pour out my anguish and pain in a flood of tears. I had carried this child with so much love and care; I went through all this pain and anguish to give birth to this little human being, and to lose her was unbearable.

Months later, my father told me that he was handed this little nameless, lifeless daughter in a long white hospital gown. Lobsang stayed with me because I was so weak and depressed. Pala got a Buddhist prayer book and drove to the Ghat, on the banks of the Brahmaputra River, to the cremation grounds. He sat in the car reading the scripture while our driver Norbu took the baby, still in her white hospital gown, well wrapped in a white sheet, to the spot where a bundle of wood was ready to be lit by some caretakers of the ground. Even before the fire could be lit, beggars rushed from all directions to fight over the sheet and the gown like a bunch of vultures. Pala and Norbu were shocked and unprepared for such inhuman behavior. After hearing of this incident, which my father had carried and needed to release, I was deeply saddened to think about what people do when they are hungry and in need. We can only have compassion for such suffering. The poverty in Calcutta can be shocking, yet the superfluous spending of the rich on alcohol and entertainment in the Calcutta nightclubs and in the popular New Market is unbelievable.

The morning after my operation, I learned from my sister that tragedy had fallen on my family once again, and my parents could not come to see me. The newspaper had announced the assassination of my mother's cousin, Jigme Dorji, the Prime Minister of Bhutan. My parents had gone to see his widow, my father's sister, Aunt Tess. Their eldest son, Paljor, was studying law in London, and he had arrived in Calcutta on his way to Bhutan to attend his father's funeral the next day. In spite of his great loss, he came to see me in the hospital, and I was very touched. We shared our grief and consoled each other. I had lost a child—I could have another—but he had lost his only father and my sorrow went to him. He was very brave.

Norzin had finished school and was about to go to the United States to continue her studies with the sponsorship of our dear friend Ilya Tolstoy. I was grateful that she was with me during my days of pain. It took some time to recover from the anguish, but Norzin was a great comfort and a wonderful companion. She helped me look after Chuki when Lobsang had to return to Delhi. I look back to those days, and I am so thankful that I had such a close, loving, and caring family.

After getting back to Delhi, Lobsang and I made a visit to Dharamsala. He had some work to do, and I was to have an audience with His Holiness. I had not seen him since getting his blessings in Varanasi and Calcutta in 1956. We stayed at one side of his Palace, where Lobsang's mother, his sister Tsering Dolma, and his brother-in-law Phuntsok Tashi Taklha resided. We took Chuki with us, too. It was good to see my mother-in-law, whom I had met a number of times in Darjeeling and Calcutta. Being friends of her youngest daughter, Jetsun Pema, my sister and I used to visit her.

During my short stay in Dharamsala, I spent most of my time with my mother-in-law. She and the family ate separately on their side of the cottage. There was a kitchen attached to her room, and she would often bake bread for His Holiness. Being in the same house was not always easy, as there was an awed silence about the place. When Chuki cried, we had to send her out in the woods with her maid. Chuki was outside for most of our stay.

One day I was told by my mother-in-law that we were to have lunch with His Holiness that day. I was so nervous! Lunch was served on the veranda of the sprawling Swagashram Cottage. Lobsang had gone to visit the various offices, and my mother-in-law, known to all Tibetans as "Gyalyum Chenmo" or Great Mother of His Holiness, and I were alone with His Holiness. He was sitting on an armchair, and there were three old monk attendants nearby. He did not look as frightening as I had imagined, and soon all the tension I had built up eased away and I felt more comfortable. A young monk brought his tray, which was handed to a tall, old monk who I later learned was the master of the kitchen. He put the tray in front of His Holiness. I really don't remember what was served for lunch or what was said, because I was awestruck. After the meal, there was bright sunlight shining on the veranda through the green pine and rhododendron trees. His Holiness asked an attendant to bring out the Chinese checker board, a game my mother-in-law was very fond of, and Gyalyum and I played this game while His Holiness watched. Chuki was called in, and she was given some chocolates by His Holiness. Thereafter, we would find her running to his private quarters if we did not keep a close eye on her. One day, Gyalyum found her in His Holiness's living room, lost among the beautiful thangkas and armchairs and tables.

The loss of my second daughter was often in my thoughts, and talking to my mother-in-law about my sadness was very comforting. She was such a kind and understanding person. Often, she would tell me that it was possible I was meant to lose this child so that she could return as a son. She told me that she had had a lovely boy who was very intelligent and lively, but he choked and died in a coughing spasm. A priest told the family that they should put a small piece of butter on the buttock of the dead child before the funeral, and the child would return to the family. The following year, another son was born with a white mark on the same spot where the butter was smeared on the child she had lost. The later child returned as my youngest brother-in-law, Tenzin Choegyal.

Another new experience for me in Dharamsala was meeting a traditional Tibetan physician. Dr. Yeshi Dhonden, a monk, had just taken His Holiness's pulse and tested his urine. Then he visited Gyalyum, who requested that he take my pulse. Dr. Dhonden told me that I was pregnant with a boy. He advised me not to eat pork and to be careful about everything else that I ate. This was my first encounter with a Tibetan physician. I was very surprised when he told me that I was pregnant, because I had no idea. Our visit soon came to an end. I still have the khata given to me by His Holiness during my audience with him.

Soon, my son, whom I named Tenzin Namdhak, was born in Calcutta. Tenzin, meaning "Holder of the Faith," and Namdhak, meaning "Perfect," was a perfect baby. The only troubles he gave me were his bouts of constipation immediately after birth. My mother was once again a great help. She prepared orange juice, forced him to take it, and urged him with a soothing voice when he was trying so hard to move his bowels. Not long after Tenzin's birth, we had to leave to go abroad, as Lobsang was sent to work at the Office of Tibet in Geneva, Switzerland.

The people of Switzerland had opened their hearts to the Tibetan refugees. Refugees were selected from the road camps and sent to work in factories in the Swiss Alps. The staff at the Bureau in Delhi had to prepare Indian travel documents for these refugees, obtain their visas, see that they were inoculated, and prepare them for entry into a new world. We had to teach them to bathe often, to use a fork and a knife, not to pee on the road, and not to stick their tongues out as a gesture of respect, as Westerners found this gesture rude. It is very difficult to change old habits. When the emigrants boarded the plane, we could see that our lessons had failed for the majority of them. Their hair was uncombed, their clothes dirty, and they stuck out their tongues as a show of respect as they wished us good-bye.

January 3, 1965, was the day Lobsang and I bid a sad farewell to Lobsang's mother in Delhi. We were on our way to Switzerland to work in the Office of Tibet. By then, I had grown very fond of Gyalyum Chenmo, a wonderful mother-in-law and a great teacher and friend. She was sad to see us leave. Chuki looked so cute in her pink overcoat I bought from a shop in Calcutta. The outfit was made abroad, and it looked new and as if it had been made just for Chuki. There were a matching hat and mittens with white fur. Tenzin, who was two and half months old, was well wrapped in warm blankets for the cold January morning, and we carried him in a red, plastic baby basket. He was such an admired baby; he had many fans among the air hostesses.

Because the Tibetan government had no funds to send the children and me with Lobsang, we were told we had to wait behind for a year until funds could be sought. My parents and some friends came to the rescue and advanced us the money for the plane tickets. Europe seemed so far away. I had traveled by plane only twice in my life, and to see these huge iron birds and think that we would be crossing oceans and mountains gave me butterflies. To add to my anxiety, we were not sure that we would get into Switzerland. The Swiss government had at first refused our visas. We learned that the Chinese had contacted the Swiss and objected to the opening of the Office of Tibet in Switzerland. Lobsang, as the brother of the Dalai Lama, may have given the Chinese more reason to make such protests.

We were first to fly to Vienna to open an exhibit on Tibet arranged by our good friend Heinrich Harrer, the Austrian adventurer, and then to proceed to New York City, where we could apply for Swiss visas. I had traveled over endless mountains to the plains of India, and now I was to fly to the other side of the world not really knowing what lay ahead. If we were not able to obtain Swiss visas, we had decided we would settle in the United States, as my husband was a resident. Only twenty-three years old, and a mother of two, I was very concerned about this travel into the unknown. Lobsang had enough funds to carry us for a couple of months in America, but after that we had no idea where the future would lead us. At the same time, I was very excited, thinking what an adventure this could be, something to relish and to tell my children and grandchildren about in the years to come.

11 In the Belly of the Iron Bird

As I climbed the metal steps into the belly of the huge iron bird, it occurred to me that I was to fly thousands of miles, over mountains and oceans, oases and deserts, that my life was in the hands of complete strangers. I would have no control. Now someone else would be taking me beyond time and space.

It was very early in the morning when we boarded the plane and left New Delhi. When we were settled down in the scented cabin with the dimmed lights and soothing music, I tried to relax. As the plane lifted off the ground, I recited a prayer to Palden Lhamo and soon my fear and anxiety melted. Calling on my protecting deity brought me peace and even gave me the courage to look out the window. Delhi was below, a sea of glittering lights.

Miles and miles up in the sky, I thought of my journey from the high Himalayan mountains, from the Holy City of Lhasa, traveling through treacherous passes and across roaring rivers, to the vast plains of India. Now I was on my way to the Holy City of Rome and to Vienna and New York. I had learned about these cities in Mrs. De's geography class at Mount Hermon, but I had never imagined that I would really see these places. Countries outside of India and China were known as the "outer world" to Tibetans. Very few of my fellow country folk had even heard of these countries, and far fewer had ever traveled to them.

The international environment in India had exposed me to Hollywood movies, Elvis Presley, and Chubby Checker, so I felt a twinge of excitement. My excitement was mixed with the sadness of leaving my parents behind. The dividing line between these emotions was so thin that it was a little confusing.

Rome was very cold. The airport was huge and full of passengers but seemed so clean and sparkling compared to India. The scent of different perfumes in the air was lovely, but it made me light-headed. Unlike India, no one wore dirty, tattered clothing. People were nicely dressed and well mannered. The usual chaos was absent, no rush or push to reach the ticket counters. I felt a bit bewildered and self-conscious in my long Tibetan robes. Hundreds of eyes seemed to peer at me. Fortunately, Lobsang was always at my side. An experienced traveler, he knew how to handle the customs and immigration formalities and the money changing business. Travel in Tibet was really so much slower and simpler.

Driving into the city was an exciting experience. Rome was covered with snow, and the sun was blazing across the white landscape. Traffic was orderly and everyone obeyed the rules. We paid the taxi driver handfuls of Italian lira once he stopped in front of our hotel. I was glad to get to the hotel room, where I could be alone with my family and try to absorb and comprehend all the new sights and sounds. It was like needing rest after a large banquet to digest the different dishes one had tasted.

With a toddler and a two-and-a-half-month-old baby, both crying for attention, bottled milk to be prepared, and nappies to be changed, I felt tired and uneasy and stayed inside most of the time we were in Rome. I could have taken a tour bus and left my husband with the children, as he had visited Rome on an earlier occasion, but I was too shy and afraid to walk out on the foreign streets among strangers. I felt thrown out of my safe cocoon into a maze of roaring cars, revolving doors, and gliding escalators, all very new to me. I regretted not seeing much of this historic city, especially Michelangelo's great works and the Vatican.

However, I was able to see some old friends. It was wonderful to visit with Geshe Jampel Sangye Ati, a learned scholar on Tibetan Buddhism who worked with the noted Italian scholar Giuseppe Tucci at the Istituto Italiano per il Medio ed Estremo Oriente. Lobsang and I also called on Professor Tucci at the Institute. He met us in a huge, elaborately decorated lounge with walls covered by beautiful paintings. Professor Tucci was quite old, and he was dwarfed by this massive room. During a trip to Lhasa some years back, Dr. Tucci had visited my family, and I still carried the pretty glass beads he had given my grandmother. Geshe Jampel Sangye Ati was a friendly, open man, very gracious and kind. He took us to meet a few of his Italian friends who were Buddhists, and who were very curious to meet us. They fussed over our children and adored them. Unfortunately, we could not speak Italian, and they spoke no Tibetan or English. Geshe-la had been a monk of Sera, but he had an Italian girlfriend then and I later learned that he had had a son by her.

Professor Namkhai Norbu was younger and a *tulku* from Kham. He was studying and teaching at a university in the city. Both these Tibetans were fluent in Italian and were the only Tibetans in Italy at that time. Meeting their friends and dining with them was like being in the company of a group of Tibetans. Italians and Tibetans both like to eat well and drink plenty. The Italians had enormous appetites and were very jovial. For the first time, I was introduced to spaghetti, lasagna, and red wine, and I loved the new tastes. I liked the spontaneity and friendliness of the Italians we met, and I was sorry we could not converse with them.

Three days in Rome passed very quickly. From there, we flew on to Vienna and were met by Mr. Thupten Woser Phala, the Dalai Lama's representative in Europe. Lobsang's sister Jetsun Pema had arrived in the city before us. Professor Heinrich Harrer was holding an exhibition in the city, and he had invited all of us for the opening. Harrer welcomed us with his effervescent manner, and soon we were all in the lobby of the hotel laughing, joking, and reminiscing about our good old days in Lhasa. The subdued manner and formality of the other European guests in the lobby was such a contrast to our raucous group of old friends who had not seen each other for a very long time. I noticed that a few people looked at us disapprovingly.

I was very happy to see Pema. She had graduated from a finishing school in Switzerland and was now in a secretarial school in London. We had not seen each other for a couple of years, so I was filling her in on all the news from home. She was a wonderful companion in Vienna.

When our supply of Indian powdered milk came to an end, I had to change to another brand to feed Tenzin, and it gave him much stomach trouble. Chuki was also tired; she fussed incessantly and there was no way she would stay with the babysitter Harrer had kindly arranged for us. Once again, I was locked up in a hotel room in a beautiful city.

I did manage to get out of my room to attend Professor Harrer's opening night ceremonies for his Tibetan exhibition. Harrer has been one of Tibet's best ambassadors to the world. Traveling out of Tibet was so difficult, yet to see the large collection he had gathered there was amazing. For most of the guests that evening, Tibet could have been on another planet. Very little was known of the country, and people like Harrer contributed much to introducing Tibet and the Tibetans to the outside world. At the inauguration, there were a number of important-looking dignitaries. A couple of speeches were made while flashbulbs popped. A television crew was there filming us with bright spotlights, and the public response was tremendous. Pema and I wore our national costumes and were one of the "live" exhibits. Tibetans were a rare species, and we were quite an attraction. This event made us very proud of our roots and lifted our spirits. It was difficult to tear ourselves away from the museum to attend the official dinner. Remembering that Chuki was howling as I left for the ceremony, I decided I should return to the hotel. It was a good thing I did, because she still was crying and poor Christa, the babysitter, was as upset as Chuki. I was glad to be reunited with my babies.

The next day, we bade farewell to Mr. Phala in the hotel lounge. Pema flew back to London. After inquiring about our visas to Switzerland, we were told to contact the Swiss Consulate in New York City. We flew to New York, hoping to join Mr. Phala soon. Harrer had come to see us off with some of his friends. The friendly hotel staff gave us a wonderful farewell. Once again, we entered the belly of a Lufthansa jet.

We flew into Manhattan at dusk. In the fading, soft orange glow of the setting sun, myriads of lights twinkled from the land below like clusters of diamonds set on a huge brooch. Lobsang loved New York City. He had lived there earlier and was very excited to show me this great place. He was pointing out the sites, and I was lost in this fairy-tale illusion. Too soon, the announcement of our approach to the city jolted me back to reality. The seat belts needed fastening, Chuki needed to be wakened from her nap, and Tenzin in his red card-box carrier needed attention.

JFK Airport was bigger, noisier, and more chaotic than the Vienna and Rome airports. Even the people seemed louder and more boisterous. The customs and immigration checking was fast and efficient, and I was really taken aback at the informality of the people in this part of the world. The airport staff addressed you like a long lost friend. I felt small and lost.

The taxi ride to New York City was an adventure. The driver talked on and on about the New York weather, the city, and baseball, a subject unfamiliar to both Lobsang and me. He wanted to know where we came from, and when we said "Tibet," it could have been "Timbuktu." When Lobsang told him that he had lived in the city earlier, the driver went through a litany of ways the city had changed for the worse. He even said, "New York City has gone down the drain!" He seemed to love hearing his own voice. He spoke so fast that I could hardly follow the conversation. I was a complete stranger to the unfamiliar New York accent.

Overwhelmed by the numerous cars on the highway and the speed at which they were driving, it was a moment before I noticed how tall the buildings we were approaching were. I sat in awe. As we entered the city, we were met by rows and rows of gravestones. We were racing into an exciting, new world and were suddenly hit smack in the face by this final journey called death. What a strange welcome to New York City.

Lobsang booked us into Hotel Bedford, a small hotel on East 42nd Street. It was a tall, narrow, red brick building with tendrils of ivy that climbed from top to bottom. The lounge of the hotel was small and lit by bright lamps, even though it was a sunny day. It was a clean, quiet hotel where many retired people stayed as permanent residents. In our suite, we had a living room with a closet for a kitchen, a bedroom, and a bath. I was glad to unpack and to be able to rest for a while before we moved to Europe. It was also a great release of tension and frustration to be able to communicate with people in a language I knew, although I did need to accustom myself to the strange accent.

We were not too far from one of the busiest underground stations of the world, Grand Central Station. My first trip in the subway was frightening. I was still apprehensive about all the new things I had to face, and unaccustomed to a world of fast people for whom other people hardly existed. Everyone seemed to be running for their lives. Most people seemed in a perpetual rush. One only saw a few old people sitting, perhaps because they were too old and weak to keep running. Going underground in well-lit passages that lead to the trains was a spooky experience. The doors to the trains opened and closed so quickly that I was afraid I would be pinched between them and dragged through the dark tunnels. I made very sure to clutch onto Lobsang so I would not lose him. It was amazing how we could get all over Manhattan at such speed, and it was hard to imagine that right above our heads were monstrous buildings and teeming traffic.

The days that followed were full of new experiences. My first visit to the supermarket left me confused about which brand of toothpaste or soap to purchase. There were so many different kinds. Curd was called yogurt, and dime meant ten cents. Lobsang introduced me to the washing machine, which left me with the impression of a magic box. However, my next visit to the laundry in the basement of the hotel was a disaster. I used the wrong kind of detergent, and not long after, Chuki and I noticed a shiny, massive puff of soap bubbles oozing down the sides of the closed machine. Alas, I had discovered the difference between laundry detergent and dishwashing liquid. It was quite an effort to mop up the suds that had managed to shimmy their way down to the floor, making a colossal mess. Chuki was beside herself with joy, but I prayed no one would enter the room and witness the disaster.

Tenzin's stomach could not tolerate the milk formula I bought in the United States, so once again I was busy with doctors, dirty diapers, and Tenzin's distress. Lobsang was worried because we still had no news concerning our visas to Switzerland, and our funds would not last much longer unless we made other housing arrangements. It was a trying time for us. Being locked up in a small hotel room during the New York winter was depressing. I had no close friends to talk to or share my feelings with. At times I felt like crying out of frustration and anger. In spite of our difficulties, we made the best of the situation, and Lobsang's old friends were all very kind and helpful.

Thupten Tharpa Liushar was the Dalai Lama's representative in the United States. Mr. Liushar was Tibet's last foreign minister, and he was a monk official of the Tibetan government. He went into exile as a member of His Holiness's party in March of 1959. Mr. Liushar was a short man in his sixties, with a pleasant, round face, small eyes, and a drooping lower lip. Because he was a monk, his hair was shaved, and his bald pate was shiny and bright. He had a gentle, serene manner and a slow gait. He did not speak English, so there were two young Tibetan boys working with him at the Office of Tibet in New York City. Lobsang and Mr. Liushar were old friends, so we visited him quite often in the evenings. It was on one of these visits that I was introduced to the television.

From Mr. Liushar I learned how to boil rice the proper way and to make steamed dumplings. He was also adjusting to a new way of life, and he said, "When I walked out of the supermarket for the first time with a couple of grocery bags in my hand, I felt very awkward and strange. I worried that someone might recognize me. I kept looking up and down the street. I had been so used to my servants carrying everything for me in the past."

Mr. Liushar was also very kind to care for Tenzin and Chuki so that Lobsang could show me New York by night from the Empire State Building. Upon our return from sight-seeing, we were relieved to hear that Tenzin had slept through our absence and Chuki had been no trouble. It must have been the first time in Mr. Liushar's life that he had been left alone in the company of two small children. Nobody other than Lobsang would have had the courage to ask the Foreign Minister of Tibet to babysit!

We still had heard nothing from the Swiss government about our visas. We could not afford to live in a hotel for much longer, as Lobsang's funds were getting low. Lobsang had six thousand dollars in the bank, and I had no funds with me. Our plans were literally hanging in the air. Lobsang kept our spirits up. He was a very idealistic and adventurous man, a highly optimistic man, who always had a deep intuition that things would turn out fine in the end. He believed there could be nothing worse than losing one's country. I was as naive and unsure of myself as an innocent child. Fortunately, Mr. Phuntsok Thonden, who had just arrived in New York, had rented an apartment in town. His wife Pema and daughter Chemi were waiting in New Delhi, and would join him as soon as the Tibetan government was able to find funds for their plane tickets. He kindly let us use his apartment.

Other than a double bed and a baby cot, the apartment was empty of furniture. We lived in this apartment for about three weeks, eating off of paper plates and drinking from plastic cups. We even entertained sitting on the floor with the food spread out in front, and we had some wonderful meals with our friends.

While in New York, we met Ilya Tolstoy again. Ilya used to call us quite often, and he invited us to his apartment a couple of times. He lived alone and had matured. He was very concerned about us, and the Tibetans in general, and was working on a project with the Tolstoy Foundation to bring Tibetan refugees to Wyoming, a project that in the end did not materialize.

We also had the company of some of Lobsang's old friends, including Jan and Elie van Hoogstraten and Leonard Ching from the Church World Service, Dr. David Baker, Dr. Allen Rice and their families from Collegeville, Pennsylvania, where Lobsang had worked as a waiter at the campus while studying English. These friends visited us and made us feel welcome in their country. Chuki even received her first doll from Mrs. Baker, which she cherished.

Another lovely person in New York was a learned Tibetan tulku named Rato Khyongla. He was a tall, bald man with a high forehead and a lovely shy smile. He was my husband's age, and a rather quiet and unassuming man, so many of us did not know that he was a highly learned Rinpoche from Tibet. I used to ask him questions about Buddhism, but he would never give me any substantial answers. I guess he thought I was trying to make small talk. Later, I learned from my husband that Buddhists do not proselytize their faith and are not in the custom of giving teachings unless the student is known to be serious. The teacher would research his potential students' motivations before he taught them the dharma or accepted them as students.

Khyongla Rinpoche had immigrated to the States, and he worked in the packaging section of a department store. Lobsang knew him well, and they enjoyed each other's company. Lobsang also roped him into babysitting for us while we went out for another sight-seeing tour. Being a monk, he had no experience with children. He gave Tenzin a prepared bottle, but Tenzin cried and cried the entire time we were away. Rinpoche said that he felt so helpless and did not know what to do. Fortunately, we had not ventured out too far from our residence, so Rinpoche's babysitting ordeal did not last long.

Lobsang was a curious, open, and inquisitive man, who loved discovering and experimenting, and he believed this was the best way for people to learn. When we came to a new town, before we had even opened our suitcases, he would be in a hurry to explore the new area, especially to visit the local food markets. He wanted to introduce me to every fine detail of America, so he said that I must taste the special American pancake breakfast. We walked a couple of blocks from our apartment to a Pancake House, where I tasted the thick, heavy syrup on the soft, buttery cake, which melted in the mouth. It was delicious. Chuki was also very enthusiastic about these pancakes. The aromatic coffee was also a treat; I became an instant fan of these pancake houses.

My visit to Chinatown left me amazed at the freedom of America. Here we were in China. The signs of the shops were in Chinese, as were the street names. There were Chinese newspapers, too. The place was crowded with restaurants and in every lane and alley the smell of food permeated the air. Small shops sold Chinese medicinal herbs and other colorful trinkets and toys. Women in colorful pajamas poked at wriggling lobsters sold by street vendors and contemplated the different ways to serve these creatures for dinner. Fat, greasy chickens were painted red and hung upside down and naked in store windows. Young mothers scolded their youngsters in loud Chinese phrases. Here in America, I was deep in China.

We also visited Central Park and fed the pigeons and toured the zoo, which Chuki loved. It was there that Chuki, a Tibetan child, saw her first yak. Chuki was afraid of the big black beast with the shaggy fur, and the poor animal looked lost and sad, so far from the Himalayas. I really felt sorry for this poor old yak.

Lobsang also made sure that I visited Macy's, which was the largest department store in the country at that time. I was appalled at the multitude of goods. Every floor of this huge department store was filled with goods of different shapes and sizes. Bewildered, I grew light-headed as I observed the variety and multitude of toys. I felt like a child lost in a maze.

My first impression of the United States was things, things, and things. It really was a consumer's paradise. Everything anyone ever wanted could be purchased, and I wondered if one's sensual appetite could ever be satisfied with so many marketable goods. There were always new models to replace the old models and it went on and on and on. Advertising and the aura of buy, buy, buy were everywhere, and everyone was motivated to shop, shop, and shop. Without caution, it would be easy to become a pauper within a few hours. It was also very easy to be misled by the glossy advertisements, as I was soon to discover.

Cooking was a problem for me, because my husband loved food. He was an excellent cook, and he expected the same of me. It was hard to concentrate on developing my culinary expertise with two small children to take care of and new customs and surroundings to adjust to. One day at Mr. Liushar's apartment, I saw a television commercial for a delicious-looking dish called ravioli. It reminded me of a small Tibetan momo, but was cooked in a tomato sauce. I thought this was great. My labor in the kitchen could be lightened with these ready-made dishes, so I bought the dish shown in the commercial. What I ended up with looked nothing like the big, juicy ravioli on the television. It was such a disappointment. On the plate were some pieces of ravioli as big as peas. Never again did I let myself be fooled by advertisements. Lobsang was so angry with my dish that he left and went out to dinner!

We had to go downtown to the immigration office to get our green cards. It had been six years since the Dalai Lama and a large number of Tibetans had gone into exile. We saw no immediate solution to the Tibetan problem or possibility for our return to our homeland. Lobsang already had his green card, and he had decided to make the United States our new home. It was even more important to make this decision because we had the future of our two children to consider. Lobsang's brother Norbu was a citizen of the United States, and he also wanted to make America his home until he could return to Tibet. It was necessary for us to find a home away from home, so we went through the immigration procedures to obtain our documents. For three days, we lined up behind long queues of people from all corners of the world who were speaking a multitude of languages. Finally, after standing in line for a very long period, we got to talk to one of the immigration officers behind the counter. To my great distress, I was not prepared for the rudeness I encountered. These "officials" were so impolite and insensitive. They spoke to us as if we were some dumb animals from another planet. If it had not been for the important documents we needed for our future, I would not have undergone this humiliation.

We decided to take a trip to Bloomington, Indiana, to visit Lobsang's oldest brother, Thubten Jigme Norbu, who was teaching at Indiana University. Professor Norbu had been living in the United States for a number of years. His wife, Kunyang, was not a complete stranger to me. She was the daughter of the late head of the Sakya sect. She was a couple of years younger than I, and we had studied together at Mount Hermon in Darjeeling. She left India for the United States in her early teens, along with her oldest brother and his family.

We stayed with Professor Norbu and his family for almost six weeks. They had three sons. The oldest, Lhundup, was a year older than Chuki, and the youngest, Jigme, was a year older than my son Tenzin. The middle son, Kunga, was Chuki's age. They all adored Chuki. Although Mr. Norbu had married, he was a reincarnation of the former Thaktse Rinpoche, so, like every other Tibetan, I called him Rinpoche. He and Kunyang were very kind to us, and I learned much from them about shopping, cooking, and housekeeping in the American style.

Kunyang used to drive a huge station wagon, and she would adjust the pillows piled on her seat before starting the car so that she could reach the steering wheel. She used to say that there was no option but to drive this big car, because the boys were growing up and the weekly groceries had to be transported in the car. Living in the countryside, one had to drive because the shopping centers were not within walking distance from the houses. I remember telling Kunyang that I would never manage driving on these busy American highways. Her reply was, "When you are compelled to do something, there is no choice, so you put your mind to do things you thought you were incapable of doing." I think back at this comment by my petite sister-in-law, behind the wheel of a huge station wagon, and wonder at my own experience in life. I am surprised at the challenges I have had to face and how much more meaningful and interesting my life has been because of my determination to take charge of it.

Going to the supermarkets in the countryside was such an experience. Huge halls were filled with all kinds of food. Food from every corner of the world could be purchased in one of these supermarkets. I realized where the expression "Land of Plenty" came from. I was also introduced to the shopping malls and was amazed at the temptation to spend the whole day in such a place. We could eat there, shop there, and even see a movie there. We relished the hot dogs and hamburgers, but our native Amdo thukpa and momo were still everyone's favorites. The delicious American ice cream, which Lobsang always talked about, was truly luscious.

I found it very strange to see the empty streets in the countryside of America. Coming from India, where hordes of people crowd every inch of space, the quiet streets seemed odd. On the other hand, I was overwhelmed by the multitude of cars. Every family owned at least one car, often one for each member of the family.

Rinpoche was a tall, handsome man. He had a smile that made our hearts lift up with cheer. I must say that all my husband's siblings had beautiful smiles. Rinpoche was very kind and jovial, like Lobsang, and his words were direct and frank. In the evenings we would drink beer. Rinpoche loved his glass of port and his menthol cigarette. The two brothers would crack jokes, some really quite crude, but to Lobsang and Norbu they were very natural. Rinpoche would say something funny, and we would be laughing until our stomachs ached. He would laugh so hard that tears would trickle down his cheeks.

The older children had a great time. In those days, Batman was the hero on the television screen. The boys would dash around the rooms with towels or any cloth they could get hold of to make a cape. Little Batmen were flying all over the house, with Chuki running at their heels. We had quite a hard time getting them to stay in the basement where all their toys were scattered. When the weather was nice, they were out in the snow, pulling each other on sleds or making snowmen and looking like Lilliputian Eskimos. Lobsang was their favorite playmate, and he enjoyed the games just as much as the children.

Rinpoche also took us to visit his university. It was my first visit to such an institution. We met his colleagues in his department. I was surprised that a German taught the Tibetan language. Rinpoche lectured on Tibetan culture. We also visited the university cafeteria. It was impressive to see the students and the professors lined up on a "first come, first served" basis, and how quickly lunch was put on the table. The cafeteria was well organized and efficiently run. Having visited just a small part of the university, I was astonished at the size of the place and at the freedom of the students.

One day, Mr. Liushar called us with the news that our Swiss visas had been issued. We bade farewell to the Norbu family and returned to New York City. Before we left for Geneva, I invited my sister Norzin to visit us in New York for a few days. It was good to see her again. She was finding herself to be a stranger in the United States and missed home very much. She was determined to complete her graduate studies in education. Ilya Tolstoy had helped her get into William Penn College, and she was very grateful to him for giving her the opportunity to go for further studies. When Norzin married some years later, and my parents were unable to attend the wedding because it was in the United States, it was Ilya who gave her away to her husband.

Chuki was delighted to have Norzin shower her with some much-needed attention. After Tenzin's arrival and our immediate departure from India soon after his birth, poor Chuki had been deprived of her role as the center of our attention. Lobsang and I were so overwhelmed with the countless things we had to do to prepare for life in a new country and to keep things running smoothly, that we did not realize Chuki's fussing was due to more than the change in surroundings and the fatigue of travel. This was her way of asking for our attention. Norzin's presence seemed to cure Chuki's distress, and they basked in each other's company. I was very happy to see my sister again and to be able to talk to her. She was very happy to be with us, and we spent a couple of pleasant days together.

Because Norzin was a student, she had very little money to spend on entertainment or shopping. She had not yet visited the shopping malls outside of her small town, so we decided to visit Macy's one day while Lobsang looked after the children. We needed to buy overcoats, and I wanted to buy some more practical clothes, such as pants and shorter dresses. Norzin and I were both taken by the fashionable suede coats and we each bought one, not knowing that they needed special care. We returned home after exploring the city all day in our new high-heeled shoes, and only then did we realize that our feet were in extraordinary pain. We were so dazzled by the sights of New York and the beautiful things in the shops that we did not notice that we had been walking around on pinched feet.

Soon after purchasing our new overcoats, Lobsang and I decided to visit some Mongolian friends who lived in New Jersey, and especially to visit a Mongolian monk called Geshe Wangyalla, who had started a Buddhist center in Freehold Acres, New Jersey. Geshe-la was an old family friend of ours. At the home of our Mongolian friends, we were served delicious, steamy momos, so popular among the Mongolian and Tibetan communities, and during this momo feast, I bit into a fat, juicy dumpling and the greasy liquid squirted all over my new overcoat. As I was very proud of this new coat, I took it to the dry cleaners. It was not until I picked up my bedraggled mess of a jacket that I realized suede clothing must be cleaned and treated in a special way.

Geshe Wangyal-la was a most unusual man. He was an old man, a monk, but very liberal and was not bothered in the least by the differences in etiquette. He must have been a strict teacher, because a number of his students became well-known Buddhist scholars and professors in universities across the United States. Geshe Wangyal cooked his own food, shaved his own hair, stitched his own robes and was a very self-sufficient man. He was kind and loved to joke. His small twinkling eyes would shine with mirth when he was with Lobsang and Norbu, and they would always be laughing and joking, as they were very good friends.

I remember meeting Geshe-la for the first time in a small hotel in New Delhi. He was on his way to meet His Holiness the Dalai Lama in Dharamsala, and was traveling with the well-known Buddhist scholar Professor Robert Thurman, who now teaches at Columbia University. It was Bob Thurman's first visit to India. He was a tall, gawky young man with a clean-shaven head, and he was most enthusiastic about taking the monk's vows. Since Lobsang was an old friend, Geshe-la had called the Bureau, and Lobsang and I went to see him and his student.

Geshe Wangyal-la had come to Tibet from Mongolia, and had studied in one of the famous Gelukpa monasteries in Lhasa before he came to the United States. In Tibet he was not known to be a very serious scholar or Buddhist practitioner, but one cannot judge a person just from looking at him. He had for some time lived at the home of the Phala family, one of the aristocratic families in Lhasa, and he often visited my family. I remember Mr. Phala saying that Geshe Wangyal-la loved the Tibetan dice game called *sho*. He was also known to have a bad temper. When he lost a game, he would grab the dice pad, the bowl and all the shells, coins, and things needed for the game, and throw them out of the window. Yet, his temper would soon subside, and everyone would laugh at his behavior.

In the United States, he lived in a small house with two Tibetan monks, and the place served as a Buddhist temple. In the living room of this small house was an altar with many statues of Buddha, and numerous scriptures lined the cabinets. A number of Mongolians who had fled first from Russian-controlled Mongolia to Europe were now making their home in this region. There were also a couple of Tibetans living on the East Coast of the United States. To these people, Howell, New Jersey was a center for pilgrimage and worship, and this was where many young Tibetan Americans were introduced to Buddha and Buddhist rituals. Geshe-la also had a couple of American students who studied Buddhism with him. It was a visit to familiar grounds for me, and most pleasant to be with old friends.

The well-known Buddhist scholar and teacher Jeffrey Hopkins was a student there, and he actually lived at the temple. Jeffrey was such a serious student that we could only get a glimpse of him fetching his food from the kitchen. Otherwise, he was locked in his room studying.

Another wonderful friend we were able to visit on this occasion was Jentsen Dhondup, who accompanied Thubten Norbu to this land from Kumbum, Amdo. Jentsen was married to a Mongolian woman, and they had a son and a daughter. Their family soon became very good friends of our family. Jentsen worked in a factory and Barbara kept chickens at home and sold eggs. We loved visiting their chicken farm and spending time with them in later years.

Now that I was adjusted to my new environment, it was time to move on to another world. I had changed from wearing my long Tibetan robes to more comfortable Western clothes. I had changed my outlook on life as well. Before we departed from the New Delhi airport, I had always had my parents and Lobsang to lean on. There were servants to amuse the children, to cook, and to wash the dishes and the clothes. Since stepping on the plane to come to the West, I had to do most of these things for myself, and I had to make decisions for myself and my family. Lobsang was still there when I needed him, but he gently pushed me to take charge of my life. I remember my first shopping trip alone to purchase some baby food for Tenzin. Lobsang actually had to throw me out of the room. I was worried I would lose my sense of direction in the street, not know how to count the money, or how to choose from the many varieties. I was confused—like a baby discovering the world and learning to walk alone.

The informality of the Americans and the freedom in this land provided a good environment in which to grow. I was not only emancipated from my long, confining robes, but also from my own limited world. I had become more independent and more confident. I loved being anonymous in the big city and walking down the streets with no one caring what I was wearing or where I was going. Lobsang was a wonderful companion and guide in the discovery of myself in my new world.

12   Little Tibet in Switzerland

We landed in Geneva on a misty, drizzling morning in April of 1966. After New York City, the airport seemed small and quiet. The shops were arranged with good taste and care, and everything was immaculate. The Swiss people were more polite and reserved than the Americans. Mr. Phala and his interpreter, Mr. Phurphu Samdup, were waiting to take us to our new home in the Parc du Bude, a lovely residential area on the outskirts of the city, not very far from the United Nations headquarters and other international offices. There was a beautiful park and a number of huge apartment buildings. We took a small elevator to the sixth floor of one of these look-alike buildings. As soon as we stepped into the apartment and had inspected the rooms, Mr. Phala took me out on the veranda to show me the gorgeous view, the playground, the shopping center, and the farmer's market where we could get fresh fruits and vegetables. I felt I had landed in a large garden surrounded by snow-capped mountains. It was a beautiful sight. The sun filtered through the light drizzle, and the raindrops on the tree leaves glittered like jewels.

The apartment was lovely, although it was sparsely furnished. Once we had unpacked our few personal belongings, such as the gold Tara wall hangings, the silver wedding gifts from my family, the cheerful Tibetan carpets, and the colorful Bhutanese chair hangings, the apartment was transformed into a more agreeable place. Bude was a cosmopolitan community, and people from all corners of the world gathered in the supermarket across from our building. I shopped among Indian ladies elegantly dressed in saris or beside Arab men in flowing gowns. The African ladies wore colorful prints with fabulous turbans around their heads. At times, I would just sit at an outdoor cafe in the shopping center, drinking hot chocolate and watching this multicultural fashion show. The children in the park were just as varied in background as the multitudes of flowers around the park.

A total of one thousand Tibetans were invited to Switzerland as part of the resettlement project. There were also two Tibetan homes in the Pestalozzi Children's Village and about 180 children were adopted into individual Swiss homes. The Office of Tibet had been open for about a year and served to assist the Swiss Red Cross and the Swiss Friends of Tibet in the resettlement program. The office acted as a liaison between the Swiss and the Tibetans, and as a link with Tibetans in other parts of Europe.

Lobsang started work as Mr. Phala's assistant. Like Mr. Liushar in New York, Mr. Phala had been a senior monk official of the Tibetan government. He was a very influential man and one of the main organizers of the Dalai Lama's flight into exile in 1959. Mr. Phala was a tall, handsome man in his sixties, with a very confident and relaxed manner. He was always impeccably dressed in suits and ties. One would never have guessed that a few years earlier he wore only simple monk's robes. We often had him home for meals, and he was very popular with our children.

Phursam-la also worked in the office. He was a very cheerful man, calm and pleasant even in difficult situations. His parents died when he was young, and he had no immediate family members living outside of Tibet. Phursam-la had worked very hard as an interpreter in Missamari, India, when the Tibetan refugees first arrived there, and later he worked at the Tibet Bureau in New Delhi. He had been sent to Italy by the Tibetan government-in-exile to study photography on a scholarship, until a severe nerve disorder that caused his hands to shake interrupted his training. He used to say, "When I was training to take pictures,

I felt so embarrassed because my hands shook, and when there were girls around, I was even more self-conscious. I thought the girls would think I was nervous because of them. I had to leave my training, because how could I take good pictures with my trembling fingers?" We enjoyed Phursam-la's company, and whenever he and Lobsang were together, they spent their time in the kitchen drinking cans of beer and preparing feasts for dinner.

As more Tibetans came to Europe, Lobsang had to travel out of the country to meet the new arrivals. Work piled up at the office, and when Lobsang was gone, Mr. Phala, who spoke only Tibetan, was left without an interpreter. I was employed part-time to help our Swiss accountant, Madame Gillioz, a very moody lady, and to take care of the English correspondence and interpret for Mr. Phala when visitors came to the office.

The Swiss were known for their tradition of helping others in need, and they were especially sympathetic to the Tibetan refugees. In 1961, the Swiss government agreed to the immigration of a first group of twenty-three Tibetans, on the condition that the Swiss Red Cross would assist them in finding jobs, maintain a common lodging for them for the first few months, bear all the expenses needed for the rehabilitation of the new families, and see that they acclimated well to their new environment. In May of 1963, the government extended their acceptance to a total of one thousand Tibetans, subject to the consent of the cantons and communes welcoming the immigrants. The Swiss Association for Tibetan Homesteads in Switzerland was set up, and the majority of Tibetans were finally resettled in the Swiss German region of Switzerland. Jobs were found for them in factories, and some of the younger men were offered the possibility of learning a trade.

As soon these new immigrants from the Himalayas arrived, the Swiss hosts met them at the airport and housed them in "Tibeter-Heims." A Swiss national was assigned to look after their needs and to introduce them to the new surroundings. A leader for each group accompanied the families, often a monk, who could deal with the cultural and religious needs of the immigrants and also teach the children the Tibetan language and

Tibetan Buddhism. An interpreter also accompanied each group. Language courses were provided, and many men took up jobs easily. Very soon, most of the families were able to set up their own homes and managed well in these Swiss villages and towns. The Tibetans worked hard and were very popular with the industry owners.

The Tibetan resettlement project was overseen from the Swiss Red Cross headquarters by Ms. Rosemarie Schwarzenbach. Ms. Schwarzenbach often joined us during the Tibetan New Year gatherings. If there was a major problem in a Tibetan home that the Swiss representative of the home could not solve, Ms. Schwarzenbach would travel to the site with Lobsang to solve the problem. She was in her mid-fifties, and she was always slightly hunched over, as if she carried all of her responsibilities on her drooping shoulders. She had a large, long face under a crop of short curly brown hair, and she always looked very tired. When there was a problem to be solved, she would silently ponder the subject, smoking a cigarette and rubbing her fingers in the air, as if she were squeezing out the solutions. Her face would suddenly light up in a lovely smile, and we would know that she had figured out what to do. Lobsang admired her patience and her quiet efficiency, and I learned a lot in my meetings with her. Ironically, her brother was a well-known Swiss politician who was opposed to foreigners being permitted to reside and work in Switzerland.

My first contact with Tibetan refugees in Switzerland occurred about ten months after our arrival in the country. During Tibetan New Year, there were a couple of holidays for the Tibetans, and some families took extra time off from work. We closed the office for about five days, and Mr. Phala accompanied us to Zurich to meet our compatriots. Mr. Phala went to one set of settlements while we made a tour of others. We traveled by train, as none of us knew how to drive.

The countryside was dotted with wooden chalets and modern concrete cottages, beautiful flowers, and the snow-capped mountains. The whole country was squeaky clean. Switzerland was an excellent place to teach Tibetans about cleanliness. We came from a cold country, very high in the mountains, where we lived in direct contact with nature. We had no vehicles in our cities and walked or rode horses. There were no plastic bags, empty cans, or bottles to throw out, and the cool, dry air was free of germs. Paper was also so scarce that I remember my grandfather writing notes on the insides of empty cigarette boxes. We were not in the habit of cleaning and bathing very often. We had no modern sanitary arrangements, so we bathed in the streams during the summer and used the outdoors to evacuate our bowels and bladders. I remember a friend of mine telling me about an experience she had with one of my fellow countrymen in the Swiss Alps at an early period of the resettlement program. She was traveling on a train with the Tibetan man. When they got out at the station, they had to climb a small pathway to reach their common destination. The man took a few steps off the pathway and then urinated. It was quite natural for him, but my friend was shocked and embarrassed and thankful that there was no one in sight.

Most of the Tibetans lived in small towns and villages outside of Zurich. The first day of New Year was celebrated with the traditional presentation of rice with raisins, Tibetan tea, and khatas offered to the altar and to His Holiness the Dalai Lama's photo, which every family kept. The family members dressed in their national costumes and wished each other "Tashi Delek."

We had to visit every Tibetan home in the area, because we were invited to take the offering of *chema*—wheat grains, tsampa and chang. Some families brewed chang, but most used beer instead. There was much feasting, drinking, singing and playing cards or *sho*, our traditional game of dice. Our Swiss friends would join us for meals and merrymaking. They loved these gatherings, because they could let go of their reserve and relax in the company of the informal, jovial Tibetans. For Mr. Phala and Lobsang, this was the time to listen to any problems the Tibetan families faced.

I admired the patience of the Swiss people. During the initial period of the resettlement program, a number of the Tibetans were homesick and having difficulty adjusting to the foreign surroundings. Almost all the Tibetans had come to Switzerland directly from road camps in India and Nepal. Most were peasants and nomads. Some had never lived in a proper house until they arrived in Switzerland. The older women refused to wear the short Western dresses they were given, and stuck to wearing the same old clothes they brought from India, which were wearing thin. They were scandalized at the idea of showing their bare legs. A number of them even packed all the new clothes in boxes to take back to Tibet. We had to tell them to bathe more often, change their clothes, and eat new food. We had to teach them basic hygiene. There was a Tibetan liaison officer and a Swiss representative in each colony, and they found it very difficult to communicate with the older Tibetans. The womenfolk refused to go out of their homes, learn the new language, or change their old habits.

One problem for the Swiss Red Cross concerned a family living in a small town. The man kept two wives, and when the inhabitants of the village learned about this, they complained to the Red Cross. The husband would not listen to their pleas to keep only one wife and divorce the other. Even Ms. Schwarzenbach could not solve this problem, and the villagers were growing increasingly upset. Lobsang was called, and after meeting with the man, he told Ms. Schwarzenbach that the man was happily living with two women who respected each other and were good friends. Neither wife was disturbed by the arrangement. There were many men who surreptitiously kept a mistress without the knowledge of the lawful wife. Ms. Schwarzenbach was very understanding, but there was no way the Swiss village delegation would listen to this argument. The poor husband told Lobsang, "I have a moral obligation to my older wife who is a good woman, but I fell in love with the second wife. Would you please make a decision for me as to which wife I should keep?" In the end, it was decided that one wife would live with him and the other would live in a separate apartment. This seemed to appease everyone.

We visited the Tibetan homes at the Pestalozzi Children's Village in Trogen, Appenzell. The children attended the local schools with children from other countries and backgrounds, but Mr. and Mrs. Tethong Rakra and Miss Sopal Tethong were excellent house parents and saw that these children kept their Tibetan culture and language, and could pursue their Buddhist beliefs. Miss Tethong had been our matron at Mount Hermon School. The house parents were well educated and had been exposed to Western culture before coming to Europe. Mr. Rakra was a tulku, a Buddhist scholar, an artist, and the children's Tibetan and religious teacher. His wife, Dolma-la, managed one home and was a mother figure. Mr. Arthur Bill, the director of the village, and Mrs. Gyr, known to all the Tibetans as "Mola," or Grandmother, were very sympathetic to the Tibetans and concerned that they not lose their Tibetan identities.

About 180 Tibetan children were adopted into Swiss homes, but to the astonishment of a number of these parents, and to the children themselves, some of the Tibetan parents started making contact with their children. These Tibetan parents had sent their children as orphans to the Tibetan Children's Village in Dharamsala, believing that they would have better futures if they were brought up there. It was a great shock when the Swiss parents learned that their adopted child had parents in India or Nepal. Some of the Swiss parents were afraid that they would have to give up their sons and daughters to their birth parents.

In several situations, the adopted children were causing trouble for their new families. Some of these children were stealing and hoarding toys and clothes, while others had trouble identifying themselves with their Swiss families. One such girl told me recently, "I came to this Swiss family and I was showered with beautiful clothes, many toys, and plenty to eat, things I had never had in my life. I was so worried that these things would be gone one day that I used to hide them. I also hid toys and clothing belonging to other children in the family and put them aside so that I could one day take them to Tibet to give to children who did not have such lovely things, but my parents would scold me and did not understand."

One summer weekend, my family visited a camp for the children who had been adopted in Swiss homes. Geshe Thupten Wangyal was the religious instructor and camp leader of one of the Tibetan colonies, and he was there to introduce these children to the Tibetan language, culture, and the Buddhist teachings. There were about twenty children from different parts of

Switzerland. These boys and girls were from eight to fourteen years of age and spoke to each other in Swiss German, and behaved like native Swiss children. They were less shy and inhibited than the Tibetan children in the settlements. Mr. Phala and Lobsang played with them, we cooked Tibetan food for them, and a couple of their Swiss families joined us on this occasion. Not all the families who had adopted Tibetan children wanted their children to have anything to do with the other Tibetans.

At the time, there were only a few other Tibetans living in Geneva. A Catholic mission had sponsored a couple of young men who were studying or working in Geneva, and we often had them to our home. They enjoyed our company, because we would cook our native dishes and speak only in Tibetan.

Mr. Tsang was another Tibetan visitor, a most unusual character. He was a businessman from a well-known family from Kham, who had settled in Hong Kong in the early fifties and become a British subject. He was known to be very wealthy and was always suspicious of everyone. Our first meeting was a bizarre encounter. There was this short, elderly man in a shabby suit standing at the front door. When I opened the door, he walked straight into our home without saying a word. He headed into the living room, took out a newspaper from an old briefcase, and began reading. I quickly went to call Lobsang, who was in the bedroom. When Lobsang came to the living room, they greeted each other. Lobsang introduced me, and Mr. Tsang gave a nod. Mr. Tsang would drop by from time to time, but he never said much and would leave as soon as he had drunk his tea. He never spoke to the children. Poor soul, he was like a man chased by an invisible spirit. He traveled most of the time and died in a car accident. The police called our office and as Mr. Phala was a friend, the monks from Rikon Monastery were called for prayers.

As time passed, I learned from a number of people living in Geneva that under the surface of the beautiful city, the local population did not like the influx of foreigners who had invaded their territory. Some of the members of the diplomatic corps were very rude and arrogant. They abused their privileges and made the natives feel that because they had large expense accounts they could do what they wanted. The Swiss French were also very proud of their language and it bothered that them these international citizens made no effort to speak their language. The shopkeepers and postal staff used to tell me, "You are in Geneva and you should speak our language!" I made the decision to take up French once again in order to refresh my earlier studies and feel more at home.

I enjoyed my French classes at Berlitz. I especially enjoyed the coffee break between classes. During this time, I met other classmates and found out about their backgrounds. Most of the students were very young women from Scandinavia who had come to seek employment as household help and to see Switzerland. I was one of the older students, and I made friends with another older student, a Jewish lady from America who had two daughters living in Israel. One of the daughters was an air hostess, and those were the hijacking days, so my friend worried about her daughter's safety. We had a quiet, observant Russian diplomat who was also our classmate. My Jewish friend had an intense disliking of this man. When he came to know that I was from Tibet, he was very interested in talking to me. My Jewish friend wondered why I talked to him, and she discouraged my conversations with him. It was hard for me to understand how one stranger could dislike another stranger with such intensity.

By now, Lobsang and I had made some interesting acquaintances, including a very good friend by the name of Nelly Kunzi. A couple of days after our arrival in Geneva, a beautiful azalea plant in full bloom arrived from a florist with a greeting card. We were intrigued to find out who this kind person was, and how she knew about our arrival. After three or four days, a telegram arrived saying that the sender of the flower arrangement wanted to call on us. I prepared some tea, and we opened our door to a middle-aged lady with short, black hair and a pale complexion. After having tea with her, she said she was a friend of Mr. Phala and Mr. Samdup. This stranger had become fascinated with Tibet after reading Lama Govinda and Heinrich Harrer. She was delighted when she learned that Harrer had stayed in my house while in Lhasa. She was a quiet, courteous lady, who spoke excellent English. She told us that she worked as a secretary at a bank in Geneva.

Nelly seemed like a very strange lady at first. Lobsang and I both smoked, and when Lobsang offered her a cigarette, she took one. We looked at each other with curiosity, because she seemed to dislike the cigarette and was finding it very difficult to smoke. Lobsang told her that if she did not like the cigarette, she need not smoke, and she seemed relieved to throw it in the ashtray. She did not make much conversation, and as we did not know her well, there was not much to say. Thereafter, Nelly showed up at our home every Thursday. As she lived alone, she enjoyed our company and she adored our children. Lobsang and I found this visit an intrusion at first, but as the months passed by, Ms. Kunzi became Aunty Nelly to our children, and we became good friends. She visited us in India and the United States, and we are still in contact with her to this day.

Lobsang and I were meeting more important people from the international organizations and one of them, Prince Sadruddin Agha Khan, who was then the General Secretary of the United Nations High Commission for Refugees (UNHCR), was very kind to us. He invited us to his chateau for dinner on several occasions, and once he even had us over for a banquet in honor of Her Highness Princess Shah of Nepal and her husband, Prince Himalaya. The Princess was awarded an honor for her social work in Nepal as the head of the Nepalese Red Cross. Our friend, Daryle Han, a nephew of the former prime minister of Burma U Nu, drove us to the dinner. Daryle worked at the UNHCR. It was my first big formal dinner, and I was very nervous about meeting all the dignitaries. Walking into the grand banquet hall and being among such distinguished guests in long evening dresses and black ties reminded me of a Hollywood movie. There were tall, fat matrons in gorgeous flowing gowns and younger slim ladies in slinky dresses that showed every curve of their bodies. They were all decorated in fabulous jewels and looked like bright Christmas trees. The distinguished-looking men moved around in formal wear, and when a white tuxedoed butler with a fat, glistening face came to my side with a tray of drinks, I picked one up and drank from the long-stemmed glass. I did not know what it was that I was drinking, but the glass looked beautiful. I still do not know what it was that I drank, but I felt a bit giddy afterwards. The hall was filled with new faces. Daryle disappeared in the crowd, Lobsang was deep in conversation with a guest, and I frantically searched for a familiar face.

Dinner was buffet style, where one filled one's plate from the heavily laden banquet table and searched for a chair at one of the numerous round tables. Lobsang was whisked off by the hostess, Prince Sadruddin's companion, and when I saw the familiar face of Mrs. Krishnan, the wife of the Indian ambassador to the United Nations, I dashed to sit near her. On the other side of me sat the wife of the chief of the Geneva police corps. In the middle of the dinner, I realized that I was the only woman sitting between two other women. The seating was such that a man and a woman sat side by side. I was so embarrassed by my mistake that I could not wait for the dinner to come to an end.

Another funny incident was at another formal dinner in the elegant home of Count and Countess d'Escayrac. The Count was French and I think his wife was Swiss. After the drinks were served in their exquisite lounge, dinner was served outside on the lawn by two waiters dressed in white coats. It was an intimate dinner with a former Japanese ambassador to the United Kingdom. When the main course was served, I noticed the guests poking their forks on a piece of sliced lemon to get the juice on the dish of fish, so I did the same. I had never eaten fish cooked this way before, and to my embarrassment and dismay, my lemon slipped out of my fingers and dropped on the plate of the honorable Japanese gentleman. Never had I felt so stupid and sloppy. To my relief, there was a welcome drizzle and the hostess kindly suggested we move indoors.

I never really enjoyed those stiff, formal parties because of all the confusing cutlery spread out on the table and worrying about which fork was for which dish and how to eat this and how to eat that. Sometimes there was more cutlery than food on the table! For people like me who were not used to such formal affairs, I was more worried about the etiquette than enjoying the meal.

When Tenzin turned two, we sent the children to a day-care nursery. A minibus came to get them in the mornings. On the first day, I don't know who was more nervous, the children or me! I came home extra early that day to find the children very happy and excited about their new school, and I realized that my anxiety was a waste of energy. By now, my children had experienced so many changes that they smoothly slipped into another new event in their lives without much fuss.

La Ronde was a small nursery school run by a Swiss lady who was married to an Englishman working in one of the many international organizations. There were twenty to thirty children and the older children attended regular nursery classes. Chuki and Tenzin picked up French very fast, and soon the children were conversing in this language and it was very funny, because they used to fight in French and we did not understand them. We spoke to them in Tibetan, our friends spoke to them in English, and they spoke French most of the time in La Ronde. They were brought up with three languages.

The Office of Tibet had to attend a number of meetings with members of the Swiss Red Cross, the International Council for Voluntary Agencies, and the United Nations High Commission for Refugees with regard to the settlement and development projects for the Tibetan refugees. Tibetans generated much interest and assistance from the Western nations. Yet, when we did discuss our plights with these international representatives in the world bodies or with journalists we met, we were met with the words, "We are very sympathetic to the Tibetan case!" I got very tired of the sympathies. We got to know a couple of journalists rather well. When we asked them to write a few words about the Tibetan story, they said they would never get visas to China if they did.

We also had some strange guests at the office, though fortunately they were few in number. They would come with kind words and sincere intentions to help the poor Tibetan refugees. I remember a particular American gentlemen who was supposedly married to a European baroness. He had some far-fetched plans about helping the Tibetans. He made an appointment by telephone to meet Mr. Phala and Lobsang. When they met in person, his plans were so impractical, idealistic, and expensive that he was sent off with some kind words. We found out later that he left his hotel with orders to send his bills to the Office of Tibet. We were from a country that opened our doors to strangers and were very hospitable to our guests, so we had to learn that not all guests came in friendship.

During this period of our stay in Switzerland, my mother-in-law came to visit. She was a wonderful companion and such a caring person. She stayed with us for almost a year. Lobsang and I did not want her to do any work around the house, as she was quite old, and we wanted to give her a good holiday. When she came into the kitchen or dusted the living room, Lobsang would scold her. One day I discovered her in the bedroom, sewing the hems of her dress. When I questioned her as to what she was doing, she said, "Lobsang and you do not want me to do any work. Am I supposed to sit and wait for death?" I understood her then, and thereafter we let her do whatever she wanted. She started baking and cooking, even toilet training Tenzin. She thrived on her duties. I felt guilty having Gyalyum Chenmo, the Great Mother of His Holiness the Dalai Lama, cook meals for us. This was unheard of in our culture, but I noted that she was happiest being a mother and bustling around in the kitchen.

Now that many Tibetans had arrived in Switzerland and there were a number of Tibetans in other countries across Europe, a common place of worship was needed, and the Buddhist monastery at Rikon was built. We went to the ground-breaking ceremony for the monastery. It was an occasion for which all the Tibetans in Switzerland gathered. A few of the new arrivals were monks, and it seemed very strange to see Tibetan monks in their maroon robes and yellow shirts, blowing on Swiss alpine horns in the Swiss mountains. The colorful prayer flags were fluttering in the breeze among the tree tops, under a cloudless sky, and the sweet incense smoke pervaded the air. My mind went back to the tired, exhausted faces of the Tibetan refugees in India in sun-scorched, tattered, dusty clothes with tiny babies suckling empty breasts. To see these same people here at this gathering was like a dream. They looked prosperous and healthy, many even overfed and fat. The women wore their national costumes in beautiful silks and colorful aprons. They had been able to save enough money to order jewels in traditional designs from India and Nepal. The children looked robust and happy. There were a few individuals who had married Swiss nationals, and the little

Swiss-Tibetan babies were looked at with admiration and curiosity by other Tibetans. There were a few disapproving looks by some older Tibetans who felt that we should keep our race pure after the genocide of Tibetans in Tibet.

Rikon Monastery became a center for all major Tibetan activities and a place where anyone could come to study Buddhism. The monastery is situated on a secluded hilltop among beautiful pine trees and wildflowers. Just below the hill were the apartments where one of the largest concentrations of Tibetans lived in Switzerland. The families lived in immaculate apartments built by owners of the Metallwarenfabrik AG factory in Rikon. This family also donated the land and collected funds for the monastery.

During my stay in Geneva, I ate food I never dreamt of eating. One day we were in a small cafe, and our host had ordered some delicious pieces of meat, cooked in butter and spices, that tasted like chicken. It was scrumptious, and only when I got home did I learn from Lobsang that we had eaten frogs' legs. I also tried oysters for the first time in my life. One could buy horse meat and rabbits in our supermarket, but I never tried them. Someone told me that the salami we enjoyed was made from donkey meat and spices, but I never knew the truth. Tibetans would be disgusted to learn that Europeans eat horse meat and snails, but not too many Europeans eat yak meat either.

I was really eager to try fondue, a very popular Swiss dish. Lobsang found out that there was a small cafe near the office that was well known for fondue. One day he took me there to try it, and little did we know that the hot sauce we dipped the bread pieces in was made with white wine. The waiter also suggested that a bottle of white wine would go well with the fondue. We enjoyed the meal and after we had an ample share, I was so soaked with wine that I could not get up from the table. Lobsang had to phone our accountant to hold the office until we were able to join her a little later. I had a double coffee, and after a short rest managed to walk to the office.

Soon, my mother-in-law was to leave for the United States to visit her oldest son, Thubten Jigme Norbu, and his family. We were sorry to have her leave us. During her extended stay with us, I had never seen her lose her temper or speak a harsh word to anyone. She was such a warm person, and she exuded such kindness and love that our neighbors were also sorry she was leaving. My sister had come over that summer to look after our children during her break, so Gyalyum had my sister to travel with on her flight to New York. Tenzin and Chuki missed Gyalyum very much, and Lobsang and I found the house very empty after she left us.

13 On the Road

By August of 1967, there were 378 Tibetans in the resettlement program in Switzerland. About fifty new refugees arrived each year, and the Office of Tibet had the additional responsibility of looking after the needs of Tibetans living in other parts of Europe as well.

There were young Tibetans in the Pestalozzi Children's Village in Wahlwies, Germany, with a Tibetan parent and an assistant to look after them. In addition to receiving a modern education in the local schools, these young Tibetans were taught Tibetan language, history, and Buddhism. Seven young lamas were also in Germany, studying in universities or teaching Tibetan and Buddhism.

In England, there was a Pestalozzi Children's Village in Sedlescombe that was home to twenty young Tibetan boys and girls, a Tibetan house parent, a religious instructor, and an assistant. Scattered in and around London there were a few Tibetans studying or undergoing vocational training, and there were four young nurse's-aid trainees in Scotland. There were twenty young Tibetan boys and girls in the French countryside who were being sponsored by the French government. They studied in a local school and lived on the school premises. A few Tibetans were in Paris, studying, teaching, or working as research scholars.

In Norway, forty-three young men were receiving training in agriculture, mechanics, welding, or other vocations. Prince Peter of Greece and Denmark—a Tibetologist who had lived in Kalimpong—was instrumental in procuring vocational training for several young Tibetans in Denmark. Sweden accommodated forty-two girls, some of whom are now serving in Tibetan communities as kindergarten teachers or engaged in our health service programs. There were a number of other young Tibetans who were studying or receiving training in Holland, Belgium, and Italy.

In the summer of 1968, Lobsang was asked to visit the various projects assisting these young Tibetans in France and England, and the children and I were able to accompany him on this trip. We flew first to Paris, where we were met by Dagpo Rinpoche's assistant, Thupten-la. Dagpo Rinpoche was teaching at a Parisian university, and, as a tulku and a learned scholar, he was in great demand by students of Buddhism and people interested in Tibet. Rinpoche was away when we landed in Paris, but Thupten-la helped us get settled and then showed us the sights of the city. We booked a room in a small hotel, the Soleil, which ironically turned out to be dark and dingy. The room was inexpensive and not very clean, but as we were only to rest there for two nights, we thought it was fine. It was only after we left Paris that I realized some of our belongings had disappeared. In our inexperience, we had tried to save money but ended up with a greater loss than we would have had by staying in a better hotel.

Thupten-la wore a nylon jacket and a floppy fedora in the heat of the Paris summer, despite Lobsang's insistence that he take them off. Soaking with sweat, Thupten-la showed us the Eiffel Tower, the Arc de Triomphe, and a number of famous tourist sites around the city. I was completely taken with the pureness and the beauty of the Sacré Coeur chapel, but simultaneously dismayed by the squalor that surrounded it. Tourists flooded the place, and sidewalk artists and garish prostitutes flaunted their goods. The Louvre was magnificent, and we walked for hours, staring in awe at the beautiful masterpieces that were so abundant in this house of treasures. The experience was worth the fatigue and sore feet. Chuki and Tenzin had been delightful, but tired out before we could see everything we had planned.

Thupten-la was kind enough to stay with the children one evening while Lobsang showed me the Paris night life. Lobsang

The author on her mother's lap (Lhasa, 1943)

Tsarong House and garden

The author's Tsarong grandparents

The author's maternal family: the ancient family of Ragashar

The author's aunt and mother (1945)

The author's father in official winter costume

The author in Tsarong House garden in Lhasa

"Barkhor," the circumambulation path around the Central Temple in Lhasa City

Tsarong siblings in Lhasa, 1956

Introduction to Western education: author on the right, with her brother and sister

Camels from Sining—outside Tsarong House in Lhasa

China comes to invade Tibet

Tibetan refugee work crews in Manali

H.H. the Dalai Lama with orphans in Dharamsala, 1960

H.H. the Dalai Lama at a Tibetan agricultural settlement in South India

The Mount Hermon graduating class of 1961—the author holds class identification

Lobsang (left) and author (center) visiting Tibetan Moslem friends in Kashmir, 1962

Right to left: Lobsang, his mother, His Holiness's senior tutor, a child, Mr. Phala, and the author in Geneva, Switzerland

Lobsang, Tenzin Choegyal, Jetsun Pema, the author, and other family members at a birthday celebration for His Holiness

One of the author's hermit friends in the mountains above Dharamsala

A good friend and teacher—abbot N. Nyima from Mongolia

Chuki and Tenzin in a Swiss Tibetan home

Lobsang and the author with Tibetan children and foster parents in France, 1968

Lobsang, Tenzin and Chuki in New Jersey, 1976

Drikung Kyabgon arrives from Tibet—with Lobsang, the author, and her father at their home in Scotch Plains, NJ (1976)

The author with H.H. the Dalai Lama's senior physician, Dr. Choedrak (to her left) and international physicians and scientists at the Tibetan Medical Institute, Dharamsala

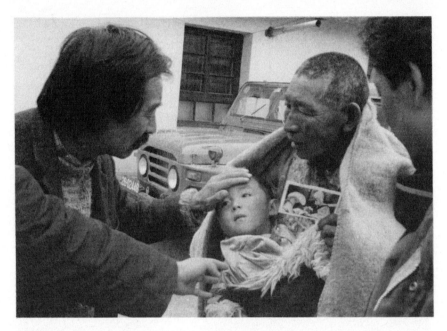

Lobsang in Amdo, Tibet, during the tour of the first delegation to Tibet in 1979

The author with health workers among Tibetan nomads in Ladakh

The author with Heinrich Harrer at the opening of the Lingkhor in Huttenberg, Austria (1994)

The author's brother, the Drikung Kyabgon

H.H. the Dalai Lama drawing the Potala rooms for M. Mathison, M. Scorsese, B. Defina, and E. Lewis for the film Kundun

The author with cast members from Kundun *in Morocco*

The author with her parents and daughter Chuki with her family, 1996

The Yabshi Taklha family offers long life prayer to His Holiness on his sixtieth birthday (Dharamsala, 1995)

The author with her grandsons

used to say, "You have had such a protected life, and you have not seen the world. You must see the world!" The Folies Bergères as a fantastic show of the beauty of the human body—nude or covered in splendid costumes. The spectacular *cancan* and *soirée au bal* were magnificent and entertaining. Lobsang also thought I should see the other popular side of Parisian night life. We walked to a particular spot, where we waited in a long line of tourists, listening to the rhythmic chatter and varied intonations of many different languages. After handing over an exorbitant entrance fee, we were finally allowed into a dark room. As the show started, a pair of skinny, rather bored-looking girls, clad only in scant patches of fabric and heavy make-up, danced up to a platform in the center of the room. Other girls in skimpy costumes and gaudy make-up circulated among the tables, pouring champagne and actively working to hook a customer. I was shocked to see a pathetic old man, well-dressed and drunk beyond his senses, cavorting with the tawdry table dancers. The odor of stale champagne and fresh cigarette smoke dimmed our senses. Rather than being entertained, I felt melancholy, as if I were a voyeur peering into a parade of human greed, weakness, and self-destruction. In truth, I was also a little disgusted by the experience. Paris was overwhelming in both its beauty and its ugliness—the best and worst of our world.

Our first official visit took place a couple of days later at a school in Bleneau in the French countryside. It was a public school for the local village children, but the Tibetan children were the only boarders. The building was old and run down, and the directress was a simple, quiet lady, whose husband drove the village bus. Mr. and Mrs. Norgay served as the Tibetan foster parents for this group of Tibetan children. In our meeting with Mr. and Mrs. Norgay, we were completely dismayed to learn of their unhappiness with the school. They feared the children would not get a proper education in such an isolated village. The location also made it impossible for this group to have contact with other Tibetans.

During our two days in Bleneau, we tried to get a sense of the situation from the children. We talked about their vocational plans and their general aims in life. Most of the students in this group were hesitant, very unsure of themselves and their futures.

We did not have a good feeling, and before leaving Bleneau, Lobsang promised to contact the French government about moving the students to a larger town, possibly some place that would allow them closer contact with other Tibetans. I felt quite sad leaving this small group of Tibetans in such a remote village.

Our next visit was to England. In London, we were met by a very kind taxi driver, who upon learning that it was my first visit to England, insisted we see a little of the city. He only charged us half the taxi fare, and left me with a very pleasant first impression of his country. A little later, we were rudely refused accommodation in a hotel.

After spending a night in London, we traveled by train to Battle and then by car to the Tibetan home in Sedlescombe. We were pleased to find a stark contrast to the situation in France. Living in a large, beautiful house with a lovely garden, these young Tibetans were frank, cheerful, and highly proficient in English. They were radiant. Many worked on farms, building projects, or at other jobs nearby to earn extra pocket money. We were able to stay in a guest room in the house, which allowed us more time with these young Tibetans. Chuki and Tenzin, much to their delight, received plenty of attention.

Lobsang met with the village director to request that another home be opened for the Tibetan children. He felt the children here were more exposed to the outside world, that their education was very broad, and that they had the support of their efficient and dedicated foster parents, Mr. and Mrs. Dupok. An additional benefit was Mr. and Mrs. Dupok's efforts to see that the children kept up their Tibetan traditions and language, and that they were taught Buddhism by a learned scholar.

Not far from the Pestalozzi village was an English family named Tomsett, who made it an annual event to invite the Tibetan students to their home for an afternoon picnic. This event happened to coincide with our visit, so we were invited to attend. The Tomsetts lived in a beautiful three-hundred-year-old home with a spacious garden. The children had a riotous time in the large swimming pool while the adults sat on the lawn under apple trees, drinking tea and talking about Tibet. Mr. Tomsett had traveled to Darjeeling, Kalimpong, and Sikkim. He even knew of my parents' home in Kalimpong, because an English friend of his had once lived in the very same house!

Next, it was on to Edinburgh. The Dupok's daughter, a nurse named Namgyal-la, offered to keep the children while we made this trip. While I knew Chuki and Tenzin would be in excellent hands, it was the first time I would be spending a night away from them. I did feel a bit apprehensive.

We landed in a small airport amid the green, rolling hills of Edinburgh. The small Scottish hotel we booked into seemed to be a local hangout. As soon as we were settled, we contacted the four Tibetan girls at the hospital where they were training and made arrangements to meet them the next day. Later in the afternoon, we took a bus tour around the beautiful, clean city and then had dinner at a Chinese restaurant. Returning to the hotel, we decided to have a drink in the hotel bar. Not only did we discover that we were the only foreigners staying in the hotel, I noticed very quickly that I was the only woman in the bar. Packed with local Scottish men, many wearing kilts and speaking a dialect that was difficult to understand, we caused quite a stir with our entrance. After the hushed silence, several of the locals began to query us about where we were from. They were extremely curious about us, especially when they learned that we were from the mountainous land of Tibet. After the question and answer session, many glasses were raised on our behalf. We found the Scots to be very warm and friendly.

Next morning, the girls arrived at our hotel and we spent the entire day with them. They introduced us to the lovely gardens and parks of Edinburgh. Although they were quite happy there, they missed their families in India.

We left clean, peaceful, and beautiful Edinburgh for busy London. There, we visited many Tibetan friends and called on the members of the Tibet Society, perhaps the oldest organization set up to help the Tibetan refugees. We also called on Trungpa Rinpoche, who was in London then, and met Mr. Marco Pallis and his friend Mr. Nicholson, who had traveled to Tibet and visited my home in Lhasa. Lunches, teas, and meetings followed. We also managed a little time for sight-seeing, although two and a half days was not enough to visit many of the monuments and

museums in this historic city. We had a memorable meeting with
Mrs. Margaret Williamson at Fifield. She had invited Lobsang
to come and choose from her collection of photos and films for
pieces to give to the Dalai Lama. Her late husband, Claude
Williamson, was a political officer in Sikkim in British India, and
had visited Tibet a couple of times. On his last visit to Lhasa, he
died there. Mrs. Williamson loved Tibet and the Tibetans. She
was quite old but kept herself very fit. A tall, trim lady, with
auburn hair streaked with white, she did all her own housework.
At first she seemed rather stern, but as we got to know her we
found her to be cheerful and warm. She lived alone in a beautiful, small cottage that peeked through masses of flowers. Entering the cottage, one was immediately transported back to Tibet.
On the walls hung thangkas and photographs of Tibet. The floor
was covered with Tibetan rugs, and all around the house were
Tibetan cups, pots, boxes, and tea stands cut from wood, silver,
and copper. There was a beautiful silver teapot, a gift from His
Holiness the Thirteenth Dalai Lama to her husband. A large
framed photo of H. H. the Thirteenth Dalai Lama hung in the
living room.

Mrs. Williamson prepared a delicious lunch of melon, cheese,
pie, and fruit followed by tea. I helped her to wash the dishes,
and then we stayed up until midnight viewing her photographs
and reels of film on Tibet. On one of the reels was a picture of
my father when he was about thirteen years old. Mrs. Williamson
was thrilled to discover that I was from the Tsarong family, because
she had met many of my family members in Lhasa.

She promised to send copies of all her films to His Holiness,
and she gave us photos, some of which were of my family. We
were sad and homesick when we talked about the present situation in Tibet. When we left the next morning, it was like parting
from an old family friend, a good friend of Tibet.

Another memorable visit on this trip was a meeting with Sir
Olaf Caroe. In the early part of the century, he had been governor general of the northwestern frontier of British India. Later,
he helped the Tibetans with refugee projects. At the time of our
visit, he was already quite old. His wife had passed away, and
his housekeeper, Ann, prepared a lovely meal for us. We had a

wonderful afternoon talking about Tibet. Sir Olaf showed us his wife's bedroom, where her gown was laid on the bed, and her presence was very much in the room. The room looked lived in, and it seemed she had just gone out of the house for some errand. Sir Olaf was very lively and active and he had kept himself well informed about the present Tibetan situation.

Returning to Sedlescombe to pick up the children, we spent another evening with the Tibetan students and staff. Several other Tibetan students had come to the village from London, one being J. T. Surkhang, an old friend of Lobsang's and mine. We stayed up until 2:00 in the morning talking about Tibet. Sometimes, we were so angry and sad that we wept. Mrs. Dupok's chang helped to cheer us. Soon, we had to say good-bye to the Tibetans in this Pestalozzi Children's Village, and Lobsang once again called on the village director to open another home for the needy Tibetan children in India and Nepal.

Back in Geneva, it was back to housekeeping, office work, and entertaining visitors. Lobsang and I had made so many international friends who were interested in Tibet that we did a great deal of entertaining. Our guests loved the informality of our home. Our menu for a small dinner was momos, a large bowl of salad, and a bottle of red wine. In our home, the generally reserved guests could put aside their stiff formality, and after a few drinks would argue, laugh, and enjoy themselves. Chuki and Tenzin were very good during these parties. They would be bathed and fed and would play quietly in their bedrooms, only occasionally peeking from the door.

Sometimes I wonder how I managed the housework, the office, and the entertaining. Fortunately, Lobsang was a wonderful partner. Before a dinner party, he would leave the office early, and we would work together. Without a husband who had no qualms about putting on an apron, cooking meals, or helping with the laundry, I would have been a nervous wreck.

The Tibetan project seemed to be working very well when we received the news that the Swiss public was growing wary of spending their tax dollars to support the refugees. Several newspaper photos and news programs showed Tibetans arriving in Switzerland not poor and needy, but well dressed and robust.

The Swiss Red Cross received numerous complaints from the public about taking in wealthy Tibetans at the expense of their tax contributions. After a number of meetings at their headquarters in Bern, the Red Cross asked Lobsang to go to India and Nepal and select only the neediest of Tibetans. Lobsang was given a Swiss Red Cross representative's identity card, and he left for India on this mission. Once in India, he visited the road camps with a representative from the Tibetan home office. There, he asked the people in the camps to decide amongst themselves who were the neediest. It was not easy, but the refugees were good at making collective decisions.

To get the few Tibetans scattered all over Europe and England together for a reunion was not very easy, but we had a couple of successful gatherings. The Tibetans from the Pestalozzi Children's Villages in England and Germany and the students in France got together at the Pestalozzi Village in Trogen, Switzerland for a week one summer. We had a small welcoming ceremony. There were performances of Tibetan folk dances and songs and plays by the children. It was very kind of the Swiss village to host this event. I remember Mr. Phala, Lobsang, and I discussing how happy we were to see these young, intelligent, good-looking Tibetans ready to face the world with the knowledge and experience they were gaining abroad. Most of these children had their families in India or Nepal, and we noted that they would experience some difficulties in adjustment when they returned to India, but we were proud of these young modern Tibetans. Many of them have now settled in Europe. The few who returned to India are serving our community as teachers, health professionals, or in development programs in settlements. The question of whether these young people being educated abroad has benefited the Tibetan population in general is often asked. There are expectations that anyone who received training abroad should return to help the community in exile. I do not think it is realistic to expect everyone to return to India or Nepal to work in our programs. These young people are supporting their families and their friends financially, educating their young relatives in India. They are good ambassadors for Tibet. Many of these young people have done much for the Tibetan cause abroad.

The director of the village, Mr. Arthur Bill, had just returned from a trip to India. He showed us a movie he shot while visiting some of the Tibetan settlements and meeting with His Holiness. On the film was a message from the Dalai Lama for the Tibetan children. Seeing His Holiness on screen and hearing his voice was very emotional for the Tibetan houseparents. Many people broke down in tears. Ms. Tethong and I were sitting near one another, and we were both overcome with sadness. We went back to her room after the film. Mrs. Kramer, the village secretary and a dear friend of Ms. Tethong, had noticed how distraught we were, and made the very kind gesture of sending us a bottle of wine. Ms. Tethong and I drank the whole bottle together and shed even more tears. When Lobsang returned, he got quite a chuckle out of Ms. Tethong and me, with our red eyes and noses, a bit tipsy after emptying the bottle of wine to console ourselves.

Another memorable event during my stay in Switzerland was the visit of the Dalai Lama's tutors, Kyabje Ling Rinpoche and Kyabje Trijang Rinpoche. This was their first visit outside of India and Tibet. They had come for the opening of the Rikon Monastery, another occasion for which many Tibetans from all over Europe gathered for a reunion. Rikon Monastery was flooded with Tibetans. Many of our Swiss friends had come, as well as friends from other countries. Everyone dressed in their best clothes; the Tibetan women wore elegant chubas with their cheery, bright aprons, and the men looked dashing in loose, long-sleeved robes and fur-trimmed caps. There were also a number of men in handsome suits and ties. A Tibetan drama society was formed, and the members proudly raised their big drums in front of their chests, with flutes and cymbals in their hands, looking very smart and festive as they played the Swiss and Tibetan national anthems. A young man carried a Swiss national flag, a simple white cross on a red background, and another carried the more colorful and elaborate Tibetan national flag.

Amidst the music of horns and the clash of the cymbals invoking the benevolent spirits, the two elderly tutors sat on beautifully decorated thrones in the main chapel in a mist of perfumed incense smoke. A recitation of prayers inaugurated the ceremony, followed by speeches from the dignitaries and the presentation of butter tea and rice with raisins. Many people lined up to receive blessings from these holy men. It was very precious and sentimental for the older Tibetans to be so close to the tutors of His Holiness and to be blessed by them. It must have been quite a strange experience for the younger generation. I could see some of the younger Tibetans giggling and acting very self-conscious as they approached the smiling holy men; it must have been the first time in their lives they had been blessed by a lama.

The tutors also stayed in Geneva for a couple of days. Mr. Phala's apartment was too small to accommodate both of them, so they traveled separately. Lobsang and I called on them and we had them both over for lunch. It was the first time I had been so close to the tutors. Once, when the senior tutor, Ling Rinpoche, was very sick in Calcutta, my father looked after him. I went to the nursing home on a couple of occasions as an interpreter when my father could not attend.

Ling Rinpoche was a simple man, but an eminent scholar and great practitioner of Buddhism. He was fat and jolly. He had a triangular-shaped face and is believed to be the manifestation of the bull-faced Yamantaka. I have heard a few people mention that the sides of his head poke out because they are in fact the horns of Yamantaka. Ling Rinpoche's humility and kindness were immense. One felt humbled and full of goodness in his presence. He laughed frequently, and he loved the leg of lamb Lobsang prepared especially for him.

Trijang Rinpoche was a tall, ascetic-looking man. He was more serious and elegant. Also a learned man and highly respected by every Tibetan, I felt more sedate in his presence. The two Rinpoches were impressed by the cleanliness and the beauty of the city. They were not as excited or carried away as some of our other guests from the East. I remember Trijang Rinpoche saying that he did not enjoy visiting the department stores because the superfluousness made him giddy.

Outside of our work and our commitment to the Tibetan cause, Lobsang and I tried to create a normal atmosphere for our family. Lobsang and I rarely argued, and we had most of our difficulties in the kitchen, because I was never a good cook. We overcame the problem by my contributions in peeling vegetables and cleaning up. Lobsang did not share my love of movies and theater, which was another small source of tension between us. I did not enjoy going out by myself. Once a year, our lawyer would send us tickets to a ballet in the Opera House in Geneva. I always had to drag Mr. Phala and Lobsang to the ballet. One year it was *Swan Lake,* and another I remember was a modern ballet on the theme of the Tibetan Book of the Dead. Lobsang would fidget in his seat and complain about getting hungry. Mr. Phala would snore, to my great embarrassment. During *Swan Lake,* Mr. Phala said, "What fun do you see in this show? Even I could get on my toes and run back and forth on the stage. This really will be my last show." Back to sleep! The following year, I remember attending the ballet with our new accountant, Madeleine, and the two gentlemen were excused.

We added a pair of lovebirds to our family of four. The male was named Tsering and the female, Dolma. The children adored the birds and loved to go out on the veranda to feed them in their cage. Feeding the birds was their way of showing love. The children were so enthusiastic about feeding them that one day Dolma died from overeating. It was so difficult to console Chuki and Tenzin. Chuki cried so hard that her eye lids were badly swollen, and there was no way she could go to school the next day.

Tsering left us one day as well. I was in the bathroom washing my hair when Tenzin and a couple of friends went out to feed Tsering. As Tenzin opened the cage to let one of his friends touch Tsering, Tsering flew away. I heard loud cries and Tenzin rushed into the bathroom in tears, crying about the bird. I dashed out of the bathroom with shampoo all over my head to find his friends in shock that Tsering had escaped.

Near the end of 1969, a social organization connected with the United Nations was putting together an international fair to support some of its charity work. The Office of Tibet was invited to take part in this fair. As all the proceedings went on in French, I was delegated to attend the organizational meeting. It was my first big meeting, and I was very nervous. It must have been the first time a Tibetan was sitting in on an international meeting in one of the grand halls of the Palais des Nations, the

UN headquarters. The meeting was attended by a few distinguished-looking Swiss men who were retired from their offices. It was chaired by a petite, attractive French lady with a pile of blonde hair and long, black, mascara-coated eyelashes, named Madame Blanchard. Her husband was the head of one of the international bodies in Geneva. There were a number of elegant ladies amidst the few, outnumbered elderly men, and the conversation took place completely in French. I had great difficulty following the meeting, but I confirmed our Tibetan participation.

What a lot of work and different experiences we landed ourselves in! We asked the Tibetan Drama Society of Switzerland to practice for the fair. We called Mrs. Dupok over from the Pestalozzi Children's Village in England to come and make her famous chang and Tibetan sweet cheese, and we asked a few of our friends from Swiss German towns to help us in the stall.

Mrs. Dupok made the chang from her recipe of rice, raisins, sugar and boiled water. This mixture was left to ferment in plastic buckets and later bottled. We had so little space for the chang production that all the buckets were stored in the children's bedroom. We hoped they would not raid it at night. The sweet cheese drops were left to dry in our bedroom, because Chuki and Tenzin could not resist putting these round, curled cheese drops in their mouths. We had labels custom-made for the chang bottles. "Chang du Tibet" was embossed on a red background, and we had about a hundred bottles lined up in the room. A few of the corks on the bottles would fly out with a big "POP!" and the sweet, sticky liquid would dribble all over the floor. This left me washing the floor on my knees every morning and evening.

Before the day of the big event, we had eighteen Tibetans sleeping on our living room sofa, on the floor and on the children's bed, while the children slept with us. When we went to put up our stall at the Palais des Expositions, people were running around everywhere, and the poor workmen who were assigned to install the counters were ordered here and there. Elegantly dressed ladies from the diplomatic corps stood around shouting orders as they gripped burning cigarettes between tight fingers. We were lucky to have Tibetans come from the settlements to help us. We all worked very hard and were so well-organized that we were one of the first groups to have our counter set up. The fair lasted two days, but our chang sold out the first day. One of our customers was the chief of the Geneva police. He asked us how we made this drink and when we told him our story, he asked, "Did you get permission from the police to make liquor?" After sampling the drink, he bought a couple of bottles to take home.

The Tibetan stall was the most colorful, with our rugs and woolen coats, named "hippy coats," and shoulder bags and other craft items. The girls who staffed the sales counter were outstanding in beautiful Tibetan dresses, and the men dashing in their robes. Chuki wore her Tibetan dress, and little chubby Tenzin was a great attraction, as always. Lobsang and I also worked at the counter, and our stall was one of the busiest.

The drama people did a lively show that was received with much applause, although the yaks came out before the announcement and really frightened the commentator. After two busy and exciting days we were all exhausted, but we had our share of joy when it was written up in the local newspapers that the best stalls were from Tibet and Israel. We were very happy, and on the last day we celebrated our hard work of introducing Tibet to the international world with a simple dinner at our apartment and a few bottles of the chang saved for this event. We partied until 4:00 in the morning, talking, laughing, and, as usual, shedding tears after talking about our country.

My parents spent a week with us on their way to America. They had gone through a lot of hardship in the heat and dust of Calcutta. The unsuccessful venture of the Gayday Iron and Steel Company had broken my father's health and mind. They had also lost much of their personal money in the Gayday project, and they wanted to immigrate to America, as my sister and two brothers were there.

It had been almost five years since I had seen my parents. My father had aged and was suffering from a severe stomach ailment. My mother was also suffering from depression, and it was sad to see them in this state. They received some medical attention in Switzerland, and I was glad to give them a week of good rest. Their spirits rose with the change of air and the cleanliness. It was also refreshing for them to be in the company of their grandchildren. Soon they left for America.

The years were whisking by so fast. The children needed to be transferred to a regular school now that they were graduating from the nursery. We had not planned to settle in Switzerland, and we did not think it wise to send them to the public school where everything was taught in French. Instead, we sent them to the international school, which took almost half of our salaries. We realized that we could not manage this in the long run. We thought of returning to India, but the Tibetan refugee schools were still not up to standard, and we could not possibly afford the fees of the private schools there. Our best option seemed to be to move to the United States. Our green cards required our presence there once every two years, and it was expensive to travel back so often. To be stateless and a refugee is a situation I would not wish on anyone. It seemed that we lived in a world where we were left hanging between heaven and earth. We could not settle down here or there. Lobsang and I felt rootless, aimless, and hopeless.

We did not know what was happening in Tibet at this time. There was no one coming out of the country, and no one was allowed in the country. Tibet was buried under a thick blanket of silence. We were very sad and frustrated about the state of affairs. Whenever a few Tibetans got together, they would ask, "What news of Tibet?" or "When can we go back to a free Tibet?" We would shake our heads despondently and tears would cloud our ordinarily sparkling eyes. We would bravely swallow the hard lumps that had surfaced in our throats.

Towards the end of 1970, we had been in Switzerland for nearly five years. We could not stay at the Office of Tibet indefinitely, and we did not want to seek asylum in Switzerland. Lobsang and I decided to take a break from service to the Tibetan government and go to the United States. It was time we put our roots down somewhere and end our nomadic life, moving from one place to another with our children and suitcases in tow.

Early in 1971, Lobsang's older brother Gyalo Thondup came to Switzerland because he was looking into the maintenance of the Offices of Tibet in Geneva and New York. We told him of our decision to leave the service of the Tibetan government and to settle in the United States. He asked us what we planned to do, and we told him that we had no definite plans, but had discussed opening a Tibetan handicraft shop. He told Lobsang, "You are an irresponsible man, taking your family to America without any plans. You may as well be jumping into the Bay of San Francisco." He wanted Lobsang to return to India and work there, but Lobsang was determined to be on his own feet now, and he wanted the children to have a proper education. We dreamt of having a place of our own, a home away from home. In May of 1971, we left for the United States.

14 On Madison Avenue

Chuki celebrated her eighth birthday in our room at the familiar Hotel Bedford. My parents had moved to the States a few months earlier and were renting a small apartment in Queens, and Norzin and her husband worked and lived in Manhattan. Chuki's birthday turned out to be a lovely family reunion. She loved the attention and the presents. With great delight, she cut her birthday cake to share with her extended family members.

We knew we could not settle permanently in the Bedford Hotel, and were pressed to find less costly living quarters. My parents had found Queens to be very expensive and were looking for more reasonable housing outside of the city. One day, my father was on the subway when an elderly gentleman approached him and asked him where he came from. My father must have looked a bit odd. Although he is a gentle and very distinguished-looking older man, he was wearing an ancient camel-hair overcoat that was several sizes too large for him. The coat had been passed down from a Mongolian friend to Lobsang, and then from Lobsang to my father. My father probably seemed a little pathetic in this unusual and ill-fitting attire. The curious stranger on the train turned out to be a real estate agent from Westfield, New Jersey, and he offered to show my father some smaller homes in a less expensive area.

When my father relayed this story to us, we grew very excited. We learned that we could buy a house with a small down payment, followed by monthly installments. The concept of mortgages was completely unknown to us. We couldn't believe our luck. My father felt that the house agent was sincere and genuinely interested in helping him, and so my parents joined the agent on a tour around Scotch Plains, New Jersey, about an hour's drive from Manhattan. They described the compact, well-maintained houses that sat on immaculate, tree-lined streets with names like Nicholl Avenue, Elm Street, and Spring Street. The public schools were nearby, as were a small shopping center with banks, a post office, public library, and several small restaurants. Buses to New York City ran every hour, and a small railway station with trains making frequent trips to the city was in the closest neighboring town.

As soon as we saw the diminutive Cape Cod with the small, tidy lawn, we knew that we had found our house. We first had to come up with enough money for the down payment. To do this, Lobsang withdrew a small sum he had in the bank, and I sold my wedding necklace and a couple of other valuable pieces of jewelry. A young lawyer who was a friend of Ilya Tolstoy worked out a good deal for us, and we spent five wonderful, happy years in this little cottage.

At first, the neighbors seemed a little suspicious of us. We noticed that we were being watched from behind closed windows, yet no one came out of their houses to greet us. Some of our friends in Europe warned us that there were white people in America who were not very friendly toward non-whites. As it turned out, we were the first non-white family to move to this street, and we wondered if we had made a mistake in choosing the neighborhood. My biggest fear was that Chuki and Tenzin might be mistreated. What if the other children called them names and taunted them? I remembered how much I had hated being called "moonface" when I was in school. I agonized over this for several weeks, until I began to notice Chuki and Tenzin playing with some of the neighborhood children. Soon we had many youngsters visiting us, and Lobsang and I even began making friends with the parents. Later we moved to a larger house not too far away, but we still remained in contact with many of these friends and visited them often. When we moved to India for good, tears were shed by many of our neighbors as we said good-bye to them.

The next great matter of urgency was to find reasonable employment. My parents were also concerned about how to support themselves. My mother had married at just fifteen and had not attended school for very long. My father had only studied in a Jesuit school in India for a few years. Lobsang had attended a Tibetan school and had taken Buddhist courses in a monastery until he was seventeen, after which he had joined the Tibetan government. He had never attended an English-medium school. They could only qualify for labor jobs or work in unskilled occupations. After much debate, we approached several of our Tibetan friends about plans to open a Tibetan handicraft shop.

Lobsang's brother Gyalo Thondup happened to be in New York during this time, and was enthusiastic about joining our business venture. He proposed that he and his wife do the buying in India and Nepal, and then send the goods to us to sell in the shop. Lobsang would manage the shop, one of our other partners, Tsering Dorji, would serve as accountant, and I would dress the window and help staff the shop along with Lobsang.

After some preparation, our arts and crafts venture went into business. We leased a space on Madison Avenue for the shop, Tibetan Arts and Crafts, as it was named, and went to work sewing labels, hanging rugs, and decorating the window. We would collect the merchandise from the customs office, label and price each piece, and indicate the country where the items had been made. We sewed labels until our fingers ached. It was very hard work, but we enjoyed the challenge and the idea that this was our business.

Every Monday morning, I changed the window display. Although I had missed my opportunity to attend the Pratt Institute and become an interior designer, I could still decorate the shop on Madison Avenue. I often received compliments from customers about the layout.

Not only was Tibetan Arts and Crafts the first Tibetan shop in Manhattan, it was the only center for people who were curious about Tibet, the country on the roof of the world. Our merchandise was very exotic to the Americans. People who wanted information on Tibet often came in to ask questions. Sometimes we had people who came in solely to argue that Tibet was a part of China. I used to get really worked up over these ignorant people. On occasion, there would be a heated exchange. At other times, people would come in to sit in front of our thangkas and meditate. Of course, there were the regular visitors who would drop by to chat and buy a card or an incense packet.

Working on Madison Avenue was thrilling. The most exclusive shops in the city were just outside our doorstep, and it was fascinating to stroll along and view the vast assortment of alluring goods for purchase. Sitting inside the shop and watching the parade of passersby was equally interesting. It amused me to see the different breeds of dogs these city people kept inside their apartments. There were sheepdogs, Afghan hounds, bull dogs, elegant poodles, even Lhasa Apsos that were well groomed and often clothed or wearing necklaces. These lucky dogs were dressed better than many humans I had been accustomed to seeing.

A number of celebrities came into our shop. I could not get over the deep blue eyes of Paul Newman. When I was at Mount Hermon School, he had been a favorite idol. I could not believe I was seeing him in person. Wanting to strike up a conversation with him, I could only muster enough courage to ask him for his autograph for my daughter. Jacqueline Kennedy Onassis sometimes strolled along Madison Avenue, looking very chic and elegant. People gawked at her as she walked. It must have been difficult to be the focus of so many inquisitive eyes.

Zsa Zsa Gabor sometimes walked by with her entourage of dogs and attendants. One of her sisters had a shop nearby. There was another lady who would amble along Madison Avenue every day in a different exotic costume. Sometimes she would dress like a character from the Chinese Opera with full stage make-up.

One day, a young lady in a long suede coat walked into the store. She wore a long, wool scarf and matching cap, under which hung ringlets of tangled blonde hair. She wore no make-up and looked pale and fragile, but she was very friendly and looked like the flower children of those days. She wanted to pay for her merchandise by credit card, and I asked to see her identification.

She must have been quite amused that we did not recognize her. In those days she was quite a celebrity. She was Julie Christie, and I hope she was not offended.

By now my parents had found a house close to us. While Lobsang and I commuted to New York City to look after our shop, my parents kept the children at their house after school. The children felt very safe and secure with their grandparents. Although we were out of town, their grandparents were always around for them. This arrangement was a great comfort for us.

The children were very happy and doing well in their studies. After school, Tenzin could be found raking leaves or cutting grass for pocket money. In the winter, he would shovel the snow from driveways. He was very enterprising. Sometimes, on our way home from work, I would look out from the bus and spot little Tenzin and an older friend busy with their money-making ventures. Chuki was a wonderful big sister and made sure that Tenzin did his homework. Eventually, my parents had to move again to find work and were not around to look after the children. Lobsang and I did not like leaving them on their own for so long after school, but we had to look after the shop in Manhattan to pay our bills. Luckily, they had many friends in the neighborhood, and there was an elderly couple across the street who kept an eye on them for us.

My parents moved first to Texas, where my father worked as an assistant to a healer, and then to Maryland where he worked as a companion to an elderly physician. They even spent two weeks as household help at the estate of the wealthy socialite Doris Duke. A friend had encouraged them to take this job because Ms. Duke spent only six weeks a year in this house and moved to her other houses with her attendants during the rest of the year. There were a couple of people who stayed on to look after the gardens and the dogs, so my parents would not be alone. It seemed an excellent arrangement, although for the first time in their lives my parents would have to be servants.

When Ms. Duke was in residence, my mother's tasks included dusting furniture and arranging the flowers. My father was to help wait on Ms. Duke. They had only been in this gorgeous seaside mansion a few weeks before Ms. Duke and her entourage

arrived. One day after Ms. Duke's arrival, my mother was repri-
manded by an assistant, Mr. Armand, about the flowers she had
arranged. My mother had never liked being criticized; no one
had ever criticized her to her face, and she replied, "Mr. Armand,
I was the head of a larger household than this with about thirty
servants, and I know how to arrange flowers!" The gentleman
was a bit shocked, but he was kind enough not to follow up on
the matter. My father, on the other hand, had never felt more
humiliated, dressing in a butler's suit and waiting on the lady of
the house. After two weeks at the estate, they graciously took
leave of Ms. Duke and the lovely environment.

Another change was in store for us as well. After spending
almost two years on Madison Avenue, we realized that we were
not making much financial progress. Two partners had already
left the business, and those of us remaining could not agree on
some terms of the financial arrangements. Lobsang and I decided to pull out of the venture and seek other means of earning
a living. Our partner and cashier, Tsering, thought this was a
good idea; he mentioned that Lobsang and I would never make
good business people.

Perhaps he was right. The Tibetan woolen rugs from India
and Nepal, as well as the other woolen items, needed constant
care. They had to be aired and treated with moth repellents. We
had a small storeroom at the back of the shop where we piled all
these items in a corner and vacuumed each and every one after
the shop closed in the evening. Despite this tedious work, the
moths loved the soft, warm wool of our beautiful carpets and
coats. The rugs that hung on the walls were even more attractive to the insects, because the heat of the spotlights encouraged
the moths to breed. When a customer liked a piece of our merchandise, we could not help but point out the often tiny defects.
Our partner, of course, thought this was no way to make money.

Shortly before we left the business, an elderly man walked
into the shop. He was not too tall, rather stout, beautifully tanned
with glistening silver hair, and very handsomely dressed. He
had on a dark blue overcoat and a matching fedora. Looking a
bit puzzled as he entered the shop, he inquired about an art gal-
lery that had leased the space before we opened our shop. He

was amazed at the unusual merchandise and curious about their origins. When we told him that the crafts were made by Tibetan refugees in India and Nepal, he was even more intrigued. He asked me if I was really from Tibet, if people really did fly from place to place, and if the natives lived on flower pills. When I gave him a short account of my country and of my arrival on Madison Avenue, he said, "Young lady, you should write your story for us." He then bade us farewell, but I never forgot what he said. I knew that one day I would write about my life and tell about the world across the Himalayas.

Of course, now we had to look around for other employment. Lobsang wanted to start a Tibetan restaurant in the city. He loved cooking, and when he was in the kitchen, it evolved into a creative, exotic corner. He would lay out all the ingredients on the table. The vegetables and the meat had to be cut in uniform shapes and sizes. Dirty dishes had to be washed or put in the sink immediately after use, and the kitchen had to be in order when the cooking was completed. As a result of his efforts, beautiful dishes were spread out on the kitchen table like a vegetable bazaar. The delicious aroma would make us salivate until we could get our chopsticks or forks into his creations.

Reluctantly, I joined Lobsang in a walk all over Manhattan, looking for a small place to open a Tibetan restaurant. We also contacted several real estate agencies. Never had I been so tired at the end of the day. In addition, I was a little unsure of taking up this project. To love cooking is one thing, but to cook in a restaurant, in front of a hot stove day in and day out, is another thing. Lobsang was not young anymore, and I was a little worried about his health. Moreover, I needed to find a regular job so that we could have health insurance for the family. I believe luck was with us, because we did not find an appropriate place.

I wanted to find a job that involved helping others. This was the kind of work I was good at, and it was where my heart was. I went to several social service agencies but discovered that without a college degree I was not qualified for such work. To me it was confusing that a college degree was more important than the desire and enthusiasm to help others. What irony. Later I met people who were employed in social services but who were only concerned with their salaries and lacked enthusiasm for their work.

In April of 1973, I found a job in a private club run by the Banker's Trust, called the Boardroom. It was a private restaurant, run mainly for large business concerns as a place to hold meetings and business discussions over meals. There were five girls running the office, and I worked in the billing section. When my colleagues went on vacation, I took over their posts, doing the payroll, the switchboard, the typing, and the reception desk.

Being a receptionist was quite entertaining. One had to have a good memory to keep up with which meetings were taking place in which rooms. We had to inform the guests where their luncheons were taking place. The businessmen were very pressured and tense and their anger was easily aroused. Japanese guests needed extra attention. They were so busy bowing to each other and deferring to their more senior executives that they never managed to get on the elevator without the assistance of our staff.

We had a manager to oversee the office, and his wife worked as the secretary. I enjoyed the camaraderie of this small group. In the kitchen, everyone referred to me as "darling" and "sweetheart." What I did not like about the job was being on the fifty-first floor, and I always wondered what would happen if there was a fire below us!

Lobsang decided to look for a job in our small town, because he hated commuting to the city. An elderly neighbor from Eastern Europe, Mr. Michael, told Lobsang of a custodial job that was open at the local junior high school. Mr. Michael had held this job at one time for many years and had since retired. Now that his two sons were out of school and holding executive posts in large companies, he and his wife were quite comfortable. He told Lobsang that it was a good place to work. Lobsang applied for and was hired for the job, which involved cleaning the office and some of the classrooms. It was the same school that our children were attending. Of course, when some of Lobsang's friends heard that he was a school janitor, they tried to persuade him to move to another city to look for a better job. They could not understand how he could take up such menial work. Lobsang was a very practical man, someone who always respected manual labor and believed that honest work was good work. He used to say, "I like this job, I cheat no one and hurt no one; this is a clean, honest way to earn a living. This machine picks up all the dirt and I just walk around the room." He did not, however, like scraping chewing gum off of desks, chairs, walls, and even from the floor, and he could not understand this dirty habit of the American people.

With this job, Lobsang was home when the children came home, and he left the house just when I returned from work. He was very enthusiastic and known to be the best janitor around. He was so thorough with his work that the town library asked him to mow their lawn and tend the garden on Saturdays. Lobsang was liked by all the staff and students. He was always bringing home baked goods from people who admired him, and wherever he went, he was greeted by "Hi, Sam." I was known as Mrs. Sam, because Lobsang was known as Lobsang Samden.

Lobsang was disappointed by the lack of discipline of many of the students at school. He thought they lacked respect for others and for school property, that they had too much freedom, and that they did what they liked to the point of destruction. Many students drank alcohol in school. The janitors would find empty whiskey and gin bottles in the toilets. Lobsang complained to the principal about the wild behavior of many of these children and suggested that discipline be more strongly enforced in the school. Lobsang was shocked to learn that the teachers got little cooperation from the parents. If disciplinary action was taken, the parents always sided with the children. We were glad that our children were not giving us any problems, but we worried about what would happen when they entered high school.

Lobsang had been a janitor for three years when a staff writer from the *New York Times* happened to find out that he was the brother of the Dalai Lama. No one in our town knew this. The reporter wanted to write about Lobsang in the *Times*, but Lobsang refused. The reporter contacted the principal of the junior high who persuaded Lobsang to talk to the reporter. When the article appeared in the *New York Times*, we had telephone calls from all over the country, many wishing us well and telling us how they admired His Holiness's brother for working as a janitor in a local school. There were offers of jobs, which Lobsang was wise not to take. Suddenly, floods of cars drove by our house, hoping to get a glimpse of us. The local people were excited, and we were fearful of losing our treasured privacy.

Not long after the article, Lobsang conceded that the custodial job was making him dull. He took a fund-raising job at the Dooley Foundation. He had known the head of this concern, Dr. Verne Chaney, for a long time, and had worked with him in India on issues relating to the health needs of Tibetan refugees in the early 1960s.

On September 27, 1977, Lobsang and I were naturalized as United States citizens; we had to proceed to the court at Elizabeth, New Jersey, with two witnesses: our friend Zurki Rinpoche, who was originally from Inner Mongolia, and our dear friend Barbara, a Kalmuck Mongolian. It was somewhat sad that we were taking up citizenship in a new country. On the other hand, because we were unable to be citizens of our own land, we were very grateful to become citizens of the United States of America.

In the late 1970s, there were no more than a hundred Tibetans in the United States, and about forty lived on the East Coast. We met during the Tibetan New Year, on March 10th, to commemorate the Tibetan uprising against the Chinese occupation of Tibet, and in July to celebrate His Holiness the Dalai Lama's birthday. We looked forward to these gatherings, and it was especially important for our children to meet other children of Tibetan parents and to be in a Tibetan environment, even if it was only for a few hours. During these gatherings, there was plenty to eat and drink. Music was essential, although American pop music was preferred, and the latest dance steps were more popular than Tibetan folk dances. Our children loved these gatherings and looked forward to the next event.

Sometimes we visited our Mongolian friends in other parts of New Jersey. Some Mongolians had built a couple of Buddhist temples. We went to pay our homage there, to acquaint the children with Buddhism, and to teach them how to prostrate in front of the statue of Buddha. We drank butter tea there and ate traditional Tibetan food. Lobsang knew many of the Mongolian monks, because they had studied in Tibetan monasteries. Geshe Wangyal-la was an especially good friend of Lobsang. We felt very much at home in these surroundings, and visited the temples quite often. My brother-in-law, Thubten Norbu, would visit us once a year with his wife and their three sons. The three Norbu boys, in the company of our son Tenzin and Tenpa Dhondup, the son of another close friend, would turn the place upside down. We later tried to spend most of these reunions at the country home of Tenpa and his family, to avoid the complaints of our neighbors. Tenpa's family lived on a chicken farm in Jackson, New Jersey, and there was plenty of space to accommodate these energetic young boys.

An extraordinary event in our lives at this time was our reunion with my brother the Rinpoche, who we had left behind in Tibet eighteen years earlier, when he was just ten years old. My father had just left for Texas and my mother was to join him soon. I went to visit my mother with my daughter one Sunday, and found her painting the garage. Upon our arrival, we went to the kitchen for a cup of coffee. Very casually she said, "I have good news." My mother was not a very emotional person, so I wondered what this good news could be. She continued, "Rinpoche has arrived in Nepal, I received a telegram." At first, I could not guess which Rinpoche she meant. When it dawned on me that the Rinpoche was the little brother we had left in Tibet, there were no words to express my happiness. I just cried. My mother cried with me. This had to be a miracle. My brother, Drikung Chetsang Rinpoche, was the head of the Drikung Kagyu school of Buddhism. It did not seem possible that he could escape from the well-guarded boundaries of Tibet. There was no one coming out of Tibet during those days. Tibet was sealed tight by the Chinese army. My father flew to India to meet him, and what a dramatic moment it was when my husband and I went to the airport to meet my father and the brother I had not seen for eighteen years. When I set eyes on him, the little chubby boy with dimples had become a tall, thin man with a serious look. He had suffered much, but when he smiled, the dimples were still visible and the twinkle in his eyes had not faded.

My brother went to live with my parents in Texas, where he went to night school to study English and worked as a dishwasher and salad chef in a Steak and Ale restaurant. When he decided to leave Texas, the manager of the restaurant wanted to give him a promotion. If only the manager of that Steak and Ale could see him now as head of several monasteries and a Master in Buddhist Studies.

In the summer of 1977, my brother Drikung Rinpoche moved to the East Coast to live with us. He had gone through much hardship in his youth. He was thrown out of the security of his monastery in Drikung when he was ten years old, and upon returning to Lhasa to Tsarong House, he found his grandfather and uncle imprisoned and the house requisitioned by the Chinese army. He searched for food, sleeping here and there in the city and facing extreme difficulties, yet there surfaced no bitterness about his past and he was always pleasant, optimistic, and smiling. We loved having him with us. He and Lobsang spent a lot of time together in the kitchen and got along very well. Tenzin took advantage of Rinpoche's good nature and used to bully him until Rinpoche would wrestle with him on the floor.

During the period my brother was with us, we received a visit from His Holiness Sakya Trizin Rinpoche from India, who was the head of the Sakya sect of Buddhism and whose ancestors had ruled Tibet in the thirteenth century. He gave a long life initiation for the Tibetan community in Manhattan, and Lobsang invited his family and another learned lama from Sakya, Dezhung Rinpoche, for lunch at our home in New Jersey. We were worried about how to bring them safely from Manhattan to our home. Drikung Rinpoche was to drive our car, and Lobsang was worried about him driving such an important person on the busy road, when unexpectedly and to our great relief my father arrived from Texas the night before the luncheon.

Sakya Trizin Rinpoche was about the same age as Drikung Rinpoche, in his early thirties, and he was a gentle, humble man of great knowledge and high status. He was such a warm person. He thoroughly enjoyed my brother's accounts of life in Tibet, and they talked about their past lineage holders, who at one period in time had fought with each other. We enjoyed serving lunch to these special people. Lobsang had prepared leg of lamb, roast potatoes, and a boiled vegetable dish, and I made a salad of assorted fresh vegetables. It was late in the day when they left our home, and it was a great honor to be in the company of such kind and warm people in our simple home. Such a visit would not have been possible in Tibet without formality and ceremony and throngs of hovering servants.

August of 1977 brought us bad news about the illness of my mother-in-law. We knew that if it had not been severe, we would not have been informed. Gyalyum never wished to inconvenience or worry anyone. On many occasions she may not have been well, but she kept the pain to herself. Lobsang experienced a strange feeling that if he went to India on this visit, he would not want to return to the United States. He also said that if he went to India this time, his eventual departure from his mother might make her illness worse. Lobsang had no worries about leaving us, as my brother was staying with us, but for some reason he did not want to travel to India. Something seemed to be holding him back from making this trip, although I never found out the reason. His brother Norbu had also decided not to make the journey, and I tried to tell Lobsang that should his mother not recover and leave us, he would regret his decision. A telegram from Tenzin Choegyal, Lobsang's youngest brother, convinced Lobsang and Norbu to make the trip to India. I was very happy.

Gyalyum recovered, Lobsang returned, and as he predicted, he talked much about returning to India. He said, "Kundun has such a heavy responsibility on his shoulders, there is so much to do in India for the Tibetan cause, and here we are living in a comfortable house, eating well and concerned just for our own well-being. I feel quite guilty living like this. I think we should go back to India, and I would like to do what I can to serve Kundun and help with the Tibetan cause."

We thought and talked a great deal about returning to India. At this stage, Tenzin was getting unruly and difficult to handle. Chuki was a beautiful girl and was pestered by many boys for dates. Her girlfriends were pressuring her to go out with these boys, but she was not at all happy with the attention. She did not look forward to entering high school the following year. We had a family meeting on this issue of moving to India, and the children were thrilled at the idea. We had just moved to a larger house, fixed it with our own labor and love, and now were thinking of leaving. Our friends were very discouraging.

All I wanted was for the family to be together and happy. With all the moves in my life and the adjustments to make from country to country, I was used to Lobsang's need for sudden changes in our lifestyle. These moves were not easy, but we saw a lot of the world. It was at this period that the Beatles were famous, and they made the Indian Guru Maharishi and his transcendental meditation very popular. I got very curious about this knowledge, which harmonized the body and the mind and made the mind clear, relaxing the meditator and producing a healthier lifestyle. I read what I could about meditation, which led me to read books on Buddhism. I realized that India was the best place to learn about Buddhism and meditation.

I was a Buddhist. I said my rosary and my "Om Mani Padme Hum" mantra, I lit lamps in the chapels and prayed for my needs, but I did not know the meaning of the mantra I recited, nor what the three Refuges meant, or to whom I prostrated. I did read a few Buddhist books that were available in English in those days; some of my fellow bus passengers used to tell me to stop reading such morbid material. I did not think Buddhism was morbid. The knowledge made me see life as it was and try to find answers to lessen suffering. With this knowledge, one could face life with courage and strength.

It was Christmas when we decided to sell our house and return to India. Over a sumptuous breakfast of Thomas's English muffins, the family's favorite bread, and crisp fried eggs, we broke the news to my parents. My aunt Tess was visiting us with her husband from India. As always, my parents did not comment. They respected our wishes now that we were adults. They also knew that I was no longer a member of their family. I had married out of the Tsarong family to join another house, and I was now a member of my husband's family. Many people thought moving to India was the worst decision of our lives, especially for the future of our children.

We sold our house to a newlywed couple, leaving our brand new washing machine and refrigerator. We sold our furniture at a garage sale and gave what was left to our Tibetan friends. We packed our books on Tibet, a few of our good kitchen utensils and clothing, and were ready for the journey. The Tibetan community gave us a wonderful farewell.

Unfortunately, we could not return as soon as we had planned. It took us an extremely long time to get our travel documents, and when we received our passports, we discovered that China was listed instead of Tibet as our place of birth. Our previous reentry document had listed Tibet. We had traveled with this paper and did not understand the sudden change. Another Tibetan from Pennsylvania, Ngawang Phakchok, was also shocked to find this similar wording on his passport. The United States government was changing its policy toward Tibetans after Nixon's trip to China. We had been fighting the illegal and forced occupation of our country by Communist China since we left our country, and we could not easily sit back and comply with this humiliating decision by the greatest democratic nation in the world. The United States challenged the violation of human rights, and now our rights were being violated. We were born in Tibet, and we had a right to have Tibet listed as our birthplace.

Ngawang came from Pennsylvania, and we met with the Office of Tibet staff and the United States Tibetan Association members to make an issue of this. The Office of Tibet staff and the Association members did a great job and organized letter writing campaigns and protests. Our American friends were also greatly concerned and helped us on this matter. The closing date of our house approached, and we had no option but to go to Maryland and leave our children with my parents while Lobsang and I traveled between New York City, Washington, D. C., and Maryland to fight for our cause. A number of our American friends mentioned that it would be impossible to have this change put on our passports, as this was a move made by the government. In Washington, D. C., Lobsang and I visited our congressman from New Jersey, Mr. Matthew Rinaldo, and the offices of other officials, including Ted Kennedy, William Goodling, Charles Percy, and Patrick Moynihan. We were given differing advice. There was the suggestion at a meeting of the Tibetan Association that some Tibetans should go to the White House and chain ourselves to the fence. This, of course, did not happen. There was a great deal of confusion among our small U. S. Tibetan community. Because Lobsang was His Holiness the Dalai Lama's brother, many Tibetans thought he could garner more support on this issue. Yet time was flying, and we had been without jobs and a home for two months. Running from place to place at our own expense was not easy, and the children were out of school.

In addition, we were getting the usual talk: "We have great sympathy for your cause!" I was really sick of hearing this phrase. Sympathy did not get us anywhere. It was a very frustrating period for Lobsang and me. At one point, we decided to give up our American passports. We went to the Indian Consulate and met the Indian ambassador to the U. N., Mr. Jaipal, and requested Indian travel documents to return to India. Ambassador Jaipal advised us to travel to India on our U. S. passports and to follow up on our case from there.

Once again we made the rounds of Washington. Congressman Bill Goodling from Pennsylvania informed us that he would put forth a bill to have Tibet reinstated on our passports as our country of birth. Our New Jersey Congressman, Mr. Rinaldo, would co-sponsor the bill. They suggested that we go on to India, and that they would notify us of this change via the American Embassy in New Delhi.

Many of our American friends and many American leaders were very supportive of this issue. They wrote to the President and the Secretary of State. There was also great solidarity among the Tibetans as the fight continued. We updated our friends in New York on our visit to the various congressmen and senators and of the latest outcomes of these meetings. The Tibetans asked us to remain in the United States until the bill was passed. It was impossible for us to do so without jobs or a roof over our heads, and we gave in to pursuing the passport issue from India.

On July 2, 1978, after attending a number of farewell parties given by our numerous friends, we bade farewell to New York City in the glow of an orange sunset. The sky was so clear that the Empire State Building was visible from the Boeing 747, and millions of lights twinkled above and below us. It was sad to leave this great country, with so many good friends and so many cherished memories.

On July 11, 1978, we received a letter from Loren E. Lawrence, Deputy Assistant Secretary for Passport Services, Department of State, stating,

> The President and the Secretary of State have asked that I respond to your recent letter regarding the use of China rather than Tibet as place of birth in the U. S. passports. In

view of the interest in this subject, as well as other place-of-birth questions that you and others have shown, we are reviewing our entire policy on an urgent basis. I will be in touch with you again when the review has been completed.

On April 30th, 1979, at the United States Embassy in New Delhi, the birthplaces on our U. S. passports were changed from China to Kumbum on Lobsang's, and to Lhasa on mine.

15 Dharamsala: Place of Refuge

Descending the steps of the airplane in New Delhi, we were hit by the intense heat which seemed to wrap itself around our lungs, leaving us breathless and drenched in perspiration. As we made our way toward the terminal, we were swallowed in a storm of locusts, many of which entered the building with us. The airport was pure chaos; amid an explosion of people and mass confusion, we managed to get through customs and hail a cab. Once in the taxi, the friendly driver put us at ease, and I sensed a slower pace of life than I had been accustomed to in recent years. Suddenly, it felt good to be back in India.

In Delhi, Lobsang called on a number of our Indian friends, including Dr. Lokesh Chandra, Professor Sondhi, and Professor Ram Rahaul. Professor Rahaul was a tall, white-haired Indian scholar with thick spectacles and a welcoming smile. He was ready with advice about how Tibetans should work with the Indian masses to solve Tibet's problems. He cautioned that although India and Tibet shared a border and a religion, the politicians would be of little help to us.

Delhi was extremely hot, and the monsoon was just entering the region. We waited anxiously for the rain to fall. The ground was parched, and the topic of when the rain would begin was on everyone's lips. As usual, Tenzin was the only one who still had the energy to race around—until he fell ill with malaria, that is. Poor Tenzin, one day he was running all over the place and the next he was shivering in the Delhi heat. His temperature rose so high that we had to rush him to a doctor.

We stayed in Delhi long enough to celebrate the Dalai Lama's birthday at the Bureau, and then we took the train to our final destination—Dharamsala. The scenery was breathtaking. The cool mountain air was such a relief after the stifling heat of the Indian plains. Climbing towards the mountains, we passed many green, lush, rice fields and sparkling streams gushing down from the hills. Small wood and stone houses with beautiful slate roofs dotted the emerald fields. Doll-like children waved as we passed them, and the banana trees swayed in the breeze. To the delight of our children, families of monkeys appeared on the road waiting patiently for the passengers to throw them bananas.

When we reached Dharamsala, we went straight to Kashmir Cottage where Gyalyum Chenmo lived, and she was waiting for us. We were delighted to see her again, yet I was sad to note that her illness had greatly aged her. She was very happy to see us. My brother Jigme and his wife Ann, Gyalo Thondup's daughter, were also there to greet us. Gyalyum was pleased that the weather was so nice; she thought it was very auspicious, because they had had rain for many days. Soon, my sister-in-law Pema arrived with her two daughters, Thenchoe and Yangzom, and her son, Tenzin Choedak. We had dinner together, and it was a lovely reunion. Lobsang's younger brother, Tenzin Choegyal, and his wife Rinchen Khando also lived in Kashmir Cottage, but they were at the hospital in Kangra because their young son was ill. We met them in the following days.

Early the next morning, we were eager to explore Dharamsala. Lobsang took us to the Dalai Lama's palace and requested an audience through his private secretary. It was a steep climb up the mountain, but the air was fresh and invigorating. Wild flowers grew in abundance. Below us was the valley of Kangra, one of the only hill stations in India where one can be so close to the snowy peaks of the Himalayas.

There were a number of people at the temple turning prayer wheels, prostrating, and circumambulating; their faith was so intense and inspiring. The people here looked very poor yet happy, relaxed, and peaceful, compared to people in the West.

We visited the Tibetan Medical Center where my brother Jigme worked as the administrator. Lobsang met many friends, and we drank so much tea that with no public toilets, we were desperate to find a place to relieve ourselves before we drank more tea; there was no way to get out of drinking so much tea.

We stopped for lunch at a small cafe run by the Dalai Lama's driver. Chuki and I could not appreciate the food, because we had a 2:00 appointment with His Holiness and we were very nervous. We returned to the temple premises, and entered the gates of the palace to be met by a couple of armed Indian police. Soon, we were ushered into a sitting room where Kundun, His Holiness, suddenly joined us. We prostrated and presented our khatas before sitting down for tea. His Holiness looked so fresh and alive, and we felt overwhelmed by his special energy. His Holiness asked Lobsang about our passport problems, and he talked to the children and me. I was so nervous I had trouble holding a cup with my trembling hands. With blessings from His Holiness, we departed from the palace. It was such an auspicious beginning to our new life in India.

I had never seen Lobsang as happy and relaxed as he was while basking in the company of his mother. Gyalyum reminded me of a pot of honey, with her family always gathered around her like a swarm of bees. She gave us a sense of belonging and being loved. Tenzin was very happy exploring the place, while Chuki, a little shy by nature, was a bit apprehensive. A few days after our arrival, she became quite ill and a Tibetan physician was called. He checked Chuki's pulse and the color of her urine, and told us that she was suffering from a bile disorder. She had eaten a lot of dried meat the day before, and this had disturbed her liver. The doctor gave her some Tibetan medicine, which worked wonders for her.

The daughter of Ngari Rinpoche and Rinchen Khando-la, Choezom, became a wonderful companion to Chuki. On Sundays, Pema and her children would join us. Sometimes Jigme and Ann had lunch with us, and it was always a joyous family get-together. There were so many of us that the children had to sit at side tables. Gyalyum loved the company of her children and grandchildren, and she looked forward to the Sunday

lunches. She made sure that everyone's favorite dishes were prepared for them. I enjoyed the long, hand-rolled noodles sprinkled
with fried onions, garlic, and soy sauce. There were always
momos and a creamy mixture of powdered peas called *chothang*,
which sounded like "cow dung" in the Lhasa dialect and looked
very similar to it as well. I did not take to this dish, although in
general, I did adapt to most of the cuisine from my husband's
birthplace.

Soon, it was time for Chuki and Tenzin to start school. We
decided that they should attend the Tibetan Children's Village.
Around this time, Lobsang and I had decided it was best for us
to move out of Kashmir Cottage, because the house could not
easily accommodate two families. We were able to lease the guest
cottage at the Children's Village, which worked out very well
for us because the children did not have to go very far to get to
school.

We spent two very interesting years in this small cottage
nestled in the woods. The children shared the bedroom, while
Lobsang and I slept in the living room. In the beginning, we
often had mice come into our beds at night. We eventually solved
this problem by keeping a cat.

The bathroom had a gap of about six inches between the wall
and the roof, which made bathing in the winter a chilly ordeal.
The kitchen was the size of a closet, and the roof leaked badly.
We cooked on a kerosene stove, so when it rained, we had to
cook under an umbrella. Oh, how I longed for the gas stove we
had in the States! The endless flow of warm water from the tap
was another luxury that we missed. Other than that, we were
quite content.

When the children were in school, Lobsang and I would clean
the house, pack a lunch with a flask of tea, and trek up into the
mountains to read and sunbathe. From the pine-and rhododen-
dron-covered hills, we would gaze down at the lush green rice
fields in the valley below. Everything was so peaceful. During
spring and autumn, the sun was very strong, and Lobsang and I
would find a cool, shady spot under a tree to eat our lunch.

On these treks, we often encountered hermits, mostly Buddhist monks but also a few nuns, who lived in small caves or

stone huts. We became friends with a number of these people and brought them food or other items that they might find useful. Talking with these hermits and sharing a cup of tea with them was a very spiritual experience. These people had no material comforts, but they seemed so content and at peace. I learned from them that happiness comes from within and not from external amusements. There was one nun in particular whom I visited often. She had been living in her cave for nine years. In her youth, she had walked all over Tibet on pilgrimage, but she now spent her days in retreat. She had a pile of stones that she covered with a bundle of old clothing and blankets to make a bed. Her only possessions were a couple of pots and pans, framed pictures of her teachers, seven brass offering bowls, and a few other religious objects she kept on a board alongside her bed. An old hermit lived not too far away in a similar cave. He and his wife had left their children behind in Tibet, and when his wife died in a road construction camp in India, he retreated to the mountains and devoted himself to a religious life. He lived with a number of small mice that he hand-fed. A monk who was on a three-year, three-month, and three-day retreat was also nearby.

Occasionally, I took the children to visit these people. I wanted them to see that these people were content despite their abject poverty. Many people in the world who had plenty of food to eat and who slept on soft mattresses covered by warm, woolen blankets and crisp, clean sheets, were often unhappy. I wanted my children to know that joy must come from the inside.

It was during this time that I met a learned monk who lived in small hut close to the Children's Village. I was having a very difficult time trying to read the Buddhist prayers in English. For each prayer, the Tibetan scripture was written in long hand with an English translation. I asked this monk if he would help me. Geshe Samdup-la agreed, and we established a practice where he would explain the commentary of these prayers from the Tibetan text, and then make me read them in Tibetan. Eventually, I graduated to receiving a couple of commentaries on short *lamrim* teachings. I was then able to attend a short teaching and a Chenrezi initiation given by His Holiness to a dozen international disciples. The teachings were translated into English by Jeffrey Hopkins, who was a professor of Buddhist Studies at the University of Virginia. Although I was not able to follow everything that was said, my teacher reminded me that I was very lucky to receive this initiation and that I should continue my dharma lessons.

I am very grateful to this teacher and the other individuals who helped me to understand the dharma and who made sure that I did not miss any of the spring teachings given by His Holiness. If I missed a teaching, my teacher and dharma friends would send word that I should not miss such an important teaching; I always turned up at the temple on the following days.

Chamdo Geshe-la was another wonderful guide and friend. This ascetic monk lived high up in the mountains in a small hut that had once been a cow shed. He was tall, had a fair complexion and a beautiful, serene face. He had suffered a stroke a few years earlier, and his right arm was immobile. Despite this handicap, he looked after himself very well. He would light the fire to make tea with his left hand when Lobsang and I came to visit. We always brought lunch to share with him, and the three of us would sit outside his hut and talk.

Geshe-la slept on a thin mattress and kept a small swatch of carpet for his visitors to sit on. Beside his bed were a couple of scriptures and a thangka of the Goddess Tara. The room was bare of furniture or other accessories. The outside room was empty except for a couple of cooking pots and a mud stove. Both rooms were immaculate, and there was a special aura about the simplicity.

One summer day in late July, 1979, Lobsang came home very excited after a visit with His Holiness. He told me that a delegation was going to Tibet, and that he had been selected to be a member. This was unbelievable; how was it possible that the Chinese were allowing a delegation of so-called traitors into Tibet? Lobsang was happy about going, but warned me not to repeat the news to anyone. It was best to keep the mission a secret until the delegation had departed from Indian soil.

At the same time Lobsang was leaving for Tibet, I was on my way to Ladakh. My brother, Drikung Kyabgon, had invited Lobsang and me to attend the eight-hundred-year anniversary celebration of the founding of the Drikung Kagyu lineage. The celebration was to be very special that year. My parents and brothers Jigme and Paljor were also attending this event.

I made the journey with Pema. We traveled by jeep to Leh, the capital of Ladakh. The scenery reminded me so much of Tibet that I felt like I could have been back in Lhasa. Caught by a sharp pang of homesickness, tears streamed down my face.

Piang Monastery was about twenty minutes from the capital, and from a distance, I caught sight of it perched majestically on a hill. Different shades of sand-covered mountains provided a huge boundary around the region. A sole strip of green rested on the foothill of the monastery, where a meandering river ran down to the valley.

Climbing the steps to the monastery was more exertion than I was accustomed to, and every step took great effort. At an altitude of 11,500 feet, I had to walk at a slow pace and rest every few steps to catch my breath. Finally, after climbing the hill and mounting the numerous stairs with my heart thumping at a frightening pace, I reached my brother's living quarters feeling absolutely breathless.

The room could have been a scene out of a Tibetan home; I could have been sitting in my grandmother's prayer room. I prostrated to Rinpoche and received his blessings. He asked me where Lobsang was, and why he was not with me. Rinpoche's treasurer and attendant were in the room, so I tried to answer nonchalantly, "Lobsang could not join me at this time." Rinpoche laughed and said, "Nothing is secret these days. Kungoe is on his way to Tibet!" What a relief; I hated making up stories. We all had a good laugh. Soon, tea was brought in and my parents joined us.

The monks were kind and simple and made me feel very much at home. During our stay, my family and I were able to visit the three main Drikung monasteries. The first was Piang, and then we traveled to Shang. To get there we had to travel on horseback along a gorge where the mountains sparkled in the sun's reflection. The mountains were made of crystal rock in a variety of shapes, sparkling purple, pink, and white. It was a gorgeous ride into Shang.

Lama Yuru Monastery was a strange place. This isolated monastery was higher than Leh, possibly over 12,000 feet. We climbed a high mountain pass and then reached the top of the world.

The ancient monastery lay deep in the valley below. The sandy mountains surrounding the village looked like huge odd-shaped cones. We traveled to the top of the mountain pass by bus and walked downhill to the monastery in the valley. The monks welcomed us just as they would have in any monastery, with religious music, incense, and khatas. The villagers were dressed in their best costumes to welcome their lama. It was a spectacular day, and as we descended to the monastery, a large rainbow circled above. The villagers were delighted at this auspicious sign. Rinpoche had spent three years, three months, and three days in retreat in this monastery a couple of years earlier. The current abbot of Drikung, Khenpo Kunchok Gyaltsen, had also done his long retreat in this monastery. That night, we were lulled to sleep by the slow beating of the *dama* and shrill sound of the *suna*, an eerie music to welcome the high lamas of the region. My parents and I slept in a small room, and shortly after I had gone to sleep, the bedbugs who were starved for a meal rushed to attack me. I turned out to be their favorite dish. I could not bear the biting and itching, and when I lit a candle and looked into my sleeping bag, I could see the skin of hundreds of brown bugs reflected in the light. I woke my mother, thinking that she might know what to do to get rid of these bugs. When she awoke, she noticed her pearl earrings were missing, and we spent much of the night searching for them. It was nearly dawn before we found her earrings under her mattress, and I went to sleep.

The next night I joined my brothers and cousin Phursam-la on the roof of the monastery. It was a chilly night, but I had a blanket over my sleeping bag and no bedbugs to bother me. The moonlight cascaded its rays on the looming, sandy mountains and the stars twinkled in the clear, dark sky like diamonds scattered on black velvet. This sight was so intoxicatingly beautiful that I lay awake for a long time. Eventually, I fell into a deep sleep and did not wake until the early morning gong chimed, calling the monks to the prayer hall.

We returned to Piang at the end of the tour, and the lama dances took place. Tongden Rinpoche, the head lama of the Drikung Kagyu monasteries in Ladakh, was the main dancer. Short and stout, he wore a black hat costume. The deer dancers leapt through the air with alacrity, and the clowns made everyone laugh. These dances are meant to show the triumph of good over evil, and to illustrate the necessity of freeing ourselves from afflictions or obstructions to peace and happiness. The dance is very spiritual, and the dancers must transform themselves into the deities and beings they represent. After the dances, the teachings took place.

I was proud and happy to see my brother sitting so majestically on his high throne, giving teachings to the several hundred people who had come for this special occasion. The day of the Powa teachings was very busy. The Drikung teachers are famous for this particular practice, which focuses on the transference of the consciousness. At death, one should be able to transfer the subtle consciousness to a higher realm or be reborn in a better form. It is the path to enlightenment. During the teaching, a number of people fell unconscious. It was said that their consciousnesses had left their bodies by the power of the teaching.

The next day, it was time for me to begin my journey home. The trip to Ladakh had been a wonderful adventure—a very interesting and spiritual experience. For a few days, I was transported back to the Tibet of my childhood. It was nice to be in the company of my parents and my brothers, but I missed my sister very much. Her husband would not let her travel without him, and he would not have been able to adapt to the monastic life we lived during this trip. My parents, both being smokers, had enough trouble adapting. They were only allowed to smoke in the confines of their room. The monks did not like smoking in the monastery, but my parents would not walk down the numerous steps to light a cigarette and then climb up again and they could not live without their cigarettes. Usually, women were not allowed to sleep in the monastery, but because we were Rinpoche's mother and sister, we were privileged to stay in these ancient quarters.

Returning to Dharamsala, I found my son covered with purple spots; he had contracted scabies. I learned that Tenzin was too shy to show the first spots to the nurses, so they spread until his body was covered with sores. A kind clinic volunteer named

Karma Lhundup treated him with purple ointment. Other than this incident, the children had fared quite well. Lobsang had written a few letters to say that all was well.

I missed Lobsang, but I kept busy with my religious studies with Geshe Samdup-la. When I felt lonely or empty, I visited His Holiness's old tutor, Kyabje Ling Rinpoche. Ling Rinpoche would insist I stay for a cup of tea. He would ask questions about my family and make jokes. Then he would ask me if I minded his jokes, because sometimes he made sarcastic remarks. I guess he wanted to study my reaction. I don't know how I could be upset with such a kind, holy man. Just spending time with him left me elated, calm, and cheerful.

Finally, Lobsang returned. It was good to have him home, but he was a changed man. He was in despair over the condition of life for Tibetans in Tibet. He said that the Chinese had made the Tibetans a community of slaves and beggars. Wherever he went, he noticed that only the Tibetans who worked in Chinese offices were decently clothed. Lobsang brought photos of hundreds of people from all parts of Tibet—Kham, Amdo, and Central Tibet, and he was able to make contacts with their families in India or abroad. I was amazed at the number of people he had met. Lobsang said he had slept only three or four hours a night because of the constant flow of visitors.

As time passed, Lobsang grew more despondent. He could not forget what he had seen in Tibet. They were placing so much hope on the Tibetans in exile. "What can we do for these people?" was the question on Lobsang's mind, day and night. Sometimes we would both weep. Often, Lobsang would say that we ought to return to Tibet to toil with our people on our own land for the future of Tibet. I was very happy when he was appointed director of the Tibetan Medical and Astrological Institute. With a job and responsibilities, Lobsang would be busy and not brood over his visit to Tibet. We needed to make some money, because we had been living off our savings from the States.

When Lobsang became director of the Institute, I was appointed to take care of the English correspondence. We started our new jobs in April of 1980, and moved into a small lodging house near the Institute in the town of McLeod Ganj. We rented two rooms, and shared a bathroom with the other tenants. Chuki lived with us, but Tenzin remained at the Children's Village, living in the boys' hostel. It was even difficult to get him home on weekends. He was the basketball star, on the school soccer team, and had a number of good friends. There was always lots going on at the Children's Village.

The Tibetan Medical Center was a small, three-storied building just below our lodge. The top floor housed the consultation rooms, the office, and the medicine-dispensing and store room. The second floor was the pharmacy, where the medicines were made. The ingredients for the medicines were dried and stored there. The ground level served as the staff quarters.

My job was to reply to the letters of patients who wanted to take Tibetan medicines. These individuals would detail their ailments in their letters, and the doctors would diagnose the problem and mail the medicines. I remember the particular case of a woman in Germany. She suffered from so many problems, and I don't know how Dr. Tamdin was able to diagnose her sickness. He prescribed medicines, she recovered, and we received a most gracious letter from her. We had corresponded with her for about six months when we received a lovely photo taken at her wedding. She said that she was now very well, and that without our help she would never have had a wedding.

Tibetan medicine was not as well known in those days as it is now. It is an ancient form of healing, an amalgamation of Greek, Indian, Persian, Chinese, and indigenous Tibetan practices, which was recorded in a text known as "The Four Medical Tantras." The medicines are made from herbs, minerals, precious gems, and animal extracts that were naturally dried or heated and then pulverized. Besides dispensing medicines, the physicians would recommend prayers and advise their patients on diet, lifestyle, and spirituality; or carry out special treatments, including medicinal baths, moxibustion, golden needle therapy, and massage.

Because the Institute was also responsible for conducting astrological calculations, I had to help with the translations. For each individual, we read from the time of birth to the time of death. I asked a number of people how accurate they found the calculations. As most people found the readings very accurate, I also made my own readings, and I must say that things have come very close to the events noted in my horoscope.

Our astrologers recommend prayers and religious activities for Buddhists, to ward off obstructions and illnesses. For non-Buddhists, we advise people to give aid to the poor and needy, to prevent animals from being killed, and to do meritorious work for the benefit of others.

We were very involved with our work in our own Tibetan community and felt a true sense of purpose. I felt especially happy when patients were healed after writing Dr. Tamdin about their illnesses. If Dr. Tamdin could not diagnose a case, I consulted the Dalai Lama's physician, Dr. Jamyang Tashi. Dr. Tashi was an elderly physician and was always laughing. If he ran across a serious condition, he would say, "Azhi Azhi," and get very concerned. He took great care in examining patients.

I am very grateful to Dr. Tashi, who was very attentive to me when I got sick. I had a severe backache due to a gynecological problem, which Tibetan medicine did not help. I went to Delhi for a checkup and the allopathic physician wanted me to undergo a small operation to cauterize a cyst on my cervix. It was a minor operation. When I awoke from the anesthesia, my aunt Daisy was visiting me in the ward with her husband, Gelek Rinpoche. She said I was crying and saying, "Doctor, people in Tibet are suffering so much." Aunt Daisy said my eyes were wide open, yet I did not seem to recognize anyone. The doctor kept telling me that the operation was over, and that I was not suffering.

During this incident, I remember awaking with Gelek Rinpoche holding my hand and praying. I saw my aunt standing at the end of the bed. The prayers and the presence of the familiar faces relaxed me enough to realize where I was. I felt drained of energy and asked Rinpoche to hand me my rosary, which had been blessed by a number of high lamas.

There was some publication work I had to wind up for the Institute, so I needed to get back. The journey to Dharamsala was very stressful, because I had made a mistake with my ticket and had to change coaches just before the train was about to leave. After I arrived home, I took a bath and was struck by a sudden, sharp headache. I took two aspirin, and then fainted in the kitchen. My husband was nearby and caught me before I hit the floor. When I woke, he was holding my hand. Dr. Tashi came and was very disturbed. He said that there was a severe disturbance in my wind energy systems, and that there was an imbalance in my life-supporting wind channel. He burnt some powdered medicine, gave me some pills, and I fell asleep for a short period.

Over the next two weeks, Dr. Tashi came to see me every day to help me combat the pain on the inside of my palms, as well as the dull, deep pain in the center of my chest. Worst of all, I could not sleep. When I slept for brief periods, I had dreams of hundreds of Tibetans with outstretched hands, shouting for help. I would wake with exhaustion and a feeling of helplessness. Only the reciting of the "Mani" mantra and my rosaries calmed me enough to lie still without waking my poor husband. The shock of hearing what was going on in Tibet, as well as the stress of the last few months, had broken me mentally. After His Holiness returned from a trip abroad, I had an audience with him, and that seemed to calm me. I was also introduced to a very kind Indian psychiatrist in Dharamsala, who prescribed some modern medicines. The Tibetan medicines were too gentle for my trauma. With the blessings of His Holiness, Dr. Khanna's medicines, Dr. Tashi's daily visits, and Lobsang's and Chuki's loving care, I recovered slowly. It took me a couple of months to regain my strength and begin working again. During the worst period of my depression, I thought that I would never be able to function as a normal person. I worried about remaining in a vegetative state and becoming a burden to my family. My husband and daughter were very patient. My mother-in-law, who was herself not in very good health, urged me to visit her when I felt better. When I did, she told me that I must eat. She said, "You are sick, so you have no appetite for food. Just force yourself to eat, because you need to regain your strength." I shall never forget her wise advice.

I resumed my work at the Tibetan Medical Institute and continued my dharma lessons. I needed a teacher closer to home. Unsure about how to go about finding one, Lobsang suggested that I seek the advice of Serkhong Tsenshab Rinpoche. I took this advice and approached Serkhong Rinpoche about introducing me to a good teacher. I told him, "I know so little of the dharma, so I do not want a teacher who is a scholar; I would like to learn from a practitioner of the dharma." I also told him that I would never be able to understand a teacher from Kham or Amdo, as I spoke the Central Tibetan dialect, and dharma language is quite different from colloquial speech. Rinpoche was kind to inform me that he would teach me. I could not believe my luck. I was so excited that I forgot to ask him when I should return to start my lessons. After a few days, I went back to visit him to inquire when our lessons would begin. I was served a delicious cup of butter tea, and after asking me about my family background and which scriptures I had studied, Rinpoche said he would let me know when I should return for my classes. I waited patiently. I went to see him again, and then I waited and waited. One day I told Lobsang, "Serkhong Rinpoche said he would give me teachings, but he has not told me when. Is it possible that he does not have the time to teach me?" Lobsang said that Rinpoche must be testing me to make sure I was really serious about my dharma studies, and that I should go and see him again. On the next visit, Serkhong Rinpoche gave me a time when I should return with the text for "The Three Principal Aspects of the Path." This was a relatively short text, but Rinpoche taught in detail and I studied under him for almost a year. He made it very clear that I should not take time off from my work for the dharma teachings, because my work was very beneficial to the sick. If my work was motivated by a desire to help suffering people, then it was as good as receiving instruction and practicing the dharma. I studied with him after work and during holidays.

Serkhong Rinpoche was responsible for my great enthusiasm and positive approach to my work and my attitude toward life. Rinpoche was a very good teacher, and he always came to the assistance of anyone who approached him for divinations, prayers, or visits to the sick. A fleshy man in his late sixties, Rinpoche had a head shaped like a soccer ball and many lines running up and down his face. His roly-poly frame shook when he laughed, and he laughed often. Sometimes, I could not hold my laughter, and we would both laugh in mutual outbursts of joy. When he talked about the sufferings of people, it often brought tears to his eyes. He was very skilled at keeping me optimistic, joyful, and looking forward to the future.

Rinpoche did not believe in extremes. Once he said, "Look at this mug of tea. If I drink one mug now, it satisfies me. If I drink two mugs, I am being greedy, and it may not be good for my health. If I do not drink anything from this mug, it is also not good for my body and I shall feel thirsty after talking to you. This is the same in whatever you want in life. Do not go to extremes." I shall never be able to repay this great teacher for all he taught me. Unfortunately, after sponsoring a Kalachakra teaching by His Holiness, he passed away.

16   Wheel of Life

Tibet finally opened up to the world after two decades of deep silence. The bamboo curtain had been lifted, and we began hearing of the horrors that had taken place during so many years of silence. We heard from the family members we had left behind. Crossing endless mountains, people came from all over Tibet to reunite with family members in India and Nepal. Some even traveled as far as Europe, Canada, and the United States. Parents were meeting young men and women who were the small children they had left behind in Tibet twenty years earlier. There were the husbands or wives who finally found their spouses after all these years of separation, only to find that they had remarried. There were also cases of relatives from Tibet who had lived through much hardship and had expected some financial assistance from their family members in exile, only to learn that these relatives were refugees and barely making ends meet themselves. Family reunions were not always joyful. Loved ones had become strangers. In one way or another, most Tibetan families experienced the repercussions of the long, forced separations.

These visitors from Tibet traveled to be blessed by the Dalai Lama, and many older people said that they were finally at peace now after seeing the face of His Holiness. They felt that they were ready to leave this world when the time came for their final departure.

Lobsang and I both had relatives who came to India during this time. First among the visitors were my cousins Jigme and

Kunsang Taring. Jigme and Kunsang were our closest cousins—children of my aunt Betty Taring. Aunt Betty and Uncle George were both in India when the Tibetan revolt broke out, and the children were in Lhasa with their grandparents. The grandparents had to flee the fighting in Lhasa in 1959, leaving the small children with their great-grandmother.

I went to Dehra Dun to meet my cousins at the Taring House in Rajpur. It was a cold winter evening when I reached the house. I climbed up the steps to the veranda, and walked into the living room where Mola was deep in conversation with Jigme-la. They did not notice that I had entered the room. Jigme-la was facing the door, and when he looked up, he hesitated, uncertain whether he should greet me or keep sitting. As I was traveling, I was not wearing my Tibetan costume, but a pair of blue jeans and a sweater, and so he did not recognize me. When I exclaimed, "Jigme-la!" he replied, "Acha Namgyal Lhamo-la." We stared at each other, and we were both in tears. Mola came over and hugged me, and I could not contain my emotions. During this tearful and joyful moment, Pola walked into the room, followed by Kunsang-la. We hugged, and more tears were shed by everyone.

It had been twenty-three years. I remember Kunsang-la as a chubby little girl of three or four. Now, she was a young woman. She was dressed in black, baggy pants with a loose sweater. Her hair was in a plait, and she wore no trace of make-up, like the women of China so often seen in magazines. She was now a mother of two young boys, and the younger son was with her. Jigme-la was a couple of years older than Kunsang-la. The cute little Jigme-la I knew was still petite, but he was very thin. He also looked sad and tired, years older than his age.

I felt like we were meeting each other in another lifetime. We talked and talked about our family members in Tibet and in exile, and it was sad to learn that their oldest sister, Nordon-la, who had often played with Norzin and me, had died. She was sent to Chamdo in Kham during the Cultural Revolution, and there she died in childbirth, leaving two small girls behind.

My cousins had suffered much because of their background. They were innocent children, but they came from an aristocratic family. Their parents and grandparents were in exile in India, so they were labeled as the children of reactionaries and traitors. Jigme-la was not allowed to get a higher education, and Kunsang-la was denied any schooling. We spent four days catching up on the news of our lives, reminiscing, laughing, crying and feeling so happy just to be together.

My cousins planned to visit me in Dharamsala because they wanted to meet His Holiness the Dalai Lama before they returned to Tibet. Their family members were waiting for their return. I am sure that they were kept in Tibet as hostages to ensure that my cousins would return, although my cousins did not say so. Were we to meet again, and if so, when? Wishing farewell was difficult, but I thought that we were all young and that there would come a day when we would see each other again and spend more time together, maybe soon in Tibet.

Many Tibetans arrived in India and Nepal. A large number of children remained in India to study at Tibetan schools because they could receive a better education in exile. I noticed that the newcomers were suspicious and temperamental. It took a very long time for these visitors from Tibet to smile, talk freely, and be open about their feelings. They needed time and understanding from others in order to heal.

Among the newcomers, a very learned Tibetan physician also arrived. As Gyalyum, my mother-in-law, was not well, Lobsang requested the Chinese authorities to allow her former physician, Dr. Tenzin Choedrak, to come to India to treat her. What great news it was when we learned that he had been granted permission to come to India. Gyalyum's younger sister and husband visited her from Tibet as well. Hearing news of the conditions in Tibet and seeing no chance of an immediate return, my mother-in-law's spirits and health deteriorated. She was quite weak and depressed when Dr. Choedrak arrived in Dharamsala at the end of 1980.

To see this physician was living proof of how Tibetan people had suffered under the Chinese. Dr. Choedrak was a simple man from a humble background who cared only for his medical profession. He was a monk, and one of the best physicians among the junior doctors at Mentsi-khang, the Tibetan Medical Center in Lhasa, prior to the Chinese occupation. In the early 1950s, he was the assistant to the Dalai Lama's physician, Dr. Khenrab Norbu. In 1959, he was accused of being a spy. The Chinese tried to force him to condemn His Holiness for deeds His Holiness had not committed. Dr. Choedrak would not lie to avoid punishment and imprisonment. He was a man of principles, so he was imprisoned. He said, "Anyone in Tibet who had an important position in the community or who had a profession was sent to labor camps, tortured, and imprisoned. They tried to weaken our spirits, so that we would become Chinese puppets."

Dr. Choedrak was sent to Chuchen, a mass labor camp on the border of northeast Tibet and China. About seventy-five men were sent to this camp, but only twenty-three returned to Lhasa. They were starved and put to hard labor. If they got sick and were too weak to survive, they were hospitalized. When they were better, they were once again put back in the camps to toil. They had to go through this torture again and again.

Dr. Choedrak was beaten so badly that one of his eyeballs had been dislocated. His teeth were knocked out during one of these beating sessions. Before he could treat anyone, he needed immediate medical attention and a new set of dentures. Despite going through such hardship and having had no occasion to practice his profession, he was anxious to get back to practicing medicine. He was a skilled healer. Patients lined up at the Medical Center, and his reputation spread far and wide. These days Dr. Choedrak is the Dalai Lama's senior physician, and he travels all over the world and receives many honors for his good work.

My uncle Phuntsok was a sad case. He returned to Tibet just before the Tibetan revolt against the Chinese in 1959. Because he was a Tibetan government official involved in the revolt, and because he had studied in an English school in India, he was imprisoned for almost twenty years. He was with Dr. Choedrak in Chuchen. Phuntsok would be sitting near us, but his thoughts were somewhere far away. He would not talk to us about his life. He would sit silently, smoking one cigarette after another. Often, he had a dazed look about him. When we questioned him about his health or his life in Tibet, his eyes would dart around the room in fear, as he relayed bits and pieces of his experience. His concentration would lapse every five to ten minutes. Then, he would put both his hands on his bowed head and draw away from the world. He was at a loss for words, and his mind had gone blank. We stopped asking him questions, but we could see that his past suffering was consuming him. He feared to tell us his story, because he was sure the Chinese would hear him and retaliate by punishing or imprisoning him again. We pieced his story together from others who knew him.

The Chinese had tried to break the spirit of our people. There were people like my uncle who were so defeated that it took every effort for them to heal and be normal again. Fortunately, my uncle survived. He is now married and has plans for the future. He was one of the lucky ones.

January of 1981 was a cold, depressing month. January is always one of the coldest periods in Dharamsala. When the snow fell on the higher peaks of the mountains, we were left in a dull, melancholy state. A hazy sunlight would try its best to shine through the heavy, dark curtain of clouds, but it was in vain. During this sad month, Gyalyum was quite ill. She had a cough with much phlegm and had difficulty clearing her lungs. She could not rest.

A few days before she left us, His Holiness came down to her residence to see her. He told her to meditate on the painting of Mahakala, the family protective deity. He knew that she was dying, and he told her, "You have lived to a good ripe age, and all your life you have helped others, so everything will be all right." The thangka was brought to her bedside from the outer room, and when she looked at the thangka of Gonpo, she became very peaceful.

It was a very sad time for all of us, yet we consoled ourselves with the knowledge that we were fortunate to have had her with us for so long. She was eighty-one years old. Never once did she complain about her illness. Instead, she apologized for causing us extra trouble. She was an extraordinary woman, always thinking of others. On January 12, she died in the arms of my husband. She was missed by everyone who came to know her, but her presence lingers on with beautiful memories.

His Holiness had left for a teaching in Bodh Gaya, but before his departure he had asked his principal secretary to take care of all of Gyalyum's funeral arrangements. He also took care of the prayers for the departed, and the public was asked to recite the "Om Mani Padme Hum" mantra. Of her six surviving children, only Lobsang was present when she left us.

In the meantime, life flowed on for us. Chuki graduated from school with a first division and honors in French. We sent her to a small college in Darjeeling, fearing she would be lost in a big city. Loreto College was a reputable girls' college, well known in Northern India, and we were happy that her guardian, my sister-in-law Chutan Thondup, lived in Darjeeling. My parents lived in Kalimpong and were not too far away. I had spent twelve happy years at Mount Hermon School in Darjeeling and thought that Chuki would be just as happy in this lovely hill station. However, it was the first time Chuki had been away from home and she was miserable. We used to get letters from her complaining about the food and the miserable, tiny room she had to share with two other girls. One day she wrote that she had a bad flu; next we heard that she was suffering from an eye infection, and before too long, she turned up in Dharamsala. What a surprise! She told Acha Chutan that she would rather die than stay in Darjeeling. Poor Acha-la was so upset that she bought Chuki a plane ticket to Delhi and packed her home. Not long after, we took Chuki to Chandigarh, where she completed her studies in psychology at the Government College for Women.

Lobsang and I were busy at the Tibetan Medical Center, which was growing quite large with the arrival of several good physicians from Tibet. Patients came from all over India, and some even traveled from abroad to seek cures from our physicians for their various ailments. With the arrival of more patients came the need for more medicines, so more ingredients had to be bought. More students were interested in studying Tibetan medicine, and the small medical school needed upgrading. We were really very, very busy.

Tenzin soon joined Chuki at Chandigarh University for his pre-university degree, and the following year joined the prestigious St. Stephen's College for Boys at Delhi University. He was on the college basketball team and was very active in the Tibetan Youth Association. The youth were engaged in social work among Tibetan communities and in the struggle for Tibetan independence. There were a small number of these youth who were impatient with the slow approach toward removing Chinese domination. Opposed to the peaceful, nonviolent stand taken by His Holiness the Dalai Lama and the Tibetan government, they wanted to take a more hard-line approach. A few of Tenzin's friends were among a group of young Tibetans who thought that we should follow the policy of the Palestinians, who were drawing world attention to their struggle by hijacking planes and taking hostages. At times I understood their frustrations, but these measures were not rational. The world is tired of violence and destruction. We need methods that do not cause more suffering for people. This is the belief followed by the Dalai Lama.

Both my children used to participate in student demonstrations in front of the Chinese Embassy. I remember one such incident that caused me great apprehension. Lobsang and I were in Delhi for work, and we had been trying to contact the children. We learned that they had both been imprisoned after joining a group of Tibetans in a demonstration over the visit of a Chinese dignitary to India. After a few telephone calls, trying to locate where Chuki and Tenzin were, we were told by the staff at the Tibetan Bureau that the girls had been rounded up and detained in a stadium on the outskirts of the city. Lobsang and I took a scooter and dashed to this place, finding no one in sight. There were a couple of people standing near the gate who told us that a group of Tibetan demonstrators had been taken to Tihar jail. Of course, we raced there only to be told to return the next morning as visiting time was over.

At that time my cousin Paljor Dorji from Bhutan happened to be in Delhi, accompanying the King of Bhutan on an official visit. We spoke to him and when he heard that my daughter was in Tihar, he said, "Namlha, Tihar jail is where all the hard-core criminals are put, and people like Charles Sobraj, the infamous serial killer, are there. This is no place for a young girl; you must get her out immediately. If there is anything I can do, please phone me." Of course, I was really worried after this phone call. I must say that Lobsang and I did not sleep very well that night.

When we reached the huge bolted gates of Tihar the next morning and got ourselves stamped on the wrist with blue ink, we were led into the visitors' room. I felt like a criminal. It took some time for Chuki to come out, and the police officers were very consoling. One warden said, "We are treating them well; please don't worry. You should be proud that your daughter is in the same ward Indira Gandhi stayed in, but please tell these girls to eat. They are not eating their meals and who in the outside world will even know if they are protesting and not eating in these cells."

I heard the clang of chains, and Chuki appeared from some inner room. When she saw us, she started crying. So did I. We told her that her cousin was eager to get her out of the prison if she wished to come out, but Chuki said that she could not leave unless all the women were let out. I felt very proud of my daughter. We urged her and her friends to eat. They told us that one of the monk leaders from the demonstration had told the crowd to refuse food in the prison.

We went to see Tenzin in the men's ward, and shortly thereafter all of the Tibetans were released from prison. Tenzin was imprisoned five times during such demonstrations, and we continued to receive notices from college mentioning that his attendance was poor because of youth meetings that were taking up a lot of his time. I had to tell him that it was not easy for us to meet his college expenses, and we could not afford it if he was to be kept back in class. We told him that he could always continue his struggle for Tibetan independence when he finished his studies; his reply was, "You should be proud of your children who are fighting for Tibet." Lobsang and I were proud, but we had to make sure that their studies were not neglected as we were paying the college bills.

Chuki had grown up to be a beautiful young woman. She had graduated from college and was attending a secretarial school in Delhi. There were so many marriage proposals for her that she was becoming slightly annoyed. We did not know that she had met an Indian boy from Himachal Pradesh during her stay in college at Chandigarh. Raj Mahant was from Manali and was a friend of Tenzin. He was a quiet, serious young man. Their courtship was not an easy task for Chuki. Many of the Tibetan boys in college and the Tibetan population were unhappy that she was serious about an Indian boy. They felt that Chuki, being the niece of the Dalai Lama, should be an example to other young Tibetan people. A marriage with a foreigner would encourage more Tibetans to court non-Tibetans, and as China was committing genocide with abortions and restrictions on population growth in Tibet, our young Tibetans in exile should marry people of their own race. I decided to send Chuki abroad for a year to Germany, so that she could get over this young man. Raj was also a Hindu Brahmin from an orthodox family, and his father and relatives were not too happy about him marrying a non-Hindu.

Lobsang had become a different man since his trip to Tibet. He had become despondent and quiet. The cheerful, optimistic, and funny side of his character was gone. His health was not very good, although a recent medical examination had revealed that he was quite fit. He had begun to drink in excess, and I was not too happy about this abuse of alcohol. When I tried to talk to Lobsang about this habit, he used to tell me that when he drank in the company of his friends, he forgot his worries and felt happy. Of course, this was not the way to face problems. We had no personal disagreements, the children were doing well in their studies, but his concern was for the future of Tibet. The present situation there gave him little reason for hope.

In the summer of 1985, we had just purchased and furnished a house in Delhi which would serve as a Tibetan medical clinic. We were on our way back to Dharamsala after six weeks of running around in the heat of Delhi. Lobsang was a perfectionist, and always wanted things well organized. He was meticulous about his work. We were both very tired, and just before we were to take the bus up to Dharamsala, His Holiness arrived in Delhi after a trip abroad. He asked Lobsang to travel with him by train. I left Delhi with two of our colleagues and was happy to have Lobsang leave for Dharamsala with Kundun, traveling in a special compartment. The compartment was comfortable and spacious, the service good, and Lobsang would get a good rest. Later I learned that he had cancelled his trip at the last minute because he wanted to follow up on the pending matter of purchasing land for building a hospital for the Institute. The Indian government official involved with this work met Lobsang on the day of his departure for Dharamsala, and he was told that the officer would be available to see him in ten days.

Ten days had turned into two weeks, and I was worried. One night I had a dream of Lobsang calling me, and he seemed to be in a very anxious state. I feared that something was wrong with him. I rushed to my sister-in-law Pema's home and called Chuki, who was in Delhi. Chuki told me that Lobsang had a bad flu and had moved to my sister-in-law's apartment after consulting a physician. I could not concentrate on my work on Monday morning. I had never had such an anxiety attack. I called Achala, and she said that Lobsang had seen a doctor that morning. He was diagnosed as suffering from jaundice. When I spoke to Lobsang, he did not sound bad, but I decided to take the bus to Delhi that same night.

I reached Delhi the next morning and found Lobsang reading a daily newspaper in the living room, dressed in the white, cotton Indian pajama suit I had brought him from Bombay. He was surprised to see me. He got up from the chair, came towards me, and hugged me tightly. We were both in tears. He looked weak and thin. I asked him why he did not inform me about his health, and he had no reply. After my arrival, he ate his food in his bedroom. He, like his mother, never wished to burden others. He was taking Tibetan medicine that was good for liver ailments before Dr. Kunga Ngarongshar came to diagnose him. His urine was the color of strong tea. On the third day after my arrival, Lobsang refused to take his pills. He began pushing us away when we came near him, and he refused to eat. Our cook, my brother Jigme, and I took Lobsang to the Holy Family Hospital. It was late in the evening when we arrived, and the senior physicians had all returned home. The physician in residence and two interns and two nurses could not handle him. He was so weak before he came to the hospital, and now five strong people could not hold him down to give him an injection.

I stayed with Lobsang in the emergency ward that night. I have never had such a difficult and agonizing night in my life. Lobsang could not pass urine. He was in severe pain, and he was violent if anyone touched him. The doctors tied him to the bed, saying he was dangerous. I pleaded with them to do something to lessen his pain, but they said they could not do anything until the chief physician came the following morning. When I was left alone with Lobsang, I untied the bandages they had used to tie him to the bed. He was sweating profusely and crying out for help. I pressed a wet towel to his forehead and recited "Mani" mantras in his ear, which seemed to calm him for a couple of hours. It was torment for me to hear Lobsang scream in pain. I was helpless. There was no place to lie down, so I tried to rest my legs by sleeping on the floor on a blanket I had carried from home. The ground was too hard. Moreover, I was so anxious and worried that I could not sit still. The nurses could do nothing without the doctor's permission, and they were busy and just as helpless as I was. I walked the corridors and helped the night nurse in the emergency ward by giving water to the helpless, suffering patients who wanted a drink. Only my prayers got me through the night. I recited different mantras and visualized the different deities to keep my mind off of Lobsang's agony.

The next morning, the senior physician arrived and gave Lobsang an injection that eased his pain and relaxed him enough for the nurse to pass a catheter to empty his bladder. The doctor told me that he was doubtful Lobsang would pull through to survive his ailment, which the doctor suspected was hepatitis. He was transferred to another medical institute in the late morning, where the doctor's diagnosis was confirmed.

Lobsang never woke from his sleep. He lay peacefully in his bed for thirteen days before he left us. On the day he died, his sister Pema, and Chuki, Tenzin, and I reached the hospital at about the same time from different corners of Delhi. Chuki and I were near his bed. It seemed he had been waiting for us to say good-bye.

I washed his body with holy water that His Holiness had sent from Dharamsala and was assisted by Tashi Tsering who had been sent from His Holiness's private office to help me. Chuki and I had just brought his white pajamas, fresh from the laundry. We dressed him in this suit and Doboom Rinpoche from Tibet House came to recite the Powa prayer, the last rites of the dead, so that Lobsang could soon be reborn to a better rebirth.

Life is so fragile. Lobsang was a young man of fifty-three, full of life, who had passed a thorough medical examination a couple of months back with the doctor saying, "He is a very fit man!" Three weeks before, Lobsang was full of vitality, and now he was gone. Throughout Lobsang's life, changes had happened so unexpectedly. We planned things, but things never ran according to our plans. His death, too, was quite unexpected. If it had not been for the Buddhist teachings on coming face to face with the realities of life and the meditations and prayers I had engaged in over the past years, I would have been another patient in the hospital. Lobsang and I were so close. Many times we thought of the same things or started to speak the same words at the same time. Our friends used to say that they could never imagine Lobsang and I without each other, and now I was alone to face life without my other half. I felt as if part of my body had been taken away. It was a very painful period for me. I was only forty-three years old, with two children who needed assistance and support as they entered adulthood.

Lobsang was cremated in Dharamsala, and the prayers kept us all occupied for some time. He was missed very much. At times I was overcome by my grief. One day, His Holiness was giving a teaching in the temple, and my mother insisted that I go to these teachings. She said, "What is the use of meeting all the visitors and repeating the story of Lobsang's death over and over again and crying? It is better that you go up and listen to His Holiness's sermon. This will help you now. Pema and I will meet all the callers who come to offer their condolences."

The teachings and the prayers were comforting, and my grief was lessened by this event. Concerned relatives and friends insisted that I should have my daughter with me for a year to keep me company at home. I had never lived alone in my life, but I did not want to burden my daughter with my despair. She had her own grief. She was very close to her father. Moreover, she needed to get through her studies and keep her mind occupied. I also thought that this was the best way to practice the teachings I had taken in these past years. I was going through the sufferings of this life, and the only way to avoid these samsaric sufferings in the wheel of life was to follow the teachings of the Lord Buddha.

I then realized that the saying of one of our learned Buddhist teachers was so true. Shantideva said, "If you want happiness, think of the welfare of others; if you want suffering, think of the welfare of yourself." The sorrier I felt for myself, the more intense my grief. When I thought of others, even making a cup of tea for a visitor or inquiring about someone else's health, it helped me to think less of my own problems.

The prayers held every seventh day for the departed also helped me deal with my grief. The prayers required a great deal of preparation, which left less time for sorrow. We Buddhists believe that after the forty-ninth day of death, one leaves the *bardo*, the world between life and death, and is reborn. A life of goodness and benefit to others leads to rebirth in a better form. A life that causes suffering or harm to others leads to rebirth in a lower form.

After Lobsang's cremation, the staff of the Tibetan Medical and Astrological Institute urged me to take Lobsang's place as director. I did not think I could handle such a responsibility, and I turned down their request. I was willing to work with a new director in the same capacity I had worked in earlier. The staff members would not listen to my pleas, and they sent a letter to His Holiness and to members of the Kashag requesting that I take up the director's post. I finally had to request my spiritual teacher to do a divination. When my teacher advised me to take the position, I gave my best to the work until I was transferred to the Department of Health in 1989.

The day I had to move my belongings from my desk to Lobsang's desk was a very painful occasion. I could not keep myself from crying. Gadong Loden-la, the General Secretary of the Institute, walked in a couple of times and walked straight out after seeing me in tears. Rosette Jean, a tiny, elderly French lady with a warm heart happened to walk into my office to inquire about becoming a member of the Institute, and when she asked me what was wrong, I poured out my story and sorrows, and the heavy lump from deep inside me just melted away. I felt much better. Rosette Jean said, "Mrs. Taklha, this is the best occasion to think on the dharma." She was a Buddhist, and she saved me from much pain that day.

An entirely new chapter in my life began. Now I was also alone for the first time. I had always had family members, servants and school friends to live with, and later Lobsang was with me. Now I had many challenges to face, including responsibilities at work and raising two children. They were yet to be settled in life and needed guidance. It was a great learning process. I always try to look at the positive side to life, and make the best of every situation. There is always a rainbow after a dull, dreary monsoon.

One morning I woke up and noticed a bright light beaming through the curtain of my bedroom window. I walked out onto my small veranda in the cold, winter morning air. In the dark, silvery sky, the stars sparkled, and a new moon was beaming down from the east. Below the moon, the orange rays of the sun blazed behind the serene dark mountains, ready to welcome a new day. The Dhauladhar ranges were covered with a powdery, white snow that looked so pure and clear. I was thankful to wake up to such a beautiful sight and glad to be alive.

17 Hollywood

After Lobsang's death, I kept myself busy with my work and my Buddhist studies. Eventually I took a new position in the Department of Health of the Tibetan government-in-exile. This job involved looking after the health care of the Tibetan people in India and Nepal, setting up training for health workers and other health staff, writing a draft for a Tibetan national health policy, giving health education on my visits to the Tibetan settlements, and making sure that adequate health care and sanitation requirements were met.

After five years of writing and visiting each other, Chuki and Raj resolved not to marry anyone if they could not marry each other. I relented, and Chuki and Raj married in October, 1988. Raj Mahant is a very kind and responsible young man, and I feel I have gained another son. On October 8, 1989, I became a grandmother. Raj and Chuki's first son was born in the small Mission Hospital in Manali. I was there to experience this miracle. Unlike the days when I had my children, the father and other family members were allowed in the delivery room. I watched in awe as the tiny baby was bathed, weighed, bundled up, and then handed over to the mother. There were none of the old segregated baby rooms, with the father longing to hold his baby in his arms. Raju decided to name the baby boy Siddhartha. Soon, another grandson, Atisha, was born. I was also with Chuki during this birth.

In the summer of 1994, I returned to Europe for a brief visit. Professor Heinrich Harrer had opened a Tibetan Museum and built a *lingkhor*, a Buddhist religious path, in his hometown in the Austrian Alps, and he had invited me to open the first stage of the lingkhor. I had not been back to Europe since 1987, and was very excited. When I arrived at the Vienna airport and walked out of customs to enter the domestic lounge, I was surprised to be greeted with a "Tashi Delek!" Lost for words, I looked around and found a young Tibetan man amongst the strangers. He was later joined by the president of the Austrian Tibetan community, Ms. Tseten Zockbauer, a Tibetan woman who was married to an Austrian rock singer. They had come to welcome me to Austria. They urged me to stay a day or so in Vienna, but Harrer and his wife Karina wanted me to join them immediately.

Professor Harrer and a friend met me at the tiny airport in Klagenfurt and drove me to Huttenberg. Coming out of the airport, I was greeted by a huge placard of my grandfather, Tsarong Pola, which was pasted on the windows of the airport to advertise the Harrer Museum. This was a touching and unexpected welcome!

We drove alongside clear streams and passed tall pine trees and herds of cows in meadows, when suddenly we were in the middle of a Tibetan landscape. There was the lingkhor with prayer flags fluttering in the wind, a majestic stone chorten built at the foot of the hills, the Guru Rinpoche statue, the Goddess Tara carved on the rock, Mani stones, and the crystal chorten sitting on the top of the mountain! I felt like I was in Tibet. Tibet had given Harrer a home, and now he was helping to preserve the culture and art of our people. I felt very grateful.

From Austria, I flew on to New York, where I was to meet with the famous movie director, Martin Scorsese, and the screenwriter Melissa Mathison Ford, the wife of actor Harrison Ford. It was an interesting chain of events that led me to this meeting.

My mother was a very practical woman and always urged me to think of my old age and my retirement needs. She would say, "How much pension will you get from the Tibetan work? We are very proud that you are working hard for the Tibetan cause, but we will die, your children will have to look after their own needs, and if you do not have any money when you get old, who will you turn to for help? You better go and work in the United States, and at least earn your social security."

Lobsang and I had served the Tibetan government all of our adult lives, with the exception of the eight years we spent in the United States. While we were in the States, we had been able to save a little money, which helped us to live a decent, yet simple life in India. Now, I was earning a little over three thousand rupees per month for my service with the Tibetan government-in-exile. I realized that I did not really have a secure future after retirement. I began to get concerned. What if I did need medical attention? Who could I ask for help? With my meager savings, I could end up a burden to my children, and they might not be in a position to help me. After some thought, I decided to take my mother's advice. I wrote to a couple of friends inquiring about employment in the States. Not long after, I was asked if I might be interested in doing research for a Hollywood movie on the life of His Holiness the Fourteenth Dalai Lama. Somehow, this offer seemed unbelievable. Karma was surely working in my favor. Perhaps my working for a good cause had reaped such a result.

It was a great honor to be asked to work on the life of such a holy person. It was also helpful that I would be earning my salary in the States and paying toward my social security while living in India, as the research was to be done here. Without the slightest hesitation, I agreed to work on the project. I got in touch with Melissa Mathison Ford and we set up a meeting with Martin Scorsese.

My friends teased me, "Wow, you are jumping from health to Hollywood!" I was exhilarated, but apprehensive about how to do research on a movie—a Hollywood movie at that! In fact, it had been five or six years since I'd seen a movie. I did not even own a television. When I arrived in New York for the meeting, my son, who was living there at the time, told me, "Now that you are to work with Martin Scorsese, a very famous director, you must see his last movie." Of course, I had no idea who Martin Scorsese was, nor had I seen *ET*, the popular film for which Melissa had written the script. Tenzin thoughtfully rented the video of Scorsese's *The Age of Innocence*. After seeing the film, I knew Martin was going to make a magnificent movie about Tibet.

When I returned to India, I read the script of *Kundun* and spent more time crying than doing any research. Memories of Lhasa, the Norbulingka Palace, attending the opera in the beautiful garden of the summer palace of the Dalai Lama, the glittering roof of the Potala, and so many other vivid memories of my earlier life overcame me each time I turned the page. I thought of my childhood and the loving family and servants who had looked after me. I thought of my aunts and cousins who were still in Tibet, locked under Chinese rule.

I thought of His Holiness the Dalai Lama, in the care of the old monks who replaced his father and mother, and what a tremendous and heavy responsibility he has carried since a very young age. Memories of my mother-in-law, who was so selfless and compassionate, and my late husband Lobsang, who is still with me in spirit, surfaced again and again in the pages of the script. Ultimately, the research became a very personal endeavor, and I experienced a range of emotions—pain, anger, sadness, and of course, great joy. It gave me great peace that people around the world would learn the real story of Tibet.

My research involved finding information that would help make the set and costumes for the movie as authentic as possible. One particularly complex task was to recreate the intricate details of the Potala and Norbulingka Palaces for the set designers. I met with the few remaining people who had actually lived in these palaces in Tibet. One was a monk at Namgyal Monastery and another was His Holiness's retired Religious Master, who had also been a caretaker of a chapel in one of the palaces in Norbulingka. They were unable to provide me with all of the details I needed, and so I worked from articles in Tibetan books and journals. I sketched a rough map of the entire Norbulingka palace and wrote down details of the layout.

One day, I suddenly remembered a photo of my father that was taken when he was very young. He was standing in front of one of the palaces of Norbulingka. I immediately wrote to him asking for this photo and inquiring if he had other photos of

Norbulingka and the Potala. He wrote back, enclosing four or five different photos of Norbulingka and noting "It's strange, I don't know how these photos came among my collection, because I did not take them. I recently found them when I was collecting some old photos of mine for the Tibetan photo archive at Amnye Machen in Dharamsala, so I am sending them for your work." What luck!

I also needed photos and details of the interior of the Potala Palace. Once again I was fortunate—or was some special spirit guiding this project? A cousin of mine had been a member of the renovation team of the Potala Palace, and he had sent my grand-aunt, Rinchen Dolma Taring, a beautiful detailed picture book of the Potala Palace after the renovation had been completed. One day she came to visit me in my retreat cottage at Dehra Dun and said, "My children do not seem to take much interest in research on Tibet, and as you show much interest in Tibet, I would like you to have this book." I could not believe it! I had been desperately searching for this information, and it just fell into my lap. When I told my aunt about my search for such details of the Potala Palace, she replied, "This is very auspicious!"

I had to find out about the characteristics of the people closest to His Holiness, and how the different ceremonies took place. This also meant doing research on the clothing and manners of the Chinese officials. I became completely immersed in the history, culture, customs, art, and people of Tibet. The richness of our traditions and our past astounded me, and made me want to learn more and more. My mind was like a blotting paper, soaking up every ounce of colorful ink.

The only task I found tedious was preparing the map of Norbulingka. The entire map had to be drawn nine times. When I thought I had everything right, someone would remember "one more detail." During the final approval from His Holiness's Chief Secretary, Reverend Tara, he mentioned that I had forgotten the camel shed and a couple of other rooms nearby. I was instructed to make a fresh drawing.

As I gathered the details needed for a particular scene, I would fax them to Melissa in New York. I drew and commissioned many sketches and made copies of many photos from different books.

We even had to have a special video made of the technique for plaiting the senior Tibetan government officials' hair. The only person who remembered this unusual and intricate hairstyle was Taring Mola, who was at the time in her late eighties. My mother was able to assist Taring Mola, as she remembered helping the special hairdresser who used to come to our home in Lhasa to do my father's hair.

Kundun was to be filmed in India. I went with a small crew to Ladakh in search of a location. This was the second location scouting. On the first, I went alone and sent photos and information to Melissa and Barbara De Fina, the producer. With my brother being the head of several monasteries in Ladakh and having influential friends in Leh, it was not too difficult.

On this second trip, we visited almost all of the monasteries in and around Leh. I made a third trip to Ladakh with the line producer, Dante Ferretti, and Melissa in late October. It was freezing. In the mornings, the water pipes were frozen, and water had to be carried to our rooms in buckets from the kitchen. Melissa and I got along very well; she was a wonderful companion.

A second Hollywood movie, on the life of Heinrich Harrer, was being planned by another Hollywood studio, and Jean-Jacques Annaud, a well known French director, was to direct this movie. Harrer's book, *Seven Years in Tibet*, was the inspiration for the movie. When Jean-Jacques and the script writer came to Dharamsala, they came to see me and asked if I would do the research for them. I told them that I was already working on the movie *Kundun*, but as I was laid off from work for a few months, I could help them until work resumed on *Kundun*. Of course, Jean-Jacques wanted me to find out from Melissa if she would agree to this arrangement. I learned from Melissa that they planned to start work on *Kundun* soon, and her team wanted me to continue my work with them.

I was completely oblivious to the workings of Hollywood. I learned that when one movie was planned, sometimes a second studio would make a similar movie. Occasionally, one of the studios would be compelled to stop work on their production. There seemed to be a great deal of cut-throat competition. Fortunately, I did not see too much of this. However, we did encounter one incident on the final scouting trip to Leh. We were about to book the hotel rooms for next summer's tentative shooting, only to discover that the representative from *Seven Years in Tibet* had already booked all the hotel rooms in town, even paying in advance. After this experience, the assistant producer, Dante Ferretti, and I dashed to Varanasi to buy the brocades we needed for the costumes and the set interiors before the other crew got there.

The two major Hollywood movies about Tibet caused great excitement among the Tibetan community worldwide. When Tibetans learned that Hollywood was hiring Tibetans to act in these two movies, many people tried to get work. By this time there was quite a lot of work to be had. My son's good friend Lhundup Dorjee, who was unemployed at the time, was hired to help me. He was to take care of our account, make lists of items needed for the movie, and gather information on people who wanted to be cast in the film. By the last stage of pre-production, he was the assistant to the casting director. By the time we were filming, he had been elevated to an assistant director position.

Martin, Barbara, Dante, Ellen Lewis (the casting director), and Melissa came with the new line producer Laura Fattori and her assistant, Antonio, to see the location sites we had chosen in and around Dharamsala. We had an audience with His Holiness as well, and Melissa asked some questions about the script. She had spent six hours with His Holiness at an earlier meeting.

During our audience, Dante asked His Holiness for some particulars of His Holiness's private rooms in the two palaces, as no other person alive knew how these rooms were furnished. His Holiness asked Dante to return the next afternoon, which was a Sunday. He invited the rest of us to come as well. Martin, Barbara, Ellen, and Melissa were extremely happy to join Dante on this next visit. On this occasion, His Holiness drew the layout of his rooms, including the positions of the bed and windows and furnishings and altars. He enjoyed the whole process of his descriptions. He even described how the mice used to climb down from the bed screen in his Potala bedroom.

As time flew by, we learned from the media about China's objections to the making of the two movies on Tibet. The Chinese were trying to stop the productions. Because of China's objections, we were unable to get approval from India to film there.

We had an Indian movie agent in Delhi who was pursuing the permit for shooting the film in India. After four months of waiting, the Indian government told the agent that due to the present circumstances, they would have to postpone issuing a permit, as the general elections were coming up soon. Hollywood could not wait this long, so it was decided that the movie would be shot in Ouarzazate, Morocco, a small town high in the Atlas Mountains where Martin had shot one of his most controversial movies, on the life of Jesus Christ.

Soon I had to leave for Morocco to work with the designer, the wardrobe head, and their crew on designing the set and creating the costumes, jewelry, and hairstyles. I also worked with the assistant directors to calculate the numbers of people required for a particular scene and to prepare the details of our customs during official meetings or ceremonies.

I flew from New Delhi to Riyadh in Saudi Arabia. In the beautiful glow of the orange and yellow sunset that was set against a steel blue horizon, the plane glided down into the brown, arid desert. The airport was shaped like a castle from *The Thousand and One Nights*, and the view was so beautiful that I was sorry when the plane landed. As soon as I entered the airport in Riyadh, my passport was taken by an airport official who led me to the main lounge. I was told to sit on a chair. I waited, but no one came back with my passport. It was quite strange to see so many men and women in flowing robes, and even stranger to see Asian women in long gowns with scarves that covered their entire heads. I realized that they were Malaysians who had come to Mecca on pilgrimage. As the only woman alone, and with an uncovered head, I felt quite uncomfortable. There was a large shopping complex, but I was nervous about venturing into it as I saw no women. My flight to Casablanca did not leave until 4:00 in the morning.

Before the Air India crew left for the city and we parted ways, one of the staff apologized and said, "Sorry, Madam, as you are traveling alone, you cannot come into the city. We can arrange for you to spend the night in a hotel and drive you to the airport tomorrow morning." I thought this man was just trying to be polite. It was only much later that I learned that women were forbidden by the laws of Moslem religion to enter the city alone in this country.

A couple of hours passed, with intermittent Moslem prayer calls over the loudspeaker, passengers arriving and leaving, mostly Moslems floating in their flowing robes and covered heads. At the call to prayer, many men got down on their knees in the airport lounge. The hours of waiting seemed to last ages, and I was still waiting for the man to reappear with my passport. The passengers were left to sit in the lounge, and the airline staff entered a door and disappeared into the womb of the terminal. There were no reception counters in the lounge where I was asked to wait. I saw an Indian youth sweeping the floor, and to his surprise, I spoke to him in Hindi. I asked him to help me get someone who could retrieve my passport. This sympathetic young man entered one of those closed doors and brought someone, who told me that I would get my passport before I got on the plane the next morning. He suggested that I take a refreshment and wait in the first class lounge for the night. I was packed off into a smaller, dark lounge with a refreshment bar and a soft couch on which I spent the night half asleep, half awake, worrying about my passport and whether I could safely get out of this unfriendly airport.

What a relief to arrive in friendly Casablanca! There was another lady passenger, covered from head to toe in her black tent-like cape, who joined me in business class. Another couple joined us too, and they all seemed to know each other. As soon as we landed, the first lady took off her black cover, and to my amazement, she was in skintight jeans and a t-shirt and plastered with make-up. She had beautiful shoulder-length hair and could have just stepped out of a fashion magazine. The other lady had thrown her sack away and was just as glamorous as the first.

On arrival in Casablanca, an agent from the movie met me at the airport and took me to a beautiful hotel to rest before flying on to our production site in Ouarzazate. I had a soothing bath, took a short nap, and went to have lunch in the hotel. There were many tourists and life was less restricted; I could have been in a five-star hotel in Bombay or Bangkok. It was a breath of fresh air to see other women uncovered and chatting away with each other or even in the company of men.

To get to the film location, I flew over high, sandy mountains speckled with tiny blotches of green. Landing in Ouarzazate at twilight, I felt very far away, in a magic land, completely cut off from the rest of the world. I was on top of the Atlas Mountains, entering the Sahara Desert. I was met by a lady who took me to small hotel. I would be in North Africa for six months.

Our location site was at a studio situated just outside of the town. We traveled to the studio in a bus. In this small Arab town, we recreated Tibet. A few months back, who would have ever thought it was possible to build Tibet in Africa? Who would have dreamt of seeing maroon-robed monks with shaved heads roaming around the streets of this small tourist town, or gazing at the golden roofs of Buddhist temples glittering in the hot African sun? By the end of our stay, the shopkeepers often greeted us with "Tashi Delek" and a few other Tibetan phrases.

Thaktse Village, the birthplace of the Dalai Lama, the Potala and Norbulingka Palaces, and the streets of Lhasa were beautifully replicated. The sets were so authentic that many of the Tibetan actors actually folded their hands in worship when they entered our Potala rooms. The costumes were beautifully constructed. Costumes for about 650 Tibetans and 300 Chinese actors were made in four months.

At the end of a long day of shooting, the Tibetan and the Moroccan actors would dash into the changing rooms and take their clothes off, hurrying off to catch the first bus back to the hotel instead of placing their clothes, hats, and shoes on their respective hangers. The Tibetans were the worst. They refused to listen to the wardrobe people, who would in turn vent their anger at me. On the next day, we had an impossible time trying to put the scattered clothes in order. Sometimes, the upcoming scene would need a crowd, and as we were understaffed, we could not sort the costumes in time. The Moroccan actors would emerge dressed in Central Tibetan robes topped with a Khampa hat, or Amdo women would turn up with the embroidered boots from

Lhasa. The crowd scenes were so enormous, one did not see the difference on the screen. The Tibetans used to have great fun exchanging their clothes. This annoyed the wardrobe people even more, because for a smaller crowd scene, shot on two different days, the actors had to wear the same clothes.

There were two old Khampa men who complained that their boots were the wrong shape and that the brocade was inferior. I told them that the boots were made by Moroccans by looking at photos and drawings. No one would ever see the details of the boots in the movie with crowds of men and women. Oh no, they refused to listen! They were so upset that the boots were not made correctly. Except for minor incidents like this, the Tibetan actors were always joking. The younger Tibetan men were like a group of mischievous schoolboys.

The Moroccan jewelers were exceptional craftsmen. I enjoyed my time working in this unit. When things got a little tense and tempers were short, I retreated to my small office and designed jewelry. I designed the jewels for His Holiness's mother, and relaxed in my little world when the noisy battles took place. Most of our crew members were Italians. They were excitable, quick to lose their tempers, and very vocal, but their tempers subsided as fast as they exploded.

About 330 Tibetans from India, Nepal, the United States, Canada, and Switzerland were selected to act in *Kundun*. It must have been quite a challenge for the director and his assistant, Scot Harris, to work with actors who had never had any training or experience. Martin and his assistant directors needed all the patience they could possibly manage.

Martin Scorsese was exceptional. He mentioned in a television interview that he was almost in retreat when he made this film. True, he would arrive at the Atlas studio in his black chauffeur-driven limousine and go directly to his trailer, which would be parked near the stage. No one entered his trailer except for the producer and his assistant and cook. He took his lunch alone in his trailer, walked back to the afternoon scene, and drove straight back to his hotel at the end of the day. He was fully concentrated on the movie and could only be seen on the set. He seemed quite happy to work with the Tibetans, and his face would light up when he passed by the Tibetan actors, who were always smiling and greeting him.

It amazed me that there were no rehearsals. Martin would go straight into the scene with Roger Deakin and his crew behind the camera. I went to the stage a couple of times to view the shooting, and Martin shot the same scene over and over until it was perfect. He was very intense and sensitive. Watching him at work was like a movie in itself. If the scene was good, he would get quite excited. The Tibetan cast revered him, and he was always very pleasant.

One of my tasks was to find out if barley grain could be found in Morocco, and if so, where to roast and grind it for tsampa. To my great surprise, Jimmy, our local casting man, mentioned that the Berbers ate roasted and powdered barley. He brought me a sample. It was just like our tsampa but darker in color. I also discovered that the Berbers used coral, turquoise, amber, and silver in their jewelry, which is also very similar to Tibetan jewelry. Another similarity was their ancient lock and key, which had the same intricate design and same system of sliding the key to open and close the lock as our old Tibetan keys and locks.

The Berbers are indigenous to Morocco, coming from the mountains in the east. The actor who played the Dalai Lama's father mentioned one day while we were traveling out of town to another location site that, "This village looks exactly like my birthplace in West Tibet. The houses are built of a similar mud construction, the roofs are flat, only the prayer flags are missing." To be in North Africa and find an environment similar to Tibet was really quite intriguing and surprising. I wondered if the Berbers had come from Tibet along the Silk Route.

I must say I was totally immersed in my new environment and my work, although it was not easy. When you look at pictures of movie stars and movie sets, it seems so glamorous that it is hard to imagine what goes on behind the scenes. In a day's work, I would move from my office to the set, to the wardrobe, to the hairdressers, and to the jewelry unit. By the end of the day, my legs ached so badly that I would leave the studio for a soak in a hot bath before collapsing into bed. We left the hotel around 7:30 in the morning and sometimes did not return from the set until 8:30 at night.

On Saturday nights, the Tibetans loved going to the disco. We even learned that some of the monks changed into jeans for a night of dancing. I went once with a group of Tibetan actors. They often invited me, but after all the standing up and running around the studio, I needed a rest.

Most of the Tibetan cast wanted the better roles and to be dressed in the better costumes. A number of the girls wanted to be dressed in the costumes of the nobility, with the heavy jewelry and brocade dresses. We were filming during summer, and they did not realize how hot they would be in these costumes on the edge of the Sahara Desert. They only saw themselves in the brocades and cascade of jewels. Several of the Tibetan actresses asked me to speak to the wardrobe head on their behalf, asking that they be cast as women of the nobility. Of course, the wardrobe head had nothing to do with casting. I told them that they should go and meet Alberto, who in the end actually chose some of these women for the roles they wanted. Once cast, these women came back from a day of filming, complaining of the heat and the weight of the jewels. They pleaded with Alberto to give them a different role. The men teased them and reminded them of the Tibetan saying, "If you want to look beautiful, you have to bear the suffering."

Interestingly, there were both Tibetan and Moroccan women who did not want to be dressed like beggars, pilgrims, or nomads in the thick sheepskin robes. It was not because of the heat that they complained, but because they felt they lost face in dressing like nomads. In addition, the Tibetan men were terrible teases. It amused me that although people were only acting a part, their self-image was diminished by the costumes that they wore.

The Moroccan actors were generally very pleasant people. They laughed at seeing each other dressed in Tibetan robes and hats. There was no verbal communication between the Tibetan and the Moroccan actors, but everyone got along very well.

One of the actors, Gya Yudon-la, was His Holiness's cousin. She was born and lived in Thaktse Village before moving to Lhasa. In the film, she was to portray the role of her sister in a scene depicting a visit His Holiness made to his birthplace after his visit to China. The Chinese authorities would not allow the sister to serve tea to the Dalai Lama. The day Gya Yudon-la arrived in Ouarzazate, she came in for her costume fitting. We dressed her in the traditional robes of her home village, and the hairdresser, a beautiful, gentle, Italian lady named Mirella, plaited her hair in the style of the women of Thaktse Village while I outfitted her in her jewelry. Gya Yudon-la seemed dazed when she glanced at herself in the mirror. Almost half a century had passed since she had worn such a costume or done her hair in this way. Tears flooded her eyes, but she put on a very brave front. Her past life seemed to be drifting back into her thoughts.

On the day we were to shoot the scene, we had to travel to a distant village where Dante and his boys had recreated Thaktse as it was in the old days. I decided to travel to the site with Gya Yudon-la, because I knew it would be a very emotional experience. When she saw the village house with the incense burner on the roof, she was overcome. The expression on her face brought me to tears. I believe that when they were shooting the scene inside the house, poor Gya Yudon-la really broke down and everyone cried, including Martin and the crew. She later told me that the setting was so authentic that she believed she really was in Thaktse, offering tea to His Holiness. Thuthob Tsarong, a grandnephew of His Holiness, was playing the role of the adult Dalai Lama, and he looked a bit like him, too.

Many parts of the filming were difficult for me as well. Throughout the movie, Lobsang was one of the main characters. Again and again, I was reminded how much I missed him. I relied on my Buddhist teachings to help me through these moments.

My Buddhist teachings were also put into practice during a strange encounter I had with one of the actors. Melissa Mathison had come to Morocco for a couple of days, and she and I were sitting in one of the tents watching Martin and his crew shoot the Norbulingka opera scene. A tall Asian man came into the tent, and Melissa informed me that he was the actor who would play Chairman Mao. This actor was from mainland China, but was now living in the United States. He took a seat alone at the back of our small tent. I had to return to the wardrobe department to see if I was needed, and I had to pass by him. I extended my hand and introduced myself as Namgyal Taklha, a Tibetan and a researcher on the movie. He smiled and introduced himself as Ben. When I returned to the tent to watch the opera, Ben was sitting near Melissa, and I joined them. Ben asked me if the scene closely resembled Lhasa. He also asked if the costumes were authentic. I told him that watching the opera scene made me feel like I was a young girl in Lhasa again.

After lunch, I returned to the wardrobe department, where I usually helped Bona plan the costumes for the next scenes. As I reached the gate that led into the wardrobe department, Ben walked out of the make-up room nearby. Mirella had shaved the front of his hair so that he had the same receding hairline as Chairman Mao. What a shock it was for me to suddenly come face-to-face with Mao. Suddenly, fear, anger, and hatred welled up inside me. Ben obviously noticed my expression. He looked very uncomfortable and said, "I don't know how I can go out like this now." Suddenly, I made myself remember that Ben had done nothing to harm the Tibetans. I remembered His Holiness the Dalai Lama's teaching, "Everyone wants happiness and not suffering." Suddenly all the tension left, and we entered the wardrobe together. I felt good enough to laugh at him and watch Bona give him his padding and dress him in his Mao suit. Now he really looked like Chairman Mao.

Ben left after a couple of days. He was to return only when the China scene was to be shot at the end of the production. I was gone by then, but I met him again in New York at the premier of *Kundun*. It was good to see him again.

My time in Hollywood came to an end when I decided to return to India after six months in Morocco. My work on the making of *Kundun* was like a dream. Before I left Morocco, the wardrobe department gave me a small farewell party, beautifully arranged in the hall where we cut and sewed the clothes and fitted the actors. They decorated our work table with different Tibetan hats and served champagne and snacks. Although I could not make conversation with Ida, Maria, Elsie and Idelwise, we spoke to each other from our hearts. They were fine, hardworking girls and Bona, our boss, was a wonderful team leader.

Sassa, the only man in our group, was teased by everyone. Of course, the Moroccan team in the wardrobe, the make-up crew, and the hairdressers joined us as well. Dante came with his wife, Francesca, the set designer. Madoka, my Japanese colleague, was there as well. Some of the Italian girls even cried when we said farewell.

18 The Setting Sun

It took me two months to recover from my work on *Kundun*. A number of the crew told me that many people "burn out" in the movie business because of the long hours and being far away from home and family. I did not burn out, but I was extremely tired when I arrived back in India. I was very happy to come home to my quiet little retreat cottage and relax. Working on the film was a very positive experience for me. I felt I had made a small contribution to telling the world about the life of a very special man and documenting a crucial period in Tibetan history, especially at a time when our culture, traditions, and lifestyle were ebbing away with the Chinese influence in Tibet and the Western and Indian influence on Tibetans in exile.

I returned to the service of the Tibetan government-in-exile, working as the secretary at the Planning Council in Dharamsala. Since then, I have visited our Tibetan settlements in Karnataka, South India, and met with some of the unemployed youth and their parents. We have placed great emphasis on the importance of educating our Tibetan children to prepare them for a better future and to see that they carry on our culture and traditions. Almost ninety-eight percent of our children are literate, which is a very positive achievement. However, we had not planned for what we would do for the children who dropped out of school. At the time of my visit, there were about three thousand unemployed Tibetan youths in the settlements. The Planning Council began providing training for some of these young Tibetans and helping others set up small businesses.

The Planning Council was also busy conducting the first demographic survey of Tibetans in exile and planning our third five-year integrated development plan for the Tibetans in exile. In the future, Tibetans will be able to use this guideline in an autonomous Tibet. This plan can also be used by the many organizations and individuals who wish to provide aid to the Tibetans.

My son brought me great joy by returning to India. After Tenzin Namdhak had completed his International Studies degree at St. Stephen's in India and a year at Georgetown University, he worked as the program officer for the Tibetan resettlement project in New York. He is now the head of the security unit for His Holiness the Dalai Lama and is his chief bodyguard. Tenzin is very protective of His Holiness and takes good care of him.

Tenzin and his wife, Tsering Dolkar, have a son named Tenzin Dhundul. With Chuki and Raj's two sons, Siddhartha and Atisha, I am very blessed to have three grandsons. I am also very fortunate to still have my wonderful parents with me. They have taught me much about kindness and compassion, and I have tried to bring the values I learned from them to my children and to my grandchildren. I miss Lobsang very much, but I try to keep doing what we wanted to achieve together—to be good parents and to serve His Holiness and our fellow Tibetans.

Now that I am approaching my late fifties, I feel the need to simplify my life. In a year or so, I will retire from the Central Tibetan Administration, having given almost thirty years of my life to the service of Tibet and the Tibetans. It has been an honor to follow in the footsteps of my father, grandfather, and great-grandfather, and to be the second woman in my family to serve the Tibetan government.

As I gaze at the setting sun, I realize that my life is also approaching this stage. I look back on my life and cherish it. It has not always been smooth, but the challenges have made me stronger and the risks have been part of the learning process. My life has been a great adventure.

I do plan a visit to Tibet after I retire. Until then, I will look forward to the day I can stand beneath the turquoise sky in Lhasa, ring the bell at the Jokhang Temple, see the Shakyamuni Buddha, and climb Chakpori Hill. Once I return to Tibet, I will have made a full circle on the wheel of life. The prayer flags will dance in the wind, and the fragrant white smoke of the burning juniper leaves will carry my prayers for friends throughout the world, across an endless rise of mountains.